ignite

ignite

ILLUMINATING THEATRE FOR YOUNG PEOPLE

edited by Heather Fitzsimmons Frey

Playwrights Canada Press
TORONTO

LIBRARY AND ARCHIVES CANADA CATALOGUING IN PUBLICATION
        Ignite : illuminating theatre for young people / Heather Fitzsimmons
Frey, editor.

A three play collection about youth.
Includes bibliographical references.
Contents: And by the way, Miss... / by URGE with the Ensemble -- Beneath the ice
    / by Eva Colmers -- The middle place / by Andrew Kushnir.
ISBN 978-1-77091-474-2 (paperback)

        1. Youth--Juvenile drama. I. Fitzsimmons Frey, Heather, editor
II. Kushnir, Andrew, 1980- . Middle place. III. Colmers, Eva M., 1953- .
Beneath the ice. IV. URGE. And by the way Miss...

PS8309.Y6I35 2015   jC812'.60809283   C2015-904091-4

We acknowledge the financial support of the Canada Council for the Arts, the Ontario Arts Council (OAC), the Ontario Media Development Corporation, and the Government of Canada through the Canada Book Fund for our publishing activities. Nous remercions l'appui financier du Conseil des Arts du Canada, le Conseil des arts de l'Ontario (CAO), la Société de développement de l'industrie des médias de l'Ontario, et le Gouvernement du Canada par l'entremise du Fonds du livre du Canada pour nos activités d'édition.

Canada Council   Conseil des arts
for the Arts   du Canada

ONTARIO ARTS COUNCIL
CONSEIL DES ARTS DE L'ONTARIO
an Ontario government agency
un organisme du gouvernement de l'Ontario

Ontario Media Development
Corporation

For my children
Leif, Meredith, Celeste, and Piers.

CONTENTS

GENERAL EDITOR'S NOTE
Bruce Barton

Ten years ago I inherited the role of General Editor with the New Canadian Drama series, then published by Borealis Press of Ottawa. At that time I proposed that the series begin to showcase the editorial skills of doctoral candidates at the (then) Graduate Centre for Study of Drama, University of Toronto, where I was a faculty member. A number of very promising projects were initiated, each edited by a Ph.D. candidate at the Centre, and each dedicated to a category of drama defined by the editor's area of inquiry and expertise. In addition, it was our hope to expand the nature and utility of published play collections in this country by surrounding the primary texts with a range of carefully selected complementary materials.

As they say, however, "the best laid plans . . . " Unfortunately, following only a single published volume in 2009, *Reluctant Texts from Exuberant Performance: Canadian Devised Theatre*, the series was cancelled by the publisher for economic reasons. As a result, several excellent play collection ideas appeared stillborn (including the present volume). However, to their huge credit, the forward-looking folks at Playwrights Canada Press were instantly enthusiastic about several of the proposed volumes. *Ignite: Illuminating Theatre for Young People* is the tangible proof of their prescience and their commitment to extending the diversity of, and the informed discourse around, dramatic publishing in this country.

I cannot speak highly enough of Blake Sproule and Annie Gibson of Playwrights Canada; their intelligence, generosity, and professionalism on this project has been unparalleled. For her part, Heather Fitzsimmons Frey has worked with unfailing commitment on this collection, resulting in a diverse and inspiring arrangement of voices. Her tireless diligence and integrity have ensured a volume that is, indeed, illuminating as well as entertaining, both through its primary texts and through its extensive critical contextualization. It has been a pleasure to accompany Heather on each stage of this ambitious project, and she should be very proud of the outcome.

ACKNOWLEDGEMENTS

Many thanks are necessary to recognize the wonderful people who have supported the journey for this book, brought me kindling, and helped to coax the flames. Thanks to Annie Gibson and Blake Sproule for embracing this project, to Bruce Barton for helping me to find a publisher, and to all the artists and writers whose work is here. Thanks to Tracy Carroll, John Mahon, Jason Matsunaga-Turnbull, and Elyne Quan, whose work with me and the Edmonton Arts Council Theatre for Young Audiences (TYA) research group originally sparked my interest in TYA. Thanks to great artists and thinkers Christine Sokaymoh Frederick, Kathleen Gallagher, Lynda Hill, and Manon van de Water for their encouragement. Enormous gratitude goes to my best support, Rod Fitzsimmons Frey, and to my wonderful children Leif, Meredith, Celeste, and Piers.

IGNITING THEATRE FOR YOUNG AUDIENCES: AN ANTHOLOGY OF CREATIVE JOURNEYS
Heather Fitzsimmons Frey

I love a campfire. In the summertime, out in the woods, my children seek out dry moss, twigs, robust grasses, and other dry wood to coax a fire to life. We always try to do it with one match (although we often use more), and even though the stakes are low since we don't actually *need* the fire for survival, there is a sense of urgency about getting the fire going before darkness falls; a thrill of excitement as we strike the match; and a kind of awe as the fire starts to take, vaporizing the kindling, smouldering on the moss, and spreading to the wood until we have a perfect, crackling fire for warmth, singing, stories, and roasting treats. The children eagerly but carefully nurture the fire so that it doesn't smother, doesn't get out of control, and doesn't fill our campsite with smoke. When the fire ignites it is risky, but fire is full of possibilities, and full of hope.

Like a good campfire, these plays were fuelled by a variety of sources of energy and inspiration, and they cast a glow of light and warmth around them that I believe draws audiences in, invites them to watch, to engage, to empathize, to contemplate, and to think critically. Each of the plays in this book is also far more than the final script that actors perform on stage—each is a story about a risky, ambitious, and hopeful journey. This volume focuses on that story. It seeks to illuminate the complex process of creating these unique works for young people, in which artists dared to imagine inspiring possibilities, and in which the voices and stories that surround the scripts you read here are as relevant as the final product. Sparks from a fire can ignite more flames, and my hope is that these scripts and the recounting of their creative journeys inspire audiences, artists, and thinkers who are interested in Canadian theatre and Theatre for Young Audiences (TYA).

When I selected the plays I wanted to share in this volume, I looked for brave, risky, and successful works that crackled with stories. I sought plays that engaged with complicated ethical questions—both in their content and in their creative process. I didn't want to share plays for young people where the bulk of the creative journey involved a playwright working in imaginative solitude with a cup of coffee, a computer, and a way with words. These plays—*The Middle Place* by Andrew Kushnir, *And by the way, Miss . . .* by URGE with the Ensemble, and *Beneath the Ice* by Eva Colmers—were only possible because of the way the artists engaged with a corner of humanity, and because they wrote, in some sense, in a collaborative way: there is a verbatim theatre piece, a collectively devised piece, and a location-specific cross-cultural research-enriched piece. The artists' carefully considered creative processes are worth revealing because they influence the words on every page.

The creators not only chose to tackle content that has a complicated ethical resonance for Canadian young people, such as youth homelessness, girlhood sexuality and violence, climate change, and North-South relations within Canada, but they chose to create and present their work in complex ways that raise questions about creative processes, collaborators, audience, and ways of knowing. I often use the words "bravery" and "courage" when referring to these artists and their works contained here, because in all the plays danger flickered constantly, both during development and during performance—danger of rejection by the plays' subjects or audiences; danger of misunderstanding or misrepresenting the communities whose voices the playwrights wanted to surface; danger of oversimplifying complex subjects or overcomplicating issues that those involved see as straightforward. None of the artists featured here were ignorant of those dangers, and all thought the topics were important enough to take the risk.

Andrew Kushnir's *The Middle Place* appealed to me for this collection because Andrew bravely engages with social justice, and his process did not shrink from gritty worlds and improbable-but-just-possible hopes of the young, homeless Canadians he met and worked with. I admired his decision to use verbatim creation methods for a play concerning young people who typically struggle to get other Canadians to hear their voices. I loved the idea of *And by the way, Miss . . .* even before I had seen an archival videotape of the production—a devised piece that incorporated the ideas of audience members as it was being developed and that was intended to be by, about, and exclusively for girls seemed like a courageous experiment to me. Writing for and, in a way, *with* a particular demographic not usually identified as a target audience meant the artists could use the piece to give stature to often invisible and inaudible girls and their voices, and in so doing raised issues about girlhood that mattered to *girl* audiences. I saw *Beneath the Ice* in Edmonton before I dreamed I would have the opportunity to share it here, and I was struck by the way Eva Colmers wove topical concerns regarding consumerism, materialism, climate change, and relations between the Canadian North and South into a play that also considered how people *know* things, and how young people learn them. When I learned about her research journey to the North and how central that was in her process, I was all the more intrigued.

All three plays address specific kinds of knowledge and ways of interpreting and seeing the world; all make use of characters that have specific relations to community members that influenced the scripts you read here; and all highlight specific ethical questions relevant to theatre practitioners and scholars for work concerning audiences of any age, regarding stories, voice, identity, and the stage.

This book is structured so that each play is accompanied by stories and voices relevant to the initial spark and the journey from spark to roaring fire. First, a scholarly essay introduces the play by engaging with issues concerning content, genre, audiences, creation ethics, and/or how the piece fits into the broader landscape of Canadian theatre. Second, there is a contextualizing piece that foregrounds the voices of playwrights, collaborators, and community stakeholders. Those sections include a discussion between a playwright and a director, the transcription of a focus group between artists, a playwright statement, and youth and community commentary. Just before the script is a creative journey timeline and fact sheet in which the artists highlight especially significant moments and people in their play-development process. Finally, there is the carefully wrought script, in which the content, themes, and playwrights' words speak for themselves.

IGNITING PROCESS

Several years ago I had a conversation with Lynda Hill, Artistic Director of Theatre Direct Canada, who spearheaded *And by the way, Miss* . . . . We were discussing the state of Canadian TYA, and she made two remarks that I keep coming back to. In the first case she argued that ambitious TYA artists who work in unusual, creative, and collaborative ways need "a willingness to risk a messy process."[1]

This is not the first volume Playwrights Canada Press has published to highlight creation processes in TYA: in Shirley Barrie and Emil Sher's *Prepare to Embark: Six Theatrical Journeys for Young Audiences* (2002), Barrie and Sher acknowledge the wide range of ways that scripts can be created and then brought to the stage. They write:

> Theatre is a voyage, a journey where actors and audiences alike are transported to a world where anything is possible and the impossible is real . . .
>
> When are the seeds of a journey first planted? . . . Sometimes the decision to pick up and go can be spontaneous, unplanned and unexpected. Other trips can take months—even years—of preparation.
>
> Playwriting is no different. The inspiration to write a play can seemingly drop in our laps out of the blue, or brew in the back of our minds for years.[2]

Their book features six plays and includes a section at the end of the book in which the playwrights' diverse script-development processes are highlighted and summarized for the benefit of middle-school readers. But what is different about this volume—besides, of course, the plays themselves—is that these plays are *all* created through unusual, messy processes. In Lynda Hill's case, she was talking about an "interdisciplinary process," because work that incorporates dance, music, and visual art, not to mention beautiful language, is the type of theatre that particularly appeals to her. However,

---

1   Lynda Hill, personal interview with the author, 6 April 2011.

2   Shirley Barrie and Emil Sher, introduction to *Prepare to Embark* (Toronto: Playwrights Canada, 2002), iii.

key to this anthology is her comment that theatre artists, who are generally risk-takers to begin with, need to be willing to risk a "messy" process.

The processes revealed in this book definitely qualify. From wading through hundreds of pages of verbatim transcriptions to craft a script, to the decision to perform a show exclusively for schoolgirls, to a white woman writing a play about an Inuit/Southerner encounter, I propose that the processes that the playwright-creators chose to make these works are *inherently* (and often intentionally) messy. These processes cannot be seen as messy because of inertia or entropy, inaction or inattention—there is so much energy and movement in the making that even as you can read, in the moments when it seems like the process is standing still, it is breathing, taking in oxygen to fan the flame.

"Messiness" is a powerful scholarly concept, frequently used in postmodern, feminist, and social science analyses. Acknowledging that some kinds of data are not "clean," and that some things may even be "unknowable" due to their complexity, it celebrates disorder as a way to arrive at ideas and possible understandings. Theorists agree that order is overrated in all kinds of sciences; that children learn better when they engage in messy play; that archival data can be perceived as "messy"; and that interactions between people can be productive but still "messy." The idea of a "messy" process foregrounds the fact that all of the artists' processes required an extended period of time, took unexpected turns, were surprising in myriad ways, and involved a significant number of voices in what is the published (but perhaps not the final) product here. Illuminating the journey and shining a light on a bit of the mess is part of the goal of offering and contextualizing the pieces in this anthology and is integral to understanding how the artists approached their work and how readers might come to share it as well.

Verbatim theatre is messy because of the vast amount of initial data, but Andrew Kushnir's decision to craft *The Middle Place* using the words of shelter youth—who live complicated, often disenfranchised lives—is especially messy because it is ethically complex. In the discussion between him and Alan Dilworth, Kushnir explains how his process with Project: Humanity helped him to get to know the young people he interviewed, how he shared his piece with the shelter community whose words he used, and how he has made peace with issues concerning voice, agency, and accountability. Through the process of developing, creating, workshopping, and presenting this play, Kushnir and Dilworth discuss how they saw the words come to life and become something "real"—an idea they and Kathleen Gallagher, who introduces *The Middle Place*, both discuss. In all its complexity, Kushnir and Dilworth challenge readers to approach the text of *The Middle Place* as an encounter in its own right.

The process of devising or collectively creating theatre is an equally but differently messy process, and the volume of scholarly analysis written about devised theatre attests to how challenging it can be to negotiate interpersonal relations, to deal with power dynamics, and to create meaningful work with a clear vision. As Michelle MacArthur and Anne Wessels point out, the multi-generational, all-female approach to creation, devising, and spectatorship in *And by the way, Miss . . .* positions the play as a part of Canadian feminist theatre history. Their analysis opens the process up to discussing opportunities that would have been unavailable had boys and men been involved, and highlights assumptions people may have about shared space and spaces where girls feel "safe." At the time this book goes to press, the final script is just over ten years old, but the artists met again recently to talk about the creation of the play. In their forum the artists discuss how girlhood and friendship were central issues for their exploration because that is what interested the girls who participated in their workshops; they go on to speculate how the content might be different if the piece were created today. They point out that they would best discover contemporary thematic shifts by remaining committed to the creation process, which they describe as complex, interdisciplinary, and multi-vocal.

Finally, creating theatre based on a particular location and on community-specific research with an "other" or non-dominant cultural group is a messy and ethically complicated decision in multiple ways, especially since *Beneath the Ice* concerns an encounter between Southern and Inuit people. Historically, Inuit have usually been represented on Southern stages by white Canadians rather than by themselves, their stories have been appropriated by Southern Canadians, and they have often been represented in historicized ways that suggest a static or even dying culture. Playwright Eva Colmers was well aware that creating this play was ethically and artistically fraught, but she wanted to take the risk and made every effort to work as respectfully as she could. Nevertheless, her process revealed even more challenges than she anticipated, and as her introduction indicates, it was not always clear to her how she should address Inuit community feedback about her work. In Sherrill Grace's introduction to *Staging the North*, Grace discusses how Herman Voaden's imagination in the 1930s focussed on impressions of the North as a way to create distinctly Canadian theatre, yet Northern people rarely create or perform plays themselves.[3] In my introduction to Colmers's script, I position her work in relation to other Southern experiments with creating plays about the North, discuss the complicated process of getting community feedback, and consider tensions among artistic impulses, community ideas, and my own desire to publish this script.

IGNITING CANADIAN THEATRE WITH TYA

The second comment Lynda Hill made during that conversation in 2011 that has really influenced my thinking here was, "We have an obligation in the TYA context to stretch creative boundaries . . . we can be innovative storytellers and we can advance our art form. We can propose new ways of thinking of theatre—in fact, we can be the *most* innovative and experimental work out there."[4] Although it has become a truism, it's worth repeating that many artists who produce TYA often feel that because their work is directed at young people, it is misunderstood, and imagined to be any number of dull adjectives: safe, conventional, overly didactic, facile, familiar, predictable, or boring. But Hill boldly asserts that TYA can be and in fact *should* be "the *most* innovative and experimental work out there." She believes that one step towards achieving that goal is to employ a messy, interdisciplinary process, but her statement does not preclude other complex creation methods; her point applies to other creative work that aims to be the most challenging and innovative in the theatre scene. And I believe it is not a stretch to say that the works featured in this volume are innovative, brave, risky, and experimental—not merely within the context of Canadian TYA, but in terms of all Canadian theatre.

---

3 Sherrill Grace, "Degrees of North," introduction to *Staging the North: Twelve Canadian Plays* (Toronto: Playwrights Canada, 1999) ix.

4 Lynda Hill, personal interview.

Even though TYA can be as complex as theatre for adult audiences, scholars rarely engage with Canadian professional TYA. In a personal correspondence with me, director and scholar Nicholas Hanson argued:

> The contemporary Canadian scholarly landscape includes abundant investigations of drama and education, with a particular emphasis on projects that foster public engagement, consider social issues, and connect various communities. Research on Theatre for Young Audiences—the performance of plays for young people—is, on the other hand, largely invisible. The paucity of TYA research is particularly striking when you consider the robust TYA activities in Canada.[5]

Joyce Doolittle and Zina Barnieh, with Hélène Beauchamp, wrote *A Mirror of Our Dreams* in 1979 (reviewed in *Theatre Research in Canada* in 1981 by Des Davis), and it remains the only survey of the Canadian TYA landscape that I am aware of. Scholarly attention to English Canadian TYA can be found in themed issues of *Canadian Theatre Review* 10 (1976) and 133 (2008); *Canadian Children's Literature* in 1977, 1990, and 1997; and in occasional articles and/or book chapters by scholars and research-practitioners like Hélène Beauchamp, Kathleen Gallagher, Annie Giannini, Nicholas Hanson, Ann Haugo, Debra McLauchlan, Monica Prendergast, Marlis Schweitzer, Jean Yoon, and Belarie Zatzman. Meanwhile, anthologies of TYA, such as *Kids Plays: Six Canadian Plays for Children* (1980), *YPThree* (1994), *Prepare to Embark* (2002), *Shakin' the Stage* (2003), *Acting Out: Scenes and Monologues from Theatre Direct Productions for Youth* (2006), *Things That Go Bump* volumes I and II (2009), *Sprouts!: An Anthology of Plays from Concrete Theatre's Sprouts New Play Festival for Kids* (2010), and *The Green Thumb Theatre Anthology* (2012), tend to present scripts and/or excerpts with little additional information or commentary, or they focus on histories of the companies that initially commissioned them. Jerry Wasserman's *Modern Canadian Plays, Vol. II* (fifth edition, 2013) recognizes that some plays like Joan McLeod's *The Shape of a Girl* are appreciated by both adult and young audiences, and in that book Wasserman offers a discussion of McLeod's trajectory as a playwright,

---

5 Nicholas Hanson, personal interview with the author, 2 May 2015.

but discusses only a little about the play itself. Like McLeod's *The Shape of a Girl*, Andrew Kushnir's *The Middle Place* has also been presented to both adult and youth audiences, and in some ways could comfortably be included in a volume like Wasserman's. However, context is extremely important to perceptions of the *Ignite* plays. This volume is a space that embraces the journey, the multiplicity, the complexity, the process, and the possibility of young people and of theatre. *Ignite* is an important break from past volumes of plays for young people in that the script, scholarly analysis, and the artist voices can all be read in one place, establishing the beginnings of a conversation between the covers of this book, which I hope ignites interest in further discussion.

THE MIDDLE PLACE

Andrew Kushnir

The play is dedicated to the residents and caseworkers at Youth Without Shelter (located in Rexdale, Ontario) who generously and courageously shared their stories, insights, and words for this play.

ACKNOWLEDGEMENTS

Wendy Horton, Judy Leroux, and Laura Lipani at Youth Without Shelter for having faith in Project: Humanity, piloting our shelter drama programming, and granting us permission to create *The Middle Place* with their youth.

Antonio Cayonne, Catherine Murray, and Dan Chapman-Smith for being the heart and soul of PH, and for believing in our venture into verbatim storytelling. An additional thank you to Catherine for all her assistance with the carefully rendered transcripts of the play.

Alan Dilworth for his vision, his ethics, his brilliance as a director and collaborator.

Thank you to Damien Atkins and Maev Beaty for being such fine partners.

Further gratitude to Kathleen Gallagher for teaching PH about what this kind of theatre can do, to Michael Rubenfeld and SummerWorks for the play's first outing, and to Andy McKim and Theatre Passe Muraille along with Matthew Jocelyn and Canadian Stage for giving the play more life in Toronto.

Thank you to the artists and supporters who helped with the development of this work: Brian Quirt, Jessica Greenberg, Kevin Walker, Akosua Amo-Adem, Paul Dunn, Aidan DeSalaiz, Monica Dottor, Kimberly Purtell, Jung-Hye Kim, Thomas Ryder Payne, Andrea Schurman, Sandi Becker, Marinda de Beer, Kinnon Elliott, Susan Stover, and Ian Arnold. Thank you, Charlie Tomlinson. And thank you to the Toronto Arts Council, the Ontario Arts Council, and the Canada Council for the Arts for support of this and other PH projects.

THE MIDDLE PLACE: CREATING INTIMACY WITH AN AUDIENCE
Kathleen Gallagher[1]

YOUTH: First of all, a documentary film wouldn't have such a, like, a set of monologues in this manner, so in the way of presentation, it is different.

INTERVIEWER: Yeah.

YOUTH: But the main difference I see between a play and a film or television documentary is that when you watch a documentary, it doesn't really feel personal to you; it's more like absorbing information.

INTERVIEWER: Yes.

YOUTH: Like you have the knowledge, it appeals to your mind, but it doesn't really appeal to your heart. Like, okay, they're homeless youths so they suffer in this way, okay! They're trying to have hope and then go on like that; great for them. It's like you can actually acknowledge those facts and you could cheer them on a little bit, but it doesn't just touch you as much.

---

1   It is an honour and a privilege to be invited to make a brief introduction to *The Middle Place* and to share something of my fortuitous encounters with its inventive and ethically-driven creator, Andrew Kushnir; its sensitive and skilful director, Alan Dilworth; and its cast of actors and Project: Humanity company members who breathed life, with precision and care, into the unforgettable voices of the young people on whose lives this unique verbatim piece of theatre is based.

INTERVIEWER: Yeah.

YOUTH: When actually you come into a play, watch it, it actually comes close to your heart much more than it would in a documentary [on a screen].

—Post-show interview conducted with youth about *The Middle Place* at Theatre Passe Muraille, Toronto, 2010

While I was conducting an ethnographic research study in a Toronto high school, I found myself in the drama classroom where Andrew Kushnir and Antonio Cayonne (of Project: Humanity) first arrived to provide a workshop for the students in the class. Entirely relevant to my study of youth engagement with theatre,[2] I watched as Kushnir and Cayonne skilfully led the students into an exploration of verbatim theatre. They introduced the students to Alan Dilworth's "punctuation walk," a technique Dilworth had used with the company of actors as they rehearsed *The Middle Place*, inviting the actors to feel the grammar of the script, the hesitations, the speech patterns, the rhythms, the idiosyncrasies of the verbatim monologues. The young people moved around the room, embodying language with delight. I was so taken by the careful pedagogy of this duo, their passion and their clear communication. That was my first introduction to *The Middle Place*, watching young people *feel* the words of others in their bodies.

After the workshop, the company brought the play to the school, where this time I observed a crammed auditorium of teenagers sit in silence, enraptured by the white oval of light on the stage, the world of the homeless shelter it evoked, and the stunning performances of the actors who carefully communicated the worries, the dreams, the hopes, the anger, the desires of the young people they were conveying. At the end of the play, students rushed the stage, hoping for a word or two with the actors. I hadn't seen a touring show move young people in that way ever.

The teacher, Naomi Savage, who had originally invited the company to the school, had herself undertaken the project of learning more about

2   See Kathleen Gallagher, *Why Theatre Matters: Urban Youth, Engagement, and a Pedagogy of the Real* (Toronto: University of Toronto Press, 2014), a book based on a five-year multi-sited SSHRC-funded ethnographic study.

verbatim theatre and finally produced a unit of study on verbatim for the Ministry of Education so that other teachers in other high schools around the province could benefit from her work.[3] With her own students, she went on to work with verbatim in her classrooms and we documented the monologues created by the young people on a blog, recording their process from interviews with their peers, through to transcription, monologue creation, and videotaping of their final monologues. The students engaged with each other's work and provided feedback through the blog. My research team and I watched the process unfold with great interest.[4] Upon hearing about the verbatim project in our Toronto school, our research collaborators in India also became very interested in this form of theatre-making; they then took up the challenge of creating a street play about domestic violence based on interviews they conducted with married women in their communities.[5] The arrival of *The Middle Place* had clearly sparked a rich pedagogical experiment for teachers and students both near and far, and provided us with a fascinating meta-research context where we were witnessing youth conduct their own research into character creation and youth subculture through verbatim techniques.

The Middle Place went on to be produced in Toronto at Theatre Passe Muraille in the fall of 2010 and at Canadian Stage in the winter of 2011. So intrigued by the experience at the school, we wondered whether we might learn more about the impact of this piece on its audiences and about the genre of verbatim theatre. We therefore discussed with Project: Humanity our interest in extending our ethnographic research into the theatres, to chart the impact of the play on audiences' perceptions of young people, and particularly young people without shelter. We developed a series of questions we wished to ask youth and adult audience members about their

3 The Council of Ontario Drama and Dance Educators (CODE) have posted the verbatim unit on their website. See http://code.on.ca/resource/verbatim-theatre.

4 For a fuller documentation of the process of this work with youth, see Kathleen Gallagher, Anne Wessels, and B. Yaman Ntelioglou, "Verbatim Theatre and Social Research: Turning Towards the Stories of Others," *Theatre Research in Canada* 33.1 (2012): 24–43.

5 The research in *Why Theatre Matters: Urban Youth, Engagement, and a Pedagogy of the Real* is based on theatre work with young people in Toronto, Canada; Lucknow, India; Taipei, Taiwan; and Boston, USA.

responses to the play, their perceptions of youth, and their reflections on verbatim as a genre. In all, we conducted seventy-five post-show interviews.

> **YOUTH:** I have never seen any theatre like this before. And it's striking because there are so few actors, and no props, costume or set changes or anything. I think that helps to make it seem more real and powerful. At times it seemed just like I was having a conversation with the person. Like listening to them. With other kinds of theatre . . . it's not the same level of closeness.

—Post-show interview conducted with youth about *The Middle Place* at Canadian Stage, Toronto, 2011

From our many interviews, we learned that people responded to the question of "the real" on multiple levels: "real" as in "lived" and resonant with one's own experiences, for those currently or having at one time lived in a shelter; a realistic acting style in which you forget they are actors; "real" because the script was developed from "real" interviews (the speech is more colloquial, authentic with minimal theatrical artifice, less obviously crafted than a fictional account).

In a conversation about their work in this book, Andrew Kushnir and Alan Dilworth also find themselves thinking about what "the real" might mean. Given the proliferation of documentary forms of theatre-making, many theatre scholars are grappling with this complex question of the real. Kushnir catches himself using the word "real" in describing the genre of verbatim, despite the fact that he acknowledges that to some extent all theatre is largely drawing from "real" encounters, relationships, and conversations. Dilworth lands upon a notion of "authenticity," despite the fact that both he and Kushnir fully appreciate the constructed-ness of verbatim theatre. Their wrestling with the term foreshadows perhaps Philip Auslander's concept of "authentic inauthenticity,"[6] which signals

6 Cited in Michael Anderson and Linden Wilkinson, "A Resurgence of Verbatim Theatre: Authenticity, Empathy and Transformation," *Australasian Drama Studies* 50 (2007): 153–169. Anderson and Wilkinson, in their article citing a resurgence of verbatim theatre, suggest that the form is well suited to intellectual and emotional complexity. At the same time, they maintain that the works are accessible because the drama is built from conversations. My sense, as I have elsewhere argued, is that

the feeling of the truthfulness of the character in full consciousness of its constructed nature. The adult audience members we interviewed were more cynical about this notion of a real, feeling that, like reality TV, documentary theatre—even that based on verbatim interviews—is nonetheless a highly constructed enterprise. The youth we interviewed seemed, on the whole, more available to the idea of a "real" they were accessing through the representations they met on stage. At first, I read this as a lack of sophistication in understanding how theatre works, but then I looked more closely.

INTERVIEWER: So, umm, let me start by asking, did the play seem real to you?

YOUTH: I'm not exactly sure how to describe it. For one thing, the play didn't seem personal, as in I could actually relate to it, but for some reason all the characters seemed so human, like they actually existed without having met them. So it felt that—also, I could almost imagine that they were there, but I couldn't actually think of them as people who actually existed, so it's kind of a funny feeling like that.

INTERVIEWER: So in a sense, then, are you saying that you felt like the actor was there but you also felt there was another presence? Like the presence of the person who said those words? Is that what you mean? Maybe I'm not understanding.

YOUTH: No. The feeling I got was, I could actually imagine the characters, through the actors, but I couldn't exactly like ahh realize that the characters were real.

INTERVIEWER: Okay.

---

verbatim also elicits ambivalence from its audience, a kind of ambivalence that continues to provoke questioning, as a productive mode of engagement. And, as the creators of *The Middle Place* hoped, it is a kind of theatre that opens up an intimate space for the imaginative leaps of its creators and its audiences.

YOUTH: But I could actually, like, see the characters, imagine how the characters would act in the little bit of knowledge I saw from the play—

INTERVIEWER: —Yes.

YOUTH: —which is pretty limited.

INTERVIEWER: Yes.

YOUTH: I could actually, like, *imagine* how the characters would be.

INTERVIEWER: Uh-huh.

YOUTH: But I didn't really like connect it that they were actually real people.

INTERVIEWER: Okay, okay, okay.

As I look at this response carefully, I see at least two important things. First, I see that the painstaking process that *The Middle Place* director and actors had engaged in was evident in how the audiences experienced the play. Theirs had not been a process of imitation or mimicry. The actors, except for Kushnir and Cayonne, had never met nor seen the real people they were depicting. Their work as *creators of lives* was an interpretive process that placed great value on how one communicates, not simply on what one says. And this left open the possibility for interpretation by the audience—exactly what Dilworth and Kushnir desire and believe possible, as they clearly articulate in their following dialogue. Secondly, I see that for many young people a sense of "the real" has deeper and fuller implications than what is commonly understood. Mary Luckhurst offers that verbatim theatre, "like other documentary forms, is always stretched on the rack between a pursuit of 'facts'—a loaded word in its own right—and an engagement with artistic representation."[7] But what

---

7   Mary Luckhurst, "Verbatim Theatre, Media Relations and Ethics," in *A Concise Companion to Contemporary British and Irish Drama*, ed. Nadine Holdsworth and

I learned from the youth we interviewed is that there is a space, a critical space, between "fact" and "representation" that demands imagination. It is not that verbatim vacillates between the demands of so-called facts and those of aesthetic representation, as Luckhurst argues, but that the work, when carefully crafted and presented, invites an audience member to enter in and make an imaginative leap, as the youth above struggles to identify. It wasn't that he was imagining a "real" person, alongside the representation by the actor. He was rather imagining "real" people based on what the play communicated to him and the consequent alchemy produced by his own imagination encountering that representation. It was a different "real," not the original one, but one of his own making, interacting as it did with all that he ever knew or felt about what he was just now seeing. So-called "reality" and skilful aesthetic representation gave his imagination a challenge, and that is a delightful and qualitatively different experience from merely encountering "facts" or authentic representations.

Some wonderful extensions of this serendipitous first encounter I had with Kusnhir and Dilworth and Project: Humanity have occurred. First, I have been able to sustain my work with Kushnir, who has now completed a draft of a new verbatim play based on the data from my ethnographic research. This new work has received two workshop readings, one by students at the Centre for Drama, Theatre and Performance Studies at the University of Toronto and the other by professional actors, directed by Dilworth and produced by Project: Humanity. The second is that through a current research project on youth homelessness and socio-spatial inequality in Canadian cities, I have again been able to witness the slow, careful pedagogical work of Kushnir, Cayonne, Daniel Chapman-Smith, and Catherine Murray of Project: Humanity, as they have been inviting new groups of homeless youth living in a shelter to take risks and pleasures with them, engaging in drama and creating, however temporarily, a space of experimentation and ensemble.[8] Lastly, I have now begun a new research project in which Kushnir's profound understanding of verbatim theatre

---

Luckhurst (Malden, MA: Blackwell, 2008), 203.

8   Our work at the shelter is part of a seven-year, multidisciplinary Social Science and Humanities Research Council of Canada–funded national Partnership Grant called Neighbourhood Inequality, Diversity, and Change: Trends, Processes, Consequences, and Policy Options for Canada's Large Metropolitan Areas (2012–2019).

will be shared across sites in Toronto, Canada; Coventry, England; Tainan, Taiwan; Lucknow, India; and Athens, Greece.[9] I am looking forward to all that we will discover about the genre of verbatim, its various techniques, the sophistication of young people's engagement with the genre, and how such stories and representations may ignite the imaginations of audiences to come.

---

9 The new multi-sited, SSHRC-funded ethnography is titled Youth, Theatre, Radical Hope and the Ethical Imaginary: An Intercultural Investigation of Drama Pedagogy, Performance and Civic Engagement (2014–2018).

CREATIVE COLLABORATORS
Creator's Voice and Director's Voice

In 2014 playwright Andrew Kushnir and director Alan Dilworth had a conversation about the nature of verbatim theatre, the creation of *The Middle Place*, and the way that the artists tried to ethically engage with shelter youth populations to create the work. The conversation considers aesthetics, "real" life, and live theatre as art and as engagement. Together they discuss some of the challenges of bringing this type of work to the stage and the ways shelter youth reacted to seeing the finished product, emphasizing the importance of this printed script still operating as "an encounter." When approached about publishing *The Middle Place*, Kushnir explained how very important context is for this kind of work: in that moment, this conversation is the context that he wanted to offer.

ANDREW: British playwright David Hare and director Max Stafford-Clark once did an interview with one another for a publication: *Verbatim Verbatim*. I figured that a verbatim dialogue between me and you—writer and director—would serve as a fitting portal to a reading of *The Middle Place*—a script that I never imagined publishing.

ALAN: Why is that?

ANDREW: I suppose I've always felt the theatre of the piece—which is to say, what happens when we do the play for an audience—would be illegible or lost in translation.

ALAN: I'm not sure about that—

ANDREW: That's not to diminish the playwriting—

ALAN: Which was carefully done—

ANDREW: But I do think to understand *The Middle Place* as theatre—well I think the text and, ultimately, the voices of the play, are served by *context*. So—as a jumping-off point—can you give me your definition of verbatim theatre?

ALAN: Verbatim theatre is . . . okay, let me start with verbatim *text*. Verbatim *text* is non-dramatic text that is non-fictional . . . and edited and shaped on a theme . . . as part of a dramatic presentation.

ANDREW: And what is non-dramatic text?

ALAN: Text that has not been written expressly to fit into a dramatic structure. So the assumption is that with verbatim text, that text has been culled and edited in a way that is outside a playwright's usual process of generating words for a play.

ANDREW: The playwright hasn't generated the dialogue between characters. And so going back, what is verbatim theatre then?

ALAN: Verbatim theatre . . . is the live, moment-to-moment experience of verbatim text around a particular question or theme . . . and the images that come with that. And it's non-fiction in nature.

ANDREW: I like that. I typically describe our verbatim theatre aesthetic as a dramatic script constructed from original interview transcripts anchored by a theme or question, performed by actors on stage. But that fails to take into account where the theatre is happening—David Hare says theatre is what happens in the air between the art and the audience.

ALAN: Yes—theatre is the meaning being made by both artists and audience.

ANDREW: Now is verbatim theatre a technique or a form? You have some practitioners like Robin Soans who conduct interviews, take thorough notes, and then compose text based on those encounters. Then you have an artist like Alecky Blythe who will have her actors listen to and replicate her original interviews with every minute detail. I believe David Hare once quipped, "I write exactly what people say. Or what they meant to say."

ALAN: Do we call that verbat*ish* theatre?

ANDREW: I would hardly mind if David Hare was the one making me more eloquent.

ALAN: You love your David Hare. I think verbatim as technique implies that it's a means to an end. The priority for an artist using verbatim techniques is the shaping of a drama. So you change things to suit your dramatic needs. Whereas an artist engaging in verbatim as a form is giving priority to exactly what has been spoken.

ANDREW: So the trade-off with that, with treating verbatim as a form, is the playwright is trying to create a clear theatrical communication with pieces that are often imperfect, human, and even unclear communications.

ALAN: And I'd argue that this very human failure to find language—both for the originators of the verbatim text and the playwright working with it—reveals other information that is of great interest to the theatre. Arguably, every character in the theatre is in some way failing to express themselves perfectly. In verbatim theatre as form, this failure is front and centre. It's the foundation for extremely dynamic, idiosyncratic, and I will dare to say human embodiment and expression. Whereas with more shaped text, no matter how brilliant the playwright, we encounter more of the playwright's voice.

ANDREW: I think all playwrights employ verbatim theatre techniques. My more traditionally written plays are rife with things I've heard people say, stories told to me by friends and relatives, ideas that other thinkers or artists have inspired me with—playwrights are constantly pilfering from their lives and the world.

ALAN: Let's say borrowing.

ANDREW: But in verbatim theatre as a form, that borrowing is fully exposed.

ALAN: That's right, there's an inherent contextualizing around the text, which we don't often do in English-speaking Canada. We don't often contextualize around a piece of writing vis-à-vis the editing, the editorial vision that surrounds a playwright's process and work. Audiences are more often encountering narrative, as opposed to narrative and how that narrative came to be.

ANDREW: The verbatim playwright is hollering, "This comes from the real world, word for word, um for um, pause for pause." In my case, I met individuals in the real world, I recorded my encounter with them, I'm sharing parts of it with an audience. Interesting, I just caught myself saying *real* world, as though there's a real world and then a less-real one we visit through art. Is verbatim theatre more "real" than other forms?

ALAN: More "real"? It's interesting—these words come up around theatre—authenticity, realness, truth.

ANDREW: And I would get that from audience members emerging from *The Middle Place*, "That was so real." Or young people in particular saying, "That was just like me and my friends." Are they fixating on the language and text alone, or is there something more to this idea of authenticity, realness, truth?

ALAN: I think that, to a degree, when people speak to those terms, with regards to the live theatre experience, it's because some meaning has been made, both by performers and by audience. The audience has participated. Some small transformation has happened. Seems to me, the more meaningful the experience, the more authentic, real, and true. It's connecting with their lives beyond their short time in the theatre. And the theatre, by virtue of its being a place of metaphor, it makes it a very fecund place for meaning-making. Research has shown that metaphor plays an extremely important role in meaning-making for the human mind and that's no surprise—how we learn, how me move ahead, shape our minds is through metaphor.

ANDREW: It's interesting you bring up metaphor and theatre being the site of metaphor. I've said before that theatre is spending time with things, characters, conflicts that aren't actually there in order to have very real feelings about them. What happens when you take verbatim words spoken by residents of a youth shelter and place them into the site of metaphor? What makes it different than placing those words in a newspaper article or magazine article?

ALAN: The transcript in verbatim play has been chosen, edited, and compressed so that the most meaningful text is highlighted.

ANDREW: But arguably that happens in a newspaper article. A journalist does that.

ALAN: But a newspaper article is written to be read. Whereas the verbatim play is written to be spoken and heard. As with all plays, the written iteration is a conduit. What we discover with *The Middle Place* is that everyday language is at home in the theatre. It becomes the poetry of the theatre. In Greek tragedy, it's not until the third great tragedian that characters of lower classes really had something to say, strong voices. And this was a shocking thing. It's rare that protagonists themselves are commoners. With *The Middle Place* young people from a shelter are front and centre, their self-expression is front and centre. The play says, "These voices, as they are, are worth your time. They are worthy of your time just like the voices of politicians and pop stars and anyone else who tends to monopolize the airwaves."

ANDREW: And not just time, these young people are worth your empathy. And that makes them great subjects for drama. That's what I was confronted with in terms of the genesis of the piece, back in 2007. Project: Humanity had been going into Youth Without Shelter in Rexdale and they wanted me to write a play to be performed back at the shelter and potentially the community at large—something that was inspired by my interface with the youth. Prior to doing sessions at the shelter, I preconceived the residents as being both more fragile and tougher than your "average" young person. And what I encountered was something far more complex; I encountered young people, away from their parents, trying to figure out their way in the "adult" world. And that was something I could relate to. That's not to say their self-actualizing or identity-building was universal—like, "These kids are just like me!" or, "Guess what, we're all the same!"—because many of these youth are facing very complicated issues—but there were many commonalities that I had failed to anticipate.

ALAN: Is it fair to say you encountered yourself at the shelter?

ANDREW: Absolutely. My prejudices, my narratives, my own privilege. The play was eventually performed at an all-girl private school in Toronto and in the post-show discussion one student said, "Those residents sound like people I know," and then moments later another said, "This play made me realize that I won the birth lottery." I certainly understand the coexistence of those feelings when encountering the shelter youth.

ALAN: How did that factor into your decision to create a verbatim play rather than write something based on your experience?

ANDREW: Well, it was based on my experience, but I didn't create text to stand in for that experience.

ALAN: Right.

ANDREW: I knew that we'd be eventually sharing it with the youth. Maybe it was a lack of courage or maybe good intuition but I didn't want to write their voices. I wanted to fashion an encounter for the audience, one that would echo what had happened to me.

ALAN: Good intuition, I'm sure. I recall in the earliest drafts of the play, the interviewer questions were delivered by the four actors playing the youth. After you and I started discussing the work, you created the Outsider character.

ANDREW: And you decided that the actor playing the Outsider would sit behind the audience, leaving the other four actors playing the youth and caseworkers on stage.

ALAN: I think having the Outsider was really key to communicating that encounter of yours, and also to creating a more ethical piece. We need the context for these voices entering the theatre. And by doing that, we were able to give *those voices* the focus. Having the Outsider implicated the audience as people who were entering the young people's world. And in a sense, through the play, the youth were speaking to us in *our* world at the same time. It made a kind of sense.

ANDREW: Now I want to talk more about process, but you bring up ethics, which I think is important terrain to cover, with regards to verbatim theatre and *The Middle Place* in particular. One of the main ethical criticisms of the form surrounds appropriation of voice—which is a legitimate concern: that an artist can parachute into a community and run off with its stories and do anything with them. As a company developing this work, Project: Humanity has always tried to keep that in mind: how do we remain accountable to the shelter and, in the end, what do the shelter youth get out of their contribution?

ALAN: Of course. That was something PH was navigating from the outset. And by the time the play was meeting general audiences, you'd still be confronted by a few audience members asking things like, "Why weren't the youth on stage performing their own lives?"

ANDREW: That's right. That's a curious question. I think I understand where it's coming from. But I'm not sure it takes into account some of the realities these youth are facing—issues around identity and labels, privacy, transience. I mean . . . I gave all the youth pseudonyms because the vast majority didn't want to be personally identified and identifiable as a homeless youth. Many didn't think they'd be at the shelter for more than a few days or weeks—they didn't perceive it as a lasting identity. They perceived it as a temporary and generally unfortunate situation. I think this concept of the youth playing themselves is predicated on *The Middle Place* being a play that shelter youth would want to perform and be unambiguously associated with; that they would be interested in standing before a high school or general audience and revisiting their experiences, word for word. I think for the young person there could be some potential value, some empowerment in doing that. But it would require an extremely high comfort level with publicly representing oneself as a shelter youth and facing whatever audience response that elicits . . . compassion, pity, anxiety, potential judgment, potential indifference—.

ALAN: Could you ensure they'd be safe in that context?

ANDREW: Well, that would be the priority, right? I think if the objective had been to put shelter youth on stage—physically on stage—I would have created a very different play—one much more led by them and populated by whatever stories they felt like telling, not necessarily the ones that capture my experience as an outsider to that community. These are already vulnerable individuals; I wouldn't want to expose them to any further stress. And who knows? Maybe they would gravitate toward much of the same content, but I wouldn't presume that to be the case.

ALAN: It's a different objective, right?

ANDREW: I think so. My objective was to help destigmatize the shelter population and humanize audiences—shelter audiences included—to the lives and experiences of homeless youth. I wanted to create something that would signal the ways in which these lives are meaningful and deserving of our attention. With that in mind, I created a script where we witness four actors embody something like twenty character voices—we witness what it means to "take a walk in another person's words," as Anna Deavere Smith puts it. And that's fundamental to the piece. The action of the play is largely about making an empathetic leap, the kind I was inspired to make in the presence of these young people, and the multi-character work is a vital part of achieving that metaphor. To have shelter youth tell their own stories is a different action, a different experience.

ALAN: A whole other show.

ANDREW: Yes. There is absolutely a theatrical experience that can feature the performances of shelter youth, even a performance of their personal narratives. I just don't think *The Middle Place* is that piece.

ALAN: You said earlier you wanted to remain accountable to the shelter and you wanted to make sure there was a tangible return with this work, right?

ANDREW: Right—and by that I mean something that extends beyond the value of the play and reflecting a community back to itself. I think, for us, it boiled down to building a careful, long-term relationship with the shelter youth population, and to be ongoing stewards of that relationship. For PH and Youth Without Shelter, it had begun with our pro-bono drama programming—

ALAN: Which you're still doing.

ANDREW: That's right—we're still regularly in the shelter doing that work.

ALAN: I think that context is valuable—that you were part of the shelter ecology in some way. I think it accounts for the candour and generosity you experienced in your interviews.

ANDREW: And with the script development, I mean, I was in an ongoing dialogue with the shelter's executive director, with caseworkers, and with the youth themselves—some of whom were brought into our rehearsal process.

ALAN: We performed the piece at the shelter, in their cafeteria—

ANDREW: Which I think was the single most important day for *The Middle Place*. I was terrified, frankly. But the level of engagement with what we had created turned out to be so intricate and live and affirming. One of the youth, who tended to be standoffish in our drama programming and had sat through the show, baseball cap shading his eyes—when we asked him what he thought of the play, his only response was, "It shows we have emotions."

ALAN: The play has a capacity to humanize its viewer. I've often said it's a "reflecting pool" for its audience.

ANDREW: It's all to say there's been lots of connection between Project: Humanity and YWS, before, during, and after *The Middle Place*. With drama programming, with the show, with fundraisers we've developed and initiated for that community. That doesn't extinguish those ethical questions around voice and story but I think it speaks to how we were conscious in our work and actively negotiating them.

ALAN: Going back to process . . . the play is deliberately constructed from moments and encounters that shifted your thinking around this demographic and community. We decided that I and the actors would only encounter your encounters through the transcripts. So we never listened to your recordings. The impetus for that came from the fact that the youth had spoken to you with a promise of anonymity, and it felt right to honour that as much as possible. The fortunate consequence was that the company got to engage in the interpretation and encounter of the language as opposed to imitation. There was a practice that we had to develop, a building of layers that maybe wouldn't have happened had we end-gamed to replicas of the original voices.

ANDREW: What I found astounding, observing those first weeks of rehearsal, was how that creative work, the building of those layers with the text, vividly evoked the people I had met.

ALAN: It was about reading through different lenses, playing games, using exercises to develop layers of understanding and meaning around what's on the page. And what was so affirming is when we took the play back to the YWS cafeteria—we had done all this imaginative work, never having heard the original interview recordings—and more than one youth came up to the actors saying, "I know who that is! That was exactly my friend!"

ANDREW: I think we embed much of ourselves in our language. The way we use language. After the shelter showing, some youth even clocked physical choices that had been made by the actors, like, "Yeah, she always held her hands like that," which was eerie. It suggests that there may be physical information contained, encoded in exactly what we say and exactly how we say it.

ALAN: Language is a powerful thing. Language can be a physical thing, too. In the theatre, it is.

ANDREW: I think we mined the power of the language without putting things on top of it, without telling the audience how to feel about it. There was so much care put into not sanctifying or vilifying any of the subjects of *The Middle Place*. There was a good deal of recognition around the simplistic binaries we create, certain narratives, and we were adamant about living in the complexity of this community, its members, and their relationships. We wanted the audience to sit in that. And the concept of sentimentality was discussed a lot—which I think can be a big danger with this sort of material—and let's—how would you define sentimentality or—

ALAN: Sentimentalism? I think it's a hanging onto a feeling, a nostalgia or romanticism. There are stereotypes implied by a kind of sentimentalism and *The Middle Place* was really about relaxing those stereotypes, if not expressly dismantling them. I find the move beyond stereotypes makes for a ferocity in the work.

ANDREW: It brings to mind the idea of audience and this concept of Theatre for Young Audiences. Though I knew full well that *The Middle Place* would play at the shelter and that we would do a high-school tour, I wasn't considering the personhood of youth to be all that different than adults. By that I mean, differences around capacities for narratives or complexity.

ALAN: You didn't simplify the ideas or the contexts.

ANDREW: And same goes for your direction of the piece. In retrospect, I think the play was at times fatiguing to some adult audiences. Because participating in the work of the play—the engagement with ambiguities, a non-linear structure, a messy kind of language—was so different than what audiences were typically seeing in the theatre. I found young people were particularly into that.

ALAN: Maybe young people aren't typically being invited to those kinds of encounters. Maybe that's why many of them felt seen or felt like they were in a room with something more real, authentic, true to them.

ANDREW: I remember doing a talkback after one of the performances at Canadian Stage, it was a mixed audience with both adult patrons and about a hundred high-school youth. An adult patron made a comment to the effect of, "I had trouble listening to these homeless youth talk about their aspirations. They seemed deluded. How can they aspire to things like new clothes and laptops when they can't hold down a job or secure a place to live?" I responded by saying that I had included those moments in the play because I felt these so-called at-risk youth were managing to aspire *in spite* of their tough circumstances—that I took that as a hopeful thing, a mark of how resilient young people are, or even, how not unlike other young people these particular youth were. I'll never forget, one of the high-school youth in the front row of the audience blurted, "We're all allowed to dream." It really pointed up for me the dialectic around hope in the piece and the fact that the complexity of what we had created was going to elicit a range of responses.

ALAN: Now you said you feel some anxiety around the publishing of the play. Is that related to a legibility of that complexity?

ANDREW: I think that's part of it. The script is trying to keep from sanctifying characters like Nevaeh and vilifying characters like Kaaliyah—

ALAN: Or vilifying the audience.

ANDREW: Yes—that kind of, "We're gonna teach you something." That's not the intention, though I recognize it can be a danger of this work. So how should someone read the play?

ALAN: Very carefully.

ANDREW: And what's a careful read, in your opinion?

ALAN: I think it's about recognizing or keeping in mind that people choose their words, how they tell those stories. Their specific lives and specific experiences can predispose them to specific language. So there is information inferred, meanings to be discovered in what is there. If one was to read the play aloud, there's no need to "make it sound more real" or decorate it in any way. I'm not a fan of the approximation of language—I'm more interested in engaging in what's there. And I'm all for the danger of being boring in order to create connections and meanings with what's on the page. If a teacher were to use this text in a class, I'd challenge them to let students wrestle with what is being said, to encourage students to read the words simply in their own voices, and to discuss possibilities as opposed to rushing to conclusions. Listen out for what is implied. For actors, there's a whole bunch of metaphorical baggage that can kick into high gear, in terms of performance—often one begins to apply interpretive objectives before taking time to explore all the possibilities of what may be implied.

ANDREW: Sometimes actors can feel very naked with this kind of text.

ALAN: And the temptation is to paste a story on top of the story. But is that how you arrive at the meaning of something? Or is that rushing or assuming meaning? I think there's value in holding off on the actions and objectives of these characters—those interpretations are often based on the culture we live in, often the community we live in, the media we consume, the stereotypes and clichés—and, very quickly, we're in danger of imposing story onto the text that may not be the case. A youth shelter in Rexdale isn't another planet, its residents are certainly touched by many cultural forces you or I may encounter. But we shouldn't assume a sameness until we encounter it.

ANDREW: You and I like the word *undergo*, right? What does it mean to *undergo* the script? Making it personal doesn't mean changing the script or its rhythms to make it feel comfortable for you to wear. Making it personal means bringing yourself to it, developing a very close relationship to the existing rhythms on the page, being in dialogue with its exact ideas.

ALAN: It means meeting the script in a very open and honest way. It's not about nailing things down to a degree where you don't have to be present. Because when that happens, I begin to feel as an audience that I'm not really necessary, that I'm not participating in the meaning-making. Not only is it not inclusive—I feel like I'm being told something as opposed to being part of a moment-to-moment experience.

ANDREW: When the audience feels necessary, the experience can feel authentic, real, and true!

ALAN: It's also about letting go of emotion. One of my teachers at York University, Erika Batdorf, used to say, "Ideally emotions are to the actor what sweat is to the athlete. It comes off you. You don't catch athletes collecting and holding on to their sweat. Just let if drop off you, and you keep going, next moment, next moment, next moment."

ANDREW: It's about being present, right? In *The Middle Place*, we encounter a group that an audience doesn't typically have access to and so there's a real responsibility with that.

ALAN: It should be an encounter rather than a simulation of an encounter—and those are two very different things to me. And we can craft an encounter by taking the time as artists, as readers, as active listeners. It's what you did in the shelter; it's what allowed you to write this powerful play.

CREATIVE JOURNEY

In the late summer/early fall of 2007, Project: Humanity (PH) started its drama programming at Youth Without Shelter (YWS). Located in one of the Greater Toronto Area's so-called "priority neighbourhoods" (the Jamestown area, Rexdale), YWS is an emergency shelter that serves homeless youth ages sixteen to twenty-five. Project: Humanity's program, which primarily consists of drama games, improvs, and moderated debates, is designed to bolster the confidence, creative expression, and communication skills of youth participants. It also aims to provide youth with much-needed decompression from their often stressful day-to-day reality.

Over a three-month span, playwright Andrew Kushnir conducted voluntary interviews with youth attending the program. Interviews were videotaped for transcribing purposes but youth could choose to have the camera lens pointed at themselves, at Andrew, or at the wall (to capture audio only). Youth were promised anonymity through a signed release, could choose their own pseudonyms, and were given full licence to pass on any questions as well as redact any comments after the fact. In this first phase in the shelter, Andrew encountered Kaaliyah, Aidan, Brussel Sprouts, and caseworker Dee.

In March 2008 a thirty-minute version of *The Middle Place* was presented at a PH fundraising event, Leaping Out.

In the summer of 2008 PH did a second stretch of drama programming at YWS, where Andrew interviewed more youth and encountered Nevaeh, Romeo, and Barbara. By then Andrew had conducted over forty interviews, which amounted to over four hundred pages of transcribed text.

From these Andrew crafted a full-length version of the play, and while his formal interview process had been completed, PH continued the drama programming at YWS. His editing process involved close attention to what he called interview "punctures"—moments in his encounters that left a lasting mark on him well after the interview was done. He also kept track of "arias"—moments when a person opened up about something they felt passionately about. These "punctures" and "arias" suggested content in service of an emotional narrative. In the case of *The Middle Place*, it became the emotional narrative of an outsider encountering for the first time a community he knew little to nothing about.

In July of 2009 *The Middle Place* started rehearsals for a first outing at the SummerWorks Theatre Festival. Over the course of this process, led by director Alan Dilworth, both caseworkers and shelter youth were invited into the rehearsal hall to watch the company's process/progress and to provide feedback. Their presence anchored the development of the writing, the aesthetic of the production, and reinforced for all involved the origins of this material.

On August 6 the play met its first audience to overwhelmingly positive critical response. On opening night several shelter youth attended, including Nevaeh.

On August 14 the play was performed at Youth Without Shelter. Thirty youth (including Romeo), caseworkers, and shelter administrative staff attended and afterwards discussed their experience of the play with Alan, Andrew, the actors, and PH's core members.

In the fall of 2009 the play went on a tour of twenty-one high schools in the Toronto District School Board (produced by PH). The show also played at numerous youth and women's shelters in the GTA.

In the 2010/2011 season, a reworked *The Middle Place* had two full-length runs in Toronto—one at the Theatre Passe Muraille Mainspace and another at Canadian Stage's Berkeley Street Theatre. The same acting company and design team carried forward from the original SummerWorks production, except Andrew took over the role of the Outsider. PH developed an "orbit" around the production entitled the Urban Youth Experience, involving a photo exhibit that captured YWS as a building, artwork created by shelter youth, playlists of songs curated by shelter youth, as well as the opportunity to do an exit interview after the show with Dr. Kathleen Gallagher and her team from the Ontario Institute for Studies in Education.

In a further effort to give back to shelter youth, in February of 2011 PH helped design Tokens4Change, a fundraiser for YWS where high school youth took over Toronto's transit system with their "artivism" (art + activism) and canvassed for TTC tokens and donations.

In March of 2011 *The Middle Place* embarked on a national tour to the Belfry Theatre, Victoria, and the Great Canadian Theatre Company, Ottawa. In Toronto (at Theatre Passe Muraille) as well as in Victoria and Ottawa, benefit performances were held in order to raise funds for local shelters.

The Toronto Arts Council, Canada Council for the Arts, and Ontario Arts Council were ongoing supporters of *The Middle Place*—in its development, production, and touring.

The Middle Place was first produced by Project: Humanity as part of the 2009 SummerWorks Theatre Festival. It featured the following cast and creative company:

Actor 1: Kevin Walker
Actor 2: Antonio Cayonne
Actress 1: Jessica Greenberg
Actress 2: Akosua Amo-Adem
The Outsider: Paul Dunn

Director: Alan Dilworth
Stage manager: Andrea Schurman
Set and costume design: Jung-Hye Kim
Lighting design: Kimberly Purtell
Sound design: Thomas Ryder Payne
Choreography: Monica Dottor
Assistant director: Susan Stover

The Middle Place garnered two SummerWorks Jury Prizes (for direction and for Akosua Amo-Adem's performance). In the *NOW Magazine* 2009 SummerWorks Festival Wrap-Up, the play was named in categories for outstanding production, outstanding ensemble, outstanding direction, and outstanding design.

The play was remounted in 2010/2011 in a co-production between Theatre Passe Muraille, Canadian Stage, and Project: Humanity. This co-production garnered the 2011 Toronto Theatre Critics' Award for Best Production of a Play as well as a Dora Mavor Moore Award nomination for Outstanding New Play for Andrew's script—to PH's knowledge, the first time a verbatim play has been nominated for the award.

NOTES ON THE TEXT

1. The words of the play come from interviews conducted by playwright Andrew Kushnir at YWS youth shelter in Rexdale, Ontario, between 2007 and 2009. All the scenes but one have been pulled verbatim from carefully rendered transcripts of recorded interviews with shelter residents and caseworkers. The scenes between Kaaliyah, Raeni, and the Outsider have been rendered from detailed notes taken by the playwright during the interview.

2. *The Middle Place* is written for four performers playing multiple roles and one performer playing the Outsider. The playwright's assignment of characters between the four actors playing multiple roles is deliberate.

3. The names have been changed to protect the privacy of the shelter residents and caseworkers originally interviewed for this documentary play. The names of the artists involved have not been changed.

4. Punctuation: A slash (/) is used to mark the start of the next speaker's line (most often before the initial speaker is done speaking). It makes for overlap and a desired cacophony. Other punctuation such as commas, dashes, and ellipses are at times used non-grammatically to best capture the rhythm of the original speaker.

NOTES ON PROJECT: HUMANITY'S ORIGINAL PRODUCTION, DIRECTED BY ALAN DILWORTH

1. Design: The set design consisted of a large white oval in the middle of the stage—the "middle place." When an actor was playing a shelter resident, they remained in the oval. When an actor was playing a caseworker, they would move freely outside the oval but still on stage. The Outsider character never stepped into the oval or onto the stage (until the curtain call).

2. Sound: Whenever a caseworker emerged or entered the oval they would raise their hand (as though waving) and a buzzer sound would go off. This signalled passage in and out of the middle place. This concept was to evoke the security doors at the shelter. A warm, institutional-sounding white noise was played under the opening and closing scenes of the play. This noise would be again heard in some internal transitions.

3. Movement: For the four actors playing residents and caseworkers, two movements were used to transition between characters: a) a drop and rebound of the head and shoulders or b) a spin.

4. Costume: All costumes were of a grey or black palate to contrast with the white oval and black void around it.

5. Approach: The director ultimately decided that he and the actors should not watch the original interview tapes—not only to maximize the anonymity of the subjects but to make the piece an interpretation of a community rather than an imitation of one. The crafting of character by the actors and director was carefully supervised by the playwright.

CHARACTERS

Characters are youth shelter residents unless otherwise noted.

Actor 1
Aidan
Queenie: a caseworker
Scott
Mike
Neill
Jamal
Tyler

Actor 2
Ama: a caseworker
Travis
Malik
Paul
Romeo

Actress 1
Monica: a caseworker
Nevaeh
Dustin
Toya
Raeni
Barbara

Actress 2
Dee: a caseworker
Kaaliyah

The Outsider: a playwright

PROLOGUE

Four actors on stage. The OUTSIDER *enters the auditorium, surveys the foursome and the audience. With his first line,* DEE, *a caseworker, steps forward. With this shift we hear a warm, institutional white noise. Not unlike the sound of air coming through a vent. Or low-volume static on a television.*

OUTSIDER: All right we're in business.

DEE: Can I look at you?

OUTSIDER: Yah look at me. You can just ignore the camera.

DEE: Yah, right?

OUTSIDER: It's interesting, some youth we've interviewed want me to turn this screen around, so they can / watch themselves—

DEE: So they can see themselves? Oh no, I don't want to see that.

OUTSIDER: I wonder what that is?

DEE: *(eyes wandering)* I don't know.

OUTSIDER: I think it's that sort of feeling of being um . . . I mean I guess it's interesting to watch yourself.

DEE: I guess, I'd rather not.

OUTSIDER: Yup.

DEE: So I'm good with that.

DEE smiles and laughs.

OUTSIDER: Okay. Um, first name?

DEE: People call me Dee.

OUTSIDER: And how long have you been here?

DEE: Uh, almost six years. Five . . . a little over five and a half.

OUTSIDER: And tell me about this place?

DEE: Um. We're the only shelter in Etobicoke, we get like, it's almost like a certain clientele.

OUTSIDER: Yah.

DEE: Um, we get kids, a lot of these kids here, their family lives around the corner. They've grown up here, they would—if they can't get in here, they're sleeping under the bridge. Cuz they refuse to go to another shelter.

OUTSIDER: Yah.

DEE: I feel they're comfortable here and they, it it's a beautiful building, I mean we newly renovated so we have a nice building, um, you know so, once they actually come in, they can kinda—and we try not to take that authoritative approach if we don't have to, so if we kind of put ourselves at the same level as them, then I don't think they're as threatened by us being *(air quotes)* authority or staff, right?

OUTSIDER: Yah.

DEE: There's some that I guess would never come out of that, you know if they've been in a position their whole life having, you know, an abusive parent who's emotionally put them down, it's hard to break that just from coming here and trying to build a relationship—

OUTSIDER: Yah.

DEE: Um, but sometimes it works, / yah.

MONICA, a caseworker, emerges.

MONICA: Everyone is everywhere . . . it's bizarre.

OUTSIDER: Like, psychologically?

MONICA: I don't know . . . it's weird, it's one of those things like you can't peg it. Like, they're not listening, uh, we're constantly redirecting them—today—everybody's everywhere. And it's Tuesday.

OUTSIDER: Do you—do you get like . . .

MONICA: Um, there's periods where we go through this. This is a really difficult house.

OUTSIDER: Right now.

MONICA: Yah. In—in regards to, behaviour.

OUTSIDER: What is—what sets it apart from—a more normal house? What is a more normal house?

MONICA: Quote, unquote? *(air quotes)*

OUTSIDER: Yep.

MONICA: Um, I don't think there is a normal house. To be honest with you. So I guess it depends on how you . . . define normal.

AMA, a caseworker, emerges.

AMA: How old are you?

MONICA: You'd be surprised some of these kids—and I don't want to say kids, but some of these youth don't know ABCDE / FG.

AMA: Is this your first time in a shelter?

DEE: I mean, you think that they all *can* get jobs, but don't want to, you know, that they're / lazy.

MONICA: Don't know how to do any of the basic life / skills.

AMA: What brings you to this shelter? Where were you before you came to the shelter? And, do you have contact with / your parents?

DEE: *(nods)* Yah, my parents worry about me doing this line of work. Especially here. The area too, that's . . .

AMA: Can you go back?

OUTSIDER: Is this a rough area?

DEE: Very. Yup. I think 2006, highest um, homicide rate in the GTA.

OUTSIDER: Okay.

DEE: Um, we had a co-worker, I think this was years ago, uh left here walked down the street and there was a man shot dead on the corner. / Very bad area. *(shrugs)* . . . Call police if we need to. Police are here quite often, so.

MONICA: They want to be everywhere. Right? So I want a job yesterday, and I don't need my resumé, and what about the ID and you know it's . . . and Andrew there's days you come out of here and you're like OH—MY—GOD *(laughing)*. Like what did I do today?! Like / someone help me!

AMA: Are you in school? Do you have any legal issues? Do / you have any medical history that we need to know about? Um, are you on medication—are you *taking* medication?

DEE: They're young. They're sixteen, they're seventeen, up to twenty-four. Why wouldn't you wanna live in a house with twenty-nine other people your same age? If I was a youth and I was in the unfortunate situation of being / homeless—

While the voices overlap, Actor 1, as AIDAN (a resident), stares down the OUTSIDER.

AMA: Give us something to work / with.

Beat.

We can't force them to like, if they don't want to go in details with it, they, they don't have to, and we tell them that. But it's just, they have to—give us something to work with.

DEE: —but I mean, a lot of the times when I tell people I work / at a youth shelter, they're like oh, "They have those?"

MONICA: They go, "Where do you work?" "At a shelter." "Wow! Why do you do that?"

Beat.

And I think like, I don't know. Why do I do it? It's just something I do.

DEE: And I'll admit it, like before I started working here I had my own judgments about homeless people, right? I just thought like, what do you mean, go get a job and get your own place, right?

OUTSIDER: Yah.

DEE: *(nodding)* Yah.

MONICA: Yah.

AMA: Yah.

A shift. The caseworkers go. The white noise slowly fades away as NEVAEH speaks.

ACT 1—IDENTITY

NEVAEH: Are the questions very hard?

OUTSIDER: They're not hard. And the rule is always if there's a question that you don't want to answer, you just say, I don't want to answer that and we move on to the next question. There's no, uh, I—I'm not gonna ask any scary *(laughing)*, don't worry.

NEVAEH: Yah *(smiling)* cuz I told, um, I told Antonio that I wanted to like, prepare for it, he's like what d'you mean prepare for it? How can you prepare if you don't even know the questions, so I was like all right whatever.

OUTSIDER: I know, it's just—it's really just about getting to know the residents, so there's nothing you can prepare cuz you're—it's your life, right? I mean it's a . . .

NEVAEH: True. It's your sad story. *(giggle)*

OUTSIDER: Well, or—

NEVAEH: Until you hear somebody else's.

OUTSIDER: Yah, yah.

NEVAEH: *(nodding)* Yah.

    Beat.

OUTSIDER: So, um, first off, if we were to give you a name in the play, that you could pick right now, cuz we take what you say and repeat it, but the names we change . . . could you pick a name?

NEVAEH: *(scrunches face)* Nevaeh?

OUTSIDER: What's that?

NEVAEH: Nevaeh?

OUTSIDER: Nevaeh?

NEVAEH: Yah, it's spelled heaven backwards *(big goofy smile)*.

    Actor 2 as PAUL *starts to pop and lock in the background.*

SCOTT: You guys getting paid to do this?

OUTSIDER: No.

SCOTT: Oh.

    Beat.

So why are you doing this?

OUTSIDER: Um.

SCOTT: If you put us in a play, no one watching would / believe it.

KAALIYAH: Sorry, I wasn't listening. *Why* you here?

MIKE: Hey, Negative! Simple: They wanna spend time with us, see what it's really like here and write a play about it.

OUTSIDER: Hear your stories.

KAALIYAH: *Stories?* Like, okay, like *shelter stories?*

She chuckles, shakes head.

You might as well make 'em up. The things that go on, okay, the amount of drama that goes on in here, no one would believe a word if you told it.

MONICA: It'd be fun for you guys to be here at eight thirty in the morning and just for an hour stay till nine thirty. Just sit back, chill out, and watch what goes on. You would die. It's like high-intense traffic in that one hour. It's like a play in itself.

KAALIYAH: *(to the OUTSIDER)* Know what, I don't trust you. You keep touching your face.

OUTSIDER: D'you have a nickname?

KAALIYAH shakes her head.

Have you ever had a nickname?

KAALIYAH shakes her head. Beat.

KAALIYAH: Fat Cow.

She laughs. Suddenly straight-faced.

Seriously. *(laughs)*

OUTSIDER: That's so rude.

KAALIYAH: I know. *(laughs)*

OUTSIDER: Uh. Kaaliyah or Kaali.

KAALIYAH: Everyone calls me Freezie.

OUTSIDER: Freezie. Why?

KAALIYAH: *(shrugs, mumbles)* I'm cold and I'm sweet.

OUTSIDER: *(clarifying)* Cuz you're cold and sweet?

KAALIYAH: *(harshly)* Yah.

> *AMA and QUEENIE, caseworkers, emerge.*

AMA: A lot of the people that—a lot of residents that live here, don't want anyone else to know they live here, right? So employers, um they don't want them to know what we are . . . if friends pick them up, they get them to pick them up down the street, like a lot of them are embarrassed, I guess to be living here.

QUEENIE: Some are. Some are and some don't care.

OUTSIDER: The ones that are ashamed, how do they . . . I mean, how do they work around that?

QUEENIE: Um, I don't know. I guess just continuing their routine, so if they're going to school or going to work, like just continue with it and I think those are the ones that you'll realize—like you'll notice that they're the ones that are trying to get out.

OUTSIDER: Hmm. The ones that haven't told their friends?

QUEENIE: Yah.

> *Shift. The caseworkers go. KAALIYAH and RAENI laugh wickedly.*

OUTSIDER: How did you two meet?

KAALIYAH: Who? Her?

OUTSIDER: Did you meet here?

KAALIYAH: In this very room.

RAENI: *(laughing)* No. We met over a ting.

KAALIYAH: Right.

They laugh.

RAENI: "Burn dat ting."

KAALIYAH: "Burn dat ting." *(suddenly straight-faced)* Yah, we met here.

RAENI: Yo, I was sitting right where he's sitting. You, over here wit dat girl.

KAALIYAH: *(mimicking)* Dat girl. Cracker, you came in here all, *(does a pout)* "I don't belong in a shelter," sat right there, thuggin' it / out.

RAENI: I was not.

KAALIYAH: Yah, thuggin' it out. On your cellphone. Talking on your cellphone like you had minutes.

RAENI: *(laughing)* I had minutes!

KAALIYAH: Her screen's blank, ain't nobody there, she's sitting there all tough on her phone talking to nobody.

RAENI: Yo, I had minutes / back then.

KAALIYAH: *Two* minutes. Sixty *seconds.*

OUTSIDER: *(to KAALIYAH)* And you were talking to some girl?

RAENI: *(laughing)* Talking! Dat girl. You were regulatin' on her like!

KAALIYAH: And this one sitting there on her cellphone with her minutes and her head starts going like this *(She pushes her chin into her neck and jolts like she's choking from laughter.)* like she having a seizure or something and I'm thinking this is serious, I'm ready to call Mark, this girl is in *trouble,* all *(does the head jolting again).*

RAENI laughs, out of control. KAALIYAH laughs with her, at her.

OUTSIDER: Sorry. What's. While you were doing what to that other girl? What's regulating?

KAALIYAH: Regulatin'. Regulatin' is like . . . okay, so you /

RAENI: Like cussin' out.

KAALIYAH: It's like, okay, if you have haggy breath, I'm gonna say something. Sh', know what I mean. It's in my nature to say something. You have a stupid haircut—

OUTSIDER: Calling people on their shit.

KAALIYAH: *(nods)* One hundred percent.

OUTSIDER: And you regulate on someone, or just regulate?

KAALIYAH: Regulate on, regulate.

OUTSIDER: And so why were you on this girl?

KAALIYAH: *(to RAENI)* Whoa, now I'm *on* the girl.

RAENI: *(laughing)* Dis girl /

KAALIYAH: Let's just say, if this girl were here she'd be flirting with you and *you* like it was nobody's business, flirting on you like it was her only business an' her business alone, especially you, and I mean, whatever . . . she had a pretty good body.

RAENI: She was a pretty girl.

KAALIYAH: She was a *decent*-looking girl.

Short beat.

But she had the *worst* kind of breath.

OUTSIDER: Haggy breath?

KAALIYAH: Saggy breath. We're talking skunk on doo-doo and then some more skunk on top of that, topped with more doo-doo.

OUTSIDER: Left in the sun.

KAALIYAH: *Seasoned by* the sun.

Beat.

And then water touched it.

All laugh.

OUTSIDER: And so you were terrorizing her /

KAALIYAH: No.

OUTSIDER: And she just sat there and took it, or?

KAALIYAH: No, she had her own lip.

OUTSIDER: She held her own?

KAALIYAH: Yah, she held it. But you know, okay, I won't have it, I don't have time for it. You wanna get into it with me? You wanna grab a shovel, get into it with me? Really?!

RAENI: You get Kaaliyah cussin' on you, you're asking for a funeral.

KAALIYAH: People walking in here, "Why are you fat?"

KAALIYAH shakes head, kisses her teeth, shocked.

Why are you homeless?!

RAENI: When Kaaliyah gets cussin' she draws a crowd.

KAALIYAH: We drove that girl out. Drove her out of Horizons, drove her out of this place. The girl was homeless, then she was home-homeless, you know what I mean. You know you're in a shelter, you're homeless, right.

You kicked out of the shelter, you're home-homeless. That girl home-home-less. No place left.

Beat.

RAENI: 'Cept Covenant House, maybe.

The girls laugh wickedly. RAENI whispers something in KAALIYAH's ear. They look at the OUTSIDER. They laugh. There is a shift. And then, roll call:

OUTSIDER: Peewee, how long have you been at this shelter?

TOYA: Three days? Four days? Since Saturday. So three days?

OUTSIDER: Richie Boy?

TRAVIS: Three weeks, month. I used to be on the other side. Got arrested.

OUTSIDER: Brussel Sprouts?

DUSTIN: Two weeks.

OUTSIDER: Mike?

MIKE: Like over a year. *(big eyes)*

OUTSIDER: Aidan?

AIDAN: Four years, on and off.

OUTSIDER: Malik?

MALIK: For like, three months now.

OUTSIDER: Barbara?

BARBARA: Yah it's Barbra Streisand to be exact *(giggles)*. Two weeks maybe, three months the first time.

OUTSIDER: Kaali?

KAALIYAH: Five months.

OUTSIDER: On and off or five months straight?

KAALIYAH: *(shakes head)* Five months straight.

OUTSIDER: Those pyjamas?

KAALIYAH: *(nods)* One hundred percent.

Actor 2, PAUL, has been upstage, gently popping and locking to his own reflection.

OUTSIDER: Paul?

PAUL is in his own world.

Paul?

PAUL stops, looks over his shoulder. Beat. Then goes back to popping.

TOYA: It's like hanging out with your friends on a weekend, you know, getting together for a weekend with / friends.

MALIK: We got cable TV and all that. And plus you have a bed to sleep on. You know . . . some roof over, / you know.

KAALIYAH: Like especially if you come here, like especially if you come here in the summertime, it's more like you feel like it's a summer camp.

OUTSIDER: And in general do you find it hospitable here? Or . . .

BARBARA: *(smiling)* Hold on! What does that mean? Hold on. *(laughing)*

AIDAN: I have to walk in two different doors—

OUTSIDER: *(chuckle)* Uh, do you find it comfortable? Are you comfortable here?

AIDAN: It's not your home. And you wake up knowing that.

BARBARA: In a sense it feels like jail, in a sense.

OUTSIDER: Bed's comfortable?

MALIK: Fff *(hell no)*. Sort of. Yah. *(kisses teeth)* Not so comfortable, though.

KAALIYAH: You come, you do whatever you wanna do, you still have your chores and things but you're new to it so it doesn't phase / you—

MALIK: Like wintertime is coming now, right, and it's getting a little chilly up in the / room, right.

KAALIYAH: But when like summer's done, cuz summer usually represents fun, when summer's done and September comes and school's here . . .

MALIK: I don't know if the heater works or not.

KAALIYAH: *(wide-eyed)* And *you're* still here.

BARBARA: I'm not comfortable. *(gestures)* I don't even know / . . . what's the word I can use for it.

MALIK: We'll soon find out.

KAALIYAH: This is not my place this is not my home this is not my bed. This is . . .

TRAVIS: I feel like this is the place.

KAALIYAH: . . . not my *walls*.

TRAVIS: I find this place the most cleanest, most supportive shelter I've ever been in.

NEILL: I'm here because there's a lot of black people here!

Beat.

I feel comfortable, like, *(looks over shoulder)*. Yah an' I, fff—see that black people treat me kinda different—other people wanna *label* me. It feel more like home an' I don't know, like . . . The the way I act it's jus', it's jus', this problem I have, it's jus', it's jus' something I can't control. Other people might see it as that but jus' for some reason wanna put a label on me man. But but when I'm around *black* people, they don't try to put no label on me. They see that it's a problem *(points finger)*. It's something I'm fighting, I guess. I hope that's all they see. Cuz that's what it is.

Beat. Then a shift.

OUTSIDER: Out of curiosity, what's the food like here?

NEVAEH: *(smiles)* Oh no.

OUTSIDER: Does it vary day to day?

NEVAEH: *(giggle)* Staff really hates me when I start talking about this topic.

OUTSIDER: Oh really?

NEVAEH: Yah, I almost got discharged.

OUTSIDER: Why? Because you said something about the food?

NEVAEH: Yah. *(shivers)* I'm not saying I said a nice comment, but um, I think I went on for two days. Yah. Like non-stop.

OUTSIDER: Do you remember what dish it was that set you off?

NEVAEH: Well, to be honest, every day something sets me off. *(laughs)* Unless it's tacos.

OUTSIDER laughs.

(shivers) But um, no, today they had fish and rice, like who eats that? Like, I don't know fish and rice. *(wince)*

OUTSIDER: What would be your dream meal? If they—if they said Nevaeh, today you get to decide the menu.

NEVAEH: Um, I'll tell them if I can cook.

OUTSIDER: And what would you make?

NEVAEH: I'll make lasagna. *(smile)*

OUTSIDER: Right.

Beat.

Can you describe your shelter room to me?

NEVAEH: Um, well in one corner it's like I told you that huge monkey from Wonderland which really cost a hundred dollars but, I won it for like fifteen. *(laugh)* My—my ex-boyfriend won it for me. So, *(shivers)* I had like another snake, a big one too and then a little, little other toys. And, I don't know, like there's a box beside my bed which is like *(shivers)* full of clothes and on the locker there's like more toys and there's like this huge poster like a collage that I did about myself. And—

OUTSIDER: A collage?

NEVAEH: Yah. And—

OUTSIDER: Sorry, is that vent bothering you, we can switch spots if you want, if that cold air . . .

NEVAEH: No, no, I'm fine.

OUTSIDER: Cuz I don't want your cold to get worse.

NEVAEH: No, / no.

OUTSIDER: Better not get me sick.

NEVAEH: No.

Beat.

It's not that kind of sick.

NEVAEH looks at the OUTSIDER briefly, then goes. KAALIYAH bursts in.

ACT 2—RELATIONSHIPS

KAALIYAH: This place is like, when you first come here, it's like okay, bringing drama, but when you like *really* really stay here, like drama *every day*.

ROMEO: It's the drama-drama-drama, that's what you find mostly in here. Like it's either, you're not dressin' a certain way, or you're dressin' a way you shouldn't be dressin'—you're rocking this colour from that colour. Or, you're in love with this girl, but this girl has this kind of boyfriend, you know what I mean?

MONICA: Let me tell you something Andrew *(reaching for him)*, I have always said this and I've been here for ten years. If it's a guy house? We have no problems. And I'm a woman. You put girls into this place? And that's where it starts.

QUEENIE: Yah. Um, it's weird. Girls don't get along with each other for long.

DEE: I don't know, I think it's difficult too because not many people at that age, were living in a house with twenty-nine other people their age. So put anyone in that situation, I would assume, you would have, an accelerated amount of drama as you would anywhere else, right?

QUEENIE: I think more girls and girls.

OUTSIDER: Mm-hm.

DEE: Um, and it's just, oh, you know, especially when there's couples, "Oh my boyfriend, your boyfriend," like, and some guys who're here have dated, more than one person—it's—they're—I couldn't even—there's so much going on here.

The caseworkers have gone.

OUTSIDER: What would be the ideal, like what are you looking for, like what would be . . . what would be a good date?

Beat. MALIK scrunches his face.

MALIK: A good date? It's, I don't know, everything goes nice, no argument, no nothing whatsoever, an' the next date is the same thing, and the next date is the same thing again, just have a nice conversation, laugh, you know, share the same feelings or like, basically, yah. Pretty much.

Long beat.

And not get *jealous*. Over little things, cuz I actually met this one girl, she actually got jealous over everything. She even get jealous me talking to the next girl. Like, you know, and we just talking, you know, just having a conversation, and then she thinks it's nice for her talk to the next guy to make *me* jealous. I'm like, I'm like come on, you know. And I'm like and she fully wanted me to come live with her, right. I didn't like, even like, I stayed with her for like two days and like fff. *(kisses teeth)* And she already losin' it an' I'm like, "Whoa, god." You know. Like. So I just like, I don't like stupid games like that, you know.

OUTSIDER: Yah.

MALIK: *(laughs)* Somethin' like that. *(quick shift)* Let's just close that topic.

OUTSIDER: Yah yah, totally.

TYLER: Being around people and not knowing who they are and what they do, or . . . you're walking into someone else's house pretty much.

OUTSIDER: Yah.

BARBARA: I know plenty of, like, youth in here that have mentalities of children /

TYLER: Into twenty other people's house /

BARBARA: And they just need that affection, they need that help. Do you know what I mean?

KAALIYAH: And then somehow your name just magically comes up into that drama and there'll be problems at your door.

MALIK: But y'know, I haven't met the right girl yet.

AIDAN and the OUTSIDER alone.

OUTSIDER: Aidan, can I ask how you and your girlfriend met?

AIDAN: Uh, through a shelter, actually.

OUTSIDER: Can you—is there a story behind that, or . . .

AIDAN: Um, *(shrug)* not really.

OUTSIDER: *(laugh)* You met at a shelter . . .

AIDAN: Yah.

OUTSIDER: Um . . .

Beat.

AIDAN: I walked in—it was Horizons, I was there I think six-and-a-half, seven-and-a-half months ago, I walked in and I was just pissed at everybody. And out of everybody in that shelter, she seemed to be the only face that lit up to me, so I walked over and then we just clicked from there.

OUTSIDER: Um, were you able to share your stories and sort of—

AIDAN: Yah.

Beat.

OUTSIDER: —um . . .

AIDAN: Like kind of—it felt like, to tell you the truth, we kind of connected right off the hop and, that's pretty much how it happened and we've been going ever since. Like don't get me wrong, it's not lovey-dovey all the time, we fight like an old married couple and we've only been together six months, but when it all comes down to it, she's the only girl I want to spend the rest of my life with, and I'm gonna be willing to do anything to make it that way.

OUTSIDER: Cool. Um—

AIDAN: And it's weird, cuz like you don't hear very many people—like if my kids ask me, I don't know what I'm gonna tell them, I met her in a shelter.

MALIK: I like somebody that's real to me, you know what I'm sayin'.

TOYA: Actually, it's funny, Paul, you know, the tall guy at the computers. I came here and thought, "I know that guy." Well I went to school with him and I came in here Saturday and I haven't seen him in like years, since like school, right. Which is funny, cuz I had a crush on him back in school, and now I see him and it's like . . . he's Paul.

KAALIYAH: *(on a tear)* And it's like, "Why you wanna fight me? I never said this or I never said that. Or I never did this. Or I never took your stuff," and it's, it's just trouble for trouble sake. Just to like prove that they're the bigger person. /

NEILL: Bigger or smaller, I'll get at you.

KAALIYAH: Like they wear the bigger drawers in the house, not knowing that *I* wear the bigger drawers, *physically*, in the house.

OUTSIDER: Sorry, I just noticed your tattoo.

MIKE: Death / Before Dishonour.

OUTSIDER: What does it say? Death Before Dishonour? Why did you pick that saying?

MIKE: I was young. And I . . .

OUTSIDER: Do you believe it?

MIKE: I used to.

KAALIYAH: *Actually—*

NEILL: They're not mental problems like I have to be in an institute, but like mental problem cuz it's not part of the norm, okay.

KAALIYAH: Someone will be standing there with this look on their face *(grimaces)*. And they'll turn on you and say, "What are *you* looking at?" And I just want to say, "Why are you twisting your face like a donkey? Where else am I supposed to look when you do that?" Y'know what I mean?

MIKE: *(about his tattoo)* It's all messed up. Actually I got, uh, I got arrested the day I got this done. So, that's like, all these white spots are places where like, scabs got ripped off.

TOYA: That guy in Malton who was shot a couple of weeks ago, he got shot cuz he gave some guy the finger.

OUTSIDER: That's all it takes?

TOYA: Yah, you disrespec' somebody and that's it. Not even. Somebody *says* that you disrespected them and you can get shot.

OUTSIDER: That's insane.

TOYA: Yah.

KAALIYAH: And they get all, "I'm gonna make a call, I'm gonna make a call." What I want to know is, okay, why can't anyone fight their own fights anymore? Hm? What ever happen to a fair fight? Nowadays, you know, you piss someone off and they don't fight back anymore, it's, "I'm going to tell my brother about this and he's gonna this and that," or, "When my cousin hears about this, you're dead." What's with everyone getting their *grandmothers* to fight / me?

OUTSIDER: Wow, Kaali.

KAALIYAH: I don't want to fight your grandmother!

Beat.

I mean, I will if I have to, don't get me wrong, I will beat on your grandmother to the curb, but come on, fight your fight.

Beat.

ROMEO: Like, anybody here they would pretty much ride or die for anybody here because we all have that one thing in common, we all have that troubled past, we all, like, my baby mother, I met her here. And the only way we clicked was because our past was exactly the same.

The residents turn their backs on the OUTSIDER. NEVAEH *appears in the vacuum created. Silence, then:*

NEVAEH: Well, my boyfriend is working right now, so we're getting our own place, hopefully soon *(giggle)*. Um, I don't work and I know that I told you I was sick, um, okay, I don't even know how to say it. I'm pregnant, that's why.

Beat.

OUTSIDER: Oh wow.

NEVAEH: But it's not, that's why when you were like, "Oh, better not get me sick," I was like I'm not gonna get you sick, trust me, like I don't think so.

OUTSIDER: *(laughing)* Yah.

NEVAEH: So, that's why like I tried to get a job, I told you I was trying to like work for a catering—oh no I told Antonio.

OUTSIDER: Oh okay.

NEVAEH: But the thing is like I can't, like I can't stand in the morning, right?

OUTSIDER: Yah.

NEVAEH: So unless it's some office job then I guess . . .

OUTSIDER: People know?

NEVAEH: Here?

OUTSIDER: Yup.

NEVAEH: Yah they do.

OUTSIDER: Yah.

NEVAEH: Like Dee tried to help me out, she told me that she has her own, supposedly pregnancy book that she's gonna give me or whatever.

OUTSIDER: Okay.

NEVAEH: To just follow up and stuff, but um, I'm happy like, a lot of people I thought they were gonna look down or whatever but they're actually accepting it and they're actually happy and it's really weird but *(giggles)*—

OUTSIDER: It's great.

NEVAEH: Yah.

OUTSIDER: It's great to have that support system. Who needs—uh the last thing you need is for people to judge you, you know?

NEVAEH: Yah.

Beat.

OUTSIDER: Do you feel lucky?

NEVAEH: Do I feel lucky?

Beat.

I do, I feel lucky and sad. Because um, my boyfriend's parents know and they're happy, um here they know and some people are happy, some are you know are telling me to think what I'm gonna do, right, cuz I'm still twenty. But um, I feel sad cuz I can't tell my parents. That's why I feel sad. Cuz, I wish I could.

OUTSIDER: And that's just not an option?

NEVAEH: Well I will, but um . . . I don't think it would be nice. I don't think the results would be great and that's what makes me sad cuz I miss them, but just we don't get along, we have like totally different visions for everything.

OUTSIDER: Yah.

NEVAEH: Like I do talk to my mom and my mom is more understanding but when it comes to my dad it's just . . . *(shakes head)*

OUTSIDER: Yah.

Beat.

NEVAEH: Like my dad got deported and then I stayed here by myself and that's how I got in the shelter. He got deported cuz of me, to be honest. He—he used to hit me.

OUTSIDER: Yah.

NEVAEH: He used to abuse me and it got pretty insane at the end, like I— how old was I? I was seventeen. Um, it was going insane, like he would hit me and he would get drunk and he would ask me to dance for his friends. It was really . . . really weird. He would threaten my ex-boyfriend, he would say that he would like cut him in pieces and send him back to his parents, like those are not nice stuff, right?

OUTSIDER: No.

A shift.

ACT 3—SURVIVAL

OUTSIDER: Are there people here you think, that could make it under the right circumstances?

KAALIYAH: Hell no.

OUTSIDER: What about this Paul guy, the one who pop and locks in front of the microwave, checking out his reflection in the glass?

KAALIYAH: No.

RAENI: *(with awe)* He used to take his tray into the lunchroom, and start singing and we would all stop and listen to him.

Short beat.

KAALIYAH: PUT PEANUT BUTTER ON THE BREAD. THE BREAD. That was his rhyme. He rhymed *bread* with *bread*. Hm, let me see here, last time I checked . . .

RAENI: *(laughing)* Pretty funny guy.

KAALIYAH: Cracker, the guy was a mess.

RAENI: Outta nowhere in the lunchroom—

KAALIYAH: *(shutting RAENI down)* Hey, Premium Plus, the guy was a mess. One band man, that guy. He's a solo act, if you know what I mean. SO-LO. Audiences Not Included. You know Lil Wayne? So you know his videos? Paul's career will max out at being that guy in the background of a Lil Wayne music video. Standing there, doing nothing, with his gold chains all—

RAENI: *(laughing)* Kaaliyah is *vicious*.

OUTSIDER: What about that guy, Scott, he told us he wanted to get into acting.

KAALIYAH: Acting?! For what? The before picture in a Colgate commercial?

KAALIYAH and RAENI laugh.

Did you see that boy's mouth? I mean, come on.

KAALIYAH laughs. Her face drops suddenly.

So, like what else you want to talk about?

OUTSIDER: You like picking fights?

Beat. KAALIYAH takes this as a challenge. Then:

KAALIYAH: *(pops and locks)* PUT PEANUT BUTTER ON THE BREAD. ON THE BREAD.

ROMEO: There was this staff here that really kinda, she really wanted to get into—to what was botherin' me so I'm that kinda person, I really, when something's botherin' me I won't really go out there and explain, I'll keep it to myself, but this time she—she went out and she bought a journal and she wrote in it so, then she'll hand it to me and she'll let me read it so then—it's like a journal where she writes something then I read it, then I write back, I write what I'm thinking about that day then she'll answer it and we just kept on doin' that until, yah.

OUTSIDER: And did you catch on right away what was going on, or did you . . . ?

ROMEO: I never—at first I never really caught onto it at first until . . . because I thought she, like she—I like doin' poetry and writin' stuff like that so, and then she wrote me a question she asked me, she wrote me a question like how was your day, like how're you feelin' and then at that time I was in a very unhappy mode so I kinda explained how I was feelin' and then yah after that I kind of caught onto it then.

They laugh.

OUTSIDER: Yah. Clever.

ROMEO: Yah it's very clever.

OUTSIDER: Um, Romeo, what are your poems about, like, um, you know, what do you like to write about?

ROMEO: Uh *(stretch)* mostly, like most of the stuff that um, when I do decide to write, it's mostly on life experience. Like, I have this one poem where I gave the title "Monster." And it's like, it's a man, but I wanna say the man, like—I based where the man's characteristics and actions is based off somebody I was close to, that I didn't like his actions and stuff, (but the man is not really about him) and I kind of extend his actions to the point when—I wish I had 'em on me, I got to go pick 'em up—it got to the point where he's actually in a battle right now with himself, that he realizes he's become a monster, there's no way of turnin' back and he's kinda feelin' sorry for himself and he's findin' ways to come back into the society cuz society cast him out so, I'm tryin' to find a way how to put him back in there and how to . . . mm . . .

MONICA: Sometimes it just takes one event . . . one thing that does or doesn't happen to you, that decides whether you're on this side or that side.

ROMEO: Mm . . . turn him from a monster to a man and not a man to a monster anymore.

NEVAEH: My dad said that he was a dentist, that we had like three houses an um supposedly I have good marks in school and that's what—we were going to go from Bulgaria to see my aunt who lives in Florida. I have no aunt in Florida. But um, we passed so we got, um, the visas. And my uncle met us at New York, and then in the morning went all the way to Niagara Falls where we got a motel, me and my dad, and he said um, he told us to stay there—my mom never came in the first place—so he told me to stay with my dad in Niagara Falls.

TYLER: It's just . . . cops and stuff like that. They don't really know me through the shelters, like the shelters do, so they don't really get along with me.

NEVAEH: He said the next day we should just cross the border, right? And tell them that we come here as a refugee and that we give up or whatever *(laughs)*. So, yah we slept there and we didn't eat the whole day because we didn't even know how to order anything, it was funny. You know what I mean, it's really hard, so he told us in the morning to get a taxi and ask how much to get to the border, right? But nobody wanted to drive us because we didn't have documents, right? So, we were wondering what to do and we would circle around the border with the luggage, and we saw a little door. *(smiling)* So we went through the door and it was ringing and we went over the bridge walking on the other side. And that's how I got to Canada. And they gave us a document as a refugee.

ROMEO: I've had my parents around until really age of fifteen, but as of age of six like, I never wanted my parents, like my parents weren't there, like my parents, to me they died mentally, like I don't know my mom. Like I just recently I talked to my mom at twenty-one, but my dad was there, but he was only there physically, like mentally, emotionally and stuff he wasn't my dad. So at the age of six, I would be in the house, and he'll think I'm in the house and I'll sneak out my window and I'll be like on the streets, I'll be on the road like doin' stuff.

TYLER: . . . Pretty much I got arrested this time, but just, I ran. They wanted to arrest me so I ran an' . . . freakin', they called the canines and stuff like that . . . *(smiles)* kicked the crap out of me *(laughs)* I kicked the dog, yah. I don't like dogs, I was always scared of dogs. I got bit by a dog when I was a kid and I never liked 'em to this day—shepherds I don't . . . I like other dogs, but shepherds I don't like . . . an' the dog was right behind me, so I kicked it and it ran away . . . and I got tackled by six other cops an' . . .

He smiles but looks like he could cry; he lists his current injuries.

Uh, three staples in my eye, four staples in my head, um, a broken rib, a fractured rib an' two black eyes . . .

TOYA: He was off at some basketball game and he called me to tell me that he's gonna be coming home late and to leave the garage door open for him. You know, boys, they go out and stay out.

ROMEO: I would call the street like my second mother.

AIDAN: Because when you go to school kids always ask you well, how's— like you have a mom right? And then they say do you have a dad and you say no, well they look at you like what the fuck. And then the first thing through their mind is we shouldn't chill with this kid, he only has one parent. So he must be a little cuck-coo cuz he only has a mom.

OUTSIDER: Right.

TOYA: And then at five o'clock in the morning, these cops come to our door. And they're asking my mom about my brother. And she's like, "What he do now?" and I go to the basement, and like Morgan not home. And so I tell the police that Morgan didn't come home last night. And they said they knew and I noticed one cop had this thing on her uniform and I was like, "Aren't you a homicide cop?" And she was, "Yah."

AIDAN: Shit that happens behind closed doors you don't really want to spread around when you're a kid, you know what I mean? And that's where most of my assault charges and everything came from because people would make fun of me for only have a mom and not a dad, "Well yah I do have a dad, he's just a dick. He decided to tuck his balls and run like an asshole." Well that's not my fault.

TOYA: And I had to identify the body for my mother.

AIDAN: Some people's lives are not like the picture perfect family you see on TV with a mom and a dad and a brother and a sister and they're all sitting around a table sharing juice. So, like . . . it's not picturesque.

Beat.

DEE: I remember we had, I think it was like two summers ago, we had a resident—he uh, had left here, on an overnight and um, him and this other guy had uh, he had been trying to get money to go visit his mom, and he couldn't get the money. I don't know. He just wanted to see his mom, like I guess he hadn't seen her in a while, I don't know maybe . . . I feel like it maybe was her birthday, I don't really remember but a lot of these youth *unfortunately* . . . have such strong feelings for their parents, but it's not, um . . . reciprocated. Like it's not going back, right? So they'll do whatever they can . . . you know, I've seen residents here give their parents money . . . *(shocked face)* that blows my mind. Like why are you giving—and some of their parents are in horrible situations too, but I—I don't understand that. And they have so much love for their family, no matter how ill-treated they've been by them, that they'll do anything for them. So him and another resident stole a van, um, that was parked you know in the community, and they got into um, a police chase and ended up crashing into a car and he passed away. So, *(sigh)* we got a bus, for, cuz a lot of people were close with him here, so we got a bus, packed it with the residents—it was out in like Brockville or Trenton, like it was some-where far, so we got a bus for the residents, all the staff went up there and his whole family was at the funeral. And, they went up and spoke about him and talked about his growing—and it just—I didn't understand it, I mean, *we* were his family.

Beat. A big shift.

ACT 4—HOPE

OUTSIDER: So, Jamal, tell me about Africa.

JAMAL: I visited there in 1999, I think it was. I was about nine years old and honestly, it wasn't what I thought, I thought it would be like the kind of Africa you see on TV. You know, the starving kids, and the—

OUTSIDER: And Sarah McLachlan and . . .

JAMAL: *(laughs)* Yah . . .

OUTSIDER: Jann Arden.

JAMAL: Yah but um. It wasn't that bad actually but um, we lived in a like upper-class kind of area—

OUTSIDER: Okay.

JAMAL: And we had servants while were living there and everything. Well . . . it'd technically be more like a slave than a servant.

OUTSIDER: Yah?

JAMAL: Yah, we had uh.

OUTSIDER: Do you provide them shelter? Like how does it? What's the?

JAMAL: Well, here's how it works: the war sprouted out a lot of orphans, a crap load of orphans. So, what the upper-class families usually do is, you have food and shelter and "you'll work for us" kind of thing, a servant thing, "while you grow up." So they get hired around nine, ten and then uh, till they're adults, or usually past that even, uh, they just work in the house . . . they just stay inside and clean. Yah.

Beat.

Well, I had a problem with that.

OUTSIDER: Did you?

JAMAL: I was a deviant little kid. When I went back to visit *(laughs)* this seems kinda funny looking back but I got in a lot of trouble for it. Um . . . I wrote an escape plan for one of the servants.

OUTSIDER: What do you mean "escape plan?" You went like, "This is how you get outta town"?

JAMAL: Yah, like, "I'll show you." But I guess they liked the way that they were living. Or. I guess it would be kind of ignorant to say that. But um, I guess, that was the best that was out there for them kind of thing. So yah.

OUTSIDER: So he didn't use your escape plan, in the end?

JAMAL: No. And when my uncle found out I got in a lot of trouble.

They laugh. PAUL begins to pop and lock, facing upstage. He stops at the end of the question.

OUTSIDER: Can you give examples of um, how they're helpin' you out here?

BARBARA: I don't know what I would do. If there was nobody like them here.

OUTSIDER: Can you imagine if that—what is that life, if there was no support system.

BARBARA: I—I don't know. I don't know, I would be like, crazy. Like seriously. Cuz, I wouldn't have nobody to talk to, or to vent at least. And there's only so much times you can vent to yourself, right? *(smiles)* Like I'm tired of looking in that mirror venting. *(laughs)* No I'm joking.

PAUL pops and locks. He stops at the end of the next line.

OUTSIDER: And uh, you're gonna be a dad.

AIDAN nods.

How do you feel about that?

AIDAN: I'm happy.

OUTSIDER: Yah? Are these your first kids, or . . .

AIDAN: Uh, yah. Well, first kids I'll actually get to see. I have one kid, but I don't get to talk to him anymore.

OUTSIDER: And um, you say kids cuz it's twins?

AIDAN nods.

Wow.

AIDAN: That's what she thinks. I'm worried about that.

OUTSIDER: Why are you worried?

AIDAN: Two kids for the price of one, man, wouldn't you be worried? *(chuckle)* It's gonna be a struggle but . . .

OUTSIDER: Are you looking forward to that?

AIDAN: *(nods)* I get to chisel somebody's life out. Figure out what I want them to be when they get older. *(shrug)* What couldn't be exciting about that?

OUTSIDER: Yah. And um, if you were to have a job . . .

BARBARA: Oh actually I do have a job. Yah. I work as a receptionist.

OUTSIDER: Okay.

BARBARA: Yah.

OUTSIDER: Where?

BARBARA: Century 21.

OUTSIDER: And do they know you're in a shelter?

BARBARA: For right now they don't know anything about me other than my name, my social insurance number, that's it.

OUTSIDER: Do you find it tricky living with a secret?

BARBARA: Sometimes, because I have like, a nosy partner secretary . . .

OUTSIDER: And what do you think would happen, let's say with this co-worker, if she found out you were in a shelter?

BARBARA: Oh, it would no—it would be no ifs ands or buts. I would probably end up getting looks, because I'm sure she would go to my boss, because she's been there three years. She would go to my boss, and already you think of shelter, you think of oh god, like dirty . . . what's coming in this place to work for us, she's gonna probably end up stealing. These are just characteristics of—I know I thought before I even came into a shelter, that's what I thought. And so if you, like if you have somebody living in a shelter working for you, you kind of contemplate, okay should I have her working for us.

OUTSIDER: Yah.

BARBARA: And then she's pregnant on top of that, oh no thank you, this is too much trouble.

OUTSIDER: Yah.

BARBARA: And then fire me, right?

Beat.

ROMEO: They automatically think oh these kids, these kids are troublesome, they're—they're nothing but dangerous and something like that so they all get this weird look and they start classifyin' them as—they're not part of society—then some if they decided to take in all that then it gets to them where they actually say, okay maybe we should become what these people want.

AIDAN: Like, cuz when I was a kid I asked teachers about questions about like sex ed and stuff and none of them would give me an answer. It was like it was so hush hush.

OUTSIDER: Why is that?

AIDAN: I don't know. They're worried, I guess. They don't want kids having sex at too young of an age, but kids are having sex because they don't know about it.

OUTSIDER: Right.

AIDAN: You know what I mean? Nobody told me that having sex leads to having babies, I figured that out on my own.

OUTSIDER: Can I ask when you're gonna *(makes an invisible motion)*—

BARBARA: January.

OUTSIDER: January.

BARBARA: Yah.

OUTSIDER: Are you hopeful?

> *Beat.* AIDAN *and* BARBARA *look to one another for the first time. Then:*

AIDAN: I feel like I'm at the lowest point of my life right now. But from the lowest point, like rock bottom, you can always climb to the next step. And once you make that first step it's just more, more, more, right?

OUTSIDER: And do you see the steps towards—I mean does it seem attainable? That sort of stability?

BARBARA: I mean slowly but surely I know—there's no ifs ands or buts, I need that stability.

OUTSIDER: Yah.

BARBARA: No matter if I break down sometimes I need to just get back up and say I need to do this. Cuz it's not for me.

> *Beat.*

AIDAN: All the staff keep telling me there's some major improvements.

> AIDAN *catches* BARBARA's *eye as they go.*

ROMEO: On the real like the staffs here . . . they're not like, like I've been to other shelters, they're really not like any other staff—

OUTSIDER: You like your caseworkers?

KAALIYAH: / No.

ROMEO: You actually get the help you're looking for and they help you till everything is completely finished and done.

RAENI: If I didn't have my caseworker, I wouldn't get anything done.

OUTSIDER: You don't like your caseworker, Kaaliyah?

KAALIYAH: He's too much.

RAENI: Your caseworker's all over you.

KAALIYAH: "Kaali, can we talk?" "Kaali, can we talk?" "Kaali, we should talk." "Can we talk Kaali?" I'm sitting on the toilet and there's a knock, "Kaali, let's talk."

RAENI: Yah, he's everywhere.

And then there's Bullet.

> RAENI *laughs.* KAALIYAH *doesn't.*

OUTSIDER: Bullet?

KAALIYAH: Yah. Picture a bullet, then turn it upside down. That's his head.

RAENI: And Monkey.

And Donkey.

> *Beat.*

OUTSIDER: Kaali, like is that it? Like, what, do you have a plan or?

> RAENI *laughs.* KAALIYAH *doesn't. Through the next sequence she takes in her fellow residents and the* OUTSIDER*'s engagement with them.*

Brussel Sprouts, what's the plan for *you* right now?

DUSTIN: I'll I'll I'll just uh I'll my main goal is to get into university and to start asking my professors difficult questions . . . and see what they have to say.

OUTSIDER: And like what interests you, like what—

DUSTIN: There are there are there are people that go into space, I'm not looking to be an astronaut but I would like to make a contribution to you know, some of the structures that are out in space. That would be my thing.

Beat.

Hopefully.

OUTSIDER: Why is that important to you?

DUSTIN: Uh.

Short beat.

Well, my ideas are really important to me. So, seeing the success of those ideas is, the success of those ideas is important to me.

OUTSIDER: Can you give an example? Or is it too . . . big?

DUSTIN: Uh. It's not too, it's not too big, it's it's it's very, it's complex. Um. My idea pertains to a structure in space that um, essentially is launched into orbit and then expands um, um, quite clever actually, using uh, panels, within the module, so instead of having a cylinder that they current uh like they consistently do um, it would expand to create a larger volume, a larger contained volume um for habitat, for humans to live. So that's cool.

OUTSIDER: That's very cool. You feel pretty inspired by it.

DUSTIN: *(as emphatic as he gets)* Yes. I'm, I, my dad says to go to university and I'm going to enter university.

TRAVIS: Right now? I wanna get enrolled in school and then uh I . . . I wanna . . . I wanna get in some kind of . . . weightlifting. I have that idea.

Beat.

But I have to quit smoking. And. It's all hard, you know.

OUTSIDER: Can I ask how much you smoke?

MALIK: Oh I smoke enough. Like given cigarettes too, like I go through like, like a pack every two days.

OUTSIDER: And . . . have you ever tried quitting or like it's . . .

MALIK: Yah. Cuz back, like I was really really athletic, right?

OUTSIDER: Yah.

DUSTIN: My dad's an engineer and I've talked to him and he says it's basically, you know, like up to me to do. Sort of thing.

MALIK: Until I got into a car accident, and like, ended up on my own, living on my own.

DUSTIN: I, I, I've sent like emails to people and like the European Space Agency, Canadian Space Agency, and I haven't heard any responses.

MALIK: And my mom passed away.

MIKE: Like this place is making me go to anger management. Cuz I have those freak-outs. But like I think I've got a lot of control over it, the last couple of years, it's taken a long time, but like, I'm more in control of myself now than I was before.

OUTSIDER: Travis, what is the weightlifting game plan, like what is, what are you thinking there?

TRAVIS: In there, I'm thinking about, uh . . . working mostly upper body and maybe doing some on legs cuz it releases a natural steroid.

OUTSIDER: Okay. Yah.

TRAVIS: I don't know if it's called circuit training when you're hopping on three things and keep / repeating it.

NEILL: I took this English program, sixty words, six chapters, ten words a chapter, ten different ways to learn the word.

OUTSIDER: An example?

NEILL: I remember *ambiguous* which is like . . . I think it's ambiguous, no? Ambiguous, ambicu, ambiguous. It means, I think, um . . . "Not so obvious?"

Beat.

Is that it?

OUTSIDER: Yah. That's totally right. Ambiguous.

NEILL: Yah! Not so obvious. Zenith . . . what else man . . . ah, squelch, uh, ah, I can't remember most of the words. If I see them, I'll know what they mean. I'm one of those learners that has to see 'em like, I can't, I can't, tss, I don't know, / ts, I can't *(points finger)*—

BARBARA: I'm not a person that's not wanting to go nowhere in life—

OUTSIDER: And are there people here you think that could make it under the right / circumstances?

MALIK: I'm gonna do some modellin', an' some actin'.

BARBARA: I am wanting to go somewhere in life.

NEILL: I don't / . . .

MALIK: I have some friends who have been, you know, extras in movies. But I don't wanna be an extra. I want main parts. As long as they don't make me cut my hair.

NEILL: I don't . . . it's . . . this mental problem I talked about, it getting in the way of a lot of things so, you know.

OUTSIDER: And are you working at all right now?

MALIK: Yah. I've been working in a factory. Manufacturin' company. But I wanna quit that job,

OUTSIDER: / Yah.

SCOTT: Hey, I wanna get into some acting, actually. /

MALIK: every time I blow my nose after work, /

NEILL: What else man—

MALIK: I see black things in it.

OUTSIDER: Yah.

SCOTT: Gonna lose some weight and look into it.

OUTSIDER: Don't have to lose any weight. It takes all shapes and / sizes.

BARBARA: My kids. Honestly.

TYLER: I got warrants out for me but . . .

TRAVIS: I want to get into that, like, upper body,

TYLER: I know I'm gonna go to jail anyway, if I stay, so / I'm just gonna go out there make a bunch of money . . .

TRAVIS: arms, chest, back, wing . . . shoulder blades.

TYLER: . . . and come back / . . .

TRAVIS: Just that stuff.

BARBARA: Just when I see them smile.

TRAVIS: And uh, trying to lose the stomach, a bit . . . *(eyes up, then down)*

TYLER: I don't know.

TRAVIS: Cuz it bothers me.

TYLER: I don't know.

KAALIYAH: I never wanna wake up.

    Beat.

OUTSIDER: You don't wanna wake up.

TYLER: Lost my job and now I'm screwed. Freakin' court cases, conditions, every week I gotta sign in at . . .

KAALIYAH: I don't wanna wake up.

TYLER: . . . bail program the first and fifteenth I gotta go sign in at the cop division, then every fucking two weeks I got court dates.

OUTSIDER: It's a feeling of?

BARBARA: Do I really have somebody in my corner?

KAALIYAH: This is not my place . . . This is not my home, this is not my bed, this is . . . not my walls.

TYLER: So I'm screwed *(laughs).*

KAALIYAH: I'm, it's like, I come here, I came here with a mission, to come here for like a month, and leave an' find my own place, and everyone tells you, you can ask anybody. But after a while, this side will drain you or make you feel like, "Okay, yah, I'm busting my ass, I'm tryin' to do this, tryin' to do that," but then you see everyone else not doing anything and then . . . like everything is coming to them but then you're working so hard and nothing is coming to you. And you can just lay back a while, and you can lay back to the point that You. Drop. Everything. You stop going to school. You stop working. *(emphatic)* And you become a big bum.

BARBARA: I wouldn't say I have family or friends. Like especially ending up in a place like this, you seem to wonder, like, there's really no one there for you.

KAALIYAH steps forward.

KAALIYAH: Y'see the thing. Sometimes I wake up and I feel so unfocused, like, feel like I'm here and I'm not doing anything, but really, yah, like I'm in school, right, I'm registered for nursing. And I'm doing nursing. But it's just. Like nursing is so hard and then like I have to come back here, and it's not even my home and I have to come here and do chores and have people telling me stuff that I really don't wanna have to hear, have to put up with orders and people's bad hygiene problems and stuff. And I'm like . . . and I'm willing to work really hard for my edication but it's just right now I come to a halt . . . in my life, where like, the shelter thing is wearing me down and tearing me down and a lot of people who will not come on this little taping thing will tell you the truth—*won't* tell you, but the truth that this place wears you and will tear you down to the dirt if you don't leave and step up.

TYLER laughs, but could just as easily cry.

Don't come here think it's gonna be easy, cuz it's not. S'gonna hit you when you wake up one morning, you'll say, "Fuck, I'm here."

KAALIYAH turns her back on the OUTSIDER. The other residents turn their backs to the OUTSIDER. After a beat, the caseworkers appear, urgently.

MONICA: Like you don't just get up one day and decide, "You know what, I'm not doing anything today. I'm not doing anything for the next *five* years." You know. Like, you don't. But yet if something or someone or some incident . . . provides that block in your life, it's, it's, they're not getting over that boulder, right?

OUTSIDER: And you have experienced youth get over that block?

MONICA: *Yah.*

OUTSIDER: Would you say that people can restart their lives?

MONICA: *(almost on top of "lives")* Oh yah. Like even though I don't know, I think, I always look at them and at some point in their life, they're gonna.

OUTSIDER: And uh, I imagine if you are sort of restarting your life, if that's what it is then it does feel like this overwhelming . . . is your, part of your job, helping them focus?

MONICA: I think in the long—like . . . on a larger scale, it is.

DEE: It's hard, it's hard. A lot of these, um, youth over the years like, I love them, like they—they like—I wanna know what's going on with them, I care about them so much and, it's hard to have that boundary with them,

I mean, I think of them as my kids sometimes and I wanna make sure that they're doing good.

MONICA: I always say like our success is earned. It's those little things, so like a client hasn't smiled for five days and they smile. And that means they're starting you know to build their relationship with you.

DEE: Everyone has a reason for why they're here and I mean everyone has a story, everyone has—I mean I guarantee some of these kids if I knew them, like, I would be friends with some of them. These guys—I mean I'm sure some of them probably went to my high school, I mean they're regular people—they're normal people, they have great personalities, I mean a lot of them—we have a lot in common. I would see myself hanging out with them, you know in my own time, so.

OUTSIDER: Yah.

DEE nods.

What is, um, you said there were residents that you can, uh, unabashedly say you love that resident—

DEE: Yah.

OUTSIDER: —and you have a real tenderness for them.

DEE: Yah—I guess that's probably the wrong word to use, but—

OUTSIDER: No no no no. But I mean . . . how do you hang onto hope?

Beat.

MONICA: Practise it.

Like *wanna* have hope.

The caseworkers leave the OUTSIDER.

ACT 5—IMAGINATION

During this sequence, a resident puts their hand up to respond. Once they've said their piece, they point at another resident who has their hand up.

OUTSIDER: Now, use your imagination. If I walked up to you in the street and said, here's ten thousand dollars, no questions asked, no strings attached, what would you do with that money?

NEILL: Ten grand?

Beat.

Ten grand is *not* a lot of money, man, but *(laughs)* let me see, what would I do yo, I would.

OUTSIDER: Anything.

NEILL: Anything, man.

BARBARA: If credit was good, right?

NEILL: Can I say clothes, liquor, chronic, an' have a hotel party? *(laughs)*

TRAVIS: I'd buy a laptop. Clothes. Lots of clothes. I'd buy, I'd prolly buy four, five, pairs of shoes. Um. Some nice gear. And I'd buy one thing for sure. That uh *(mumbled)* Absonic belt.

OUTSIDER: What?

TRAVIS: Sonic belt. *(gestures to his midsection)*

OUTSIDER: . . . ?

TRAVIS: That sonic belt thing.

OUTSIDER: I don't know what / that is—

TRAVIS: You put it on, you lose inches by the day, in your midsection.

DUSTIN: I'd go join the military.

OUTSIDER: Really? Why?

DUSTIN: If you had ten thousand dollars, you're going to need some discipline.

OUTSIDER: And that's the quick and easy way of getting it?

DUSTIN: Nothing quick and easy about it.

JAMAL: First off, I'd get my driver's licence. For / sure.

TRAVIS: I'd buy all kinds of protein stuff, shakes / you buy.

TOYA: I would buy a plane ticket—

TRAVIS: I'd buy a juice maker for sure. That's wicked.

TOYA: An' live in Jamaica.

MALIK: Ah, first thing I would do is get my driver's licence back.

BARBARA: I want something to call my own. Something that I paid for.

MALIK: And then like *(snaps fingers)* get myself an apartment.

BARBARA: Just have my kids stable—when they grow older—a car, or school, or my daughter for a wedding.

KAALIYAH has had her hand up for a while. The other residents are taken aback.

KAALIYAH: I would save it. H'automatically.

Beat. The other three residents shoot their hands up in the air.

JAMAL: To be honest, I think I'd take the rest and save it.

OUTSIDER: Really?!

DUSTIN: I would probably put it in some sort of savings account. For the future.

JAMAL: Invest it. Make my money work for me.

MALIK: Save it.

KAALIYAH: For, to be honest honest, somebody gave me ten thousand dollars *right* now.

OUTSIDER: Like right now I give you ten thousand dollars, what are you gonna—

KAALIYAH: Give it to my mom.

Beat.

OUTSIDER: Really.

KAALIYAH: Automatically.

OUTSIDER: Why?

KAALIYAH: Wouldn't take any for myself.

NEILL: Well, my cousin is going to school. So I would have to give her like at least three-four grand to do something with cuz she's a smart person and I know, if I had any, if, ever, if I had any need she would be the first, that at least, I go to and she would, if she could you know, give me whatever yo. I'd give her the money.

OUTSIDER: How would she react?

NEILL: She would react, like thank you. An' give me a hug. An' that's probably it cuz I'm not actually looking for anything back. I'm looking for . . . just the love, man, I guess man. I know I don't have to pay for it but . . . y'know, I know the love is there so I'm jus' . . . gettin' it a little fatter, I guess. I love my cousin an' she loves me.

KAALIYAH: I love my mom.

NEILL: You know, I love to fat up the love, man.

KAALIYAH: I love my mom.

NEILL: If there's love there, I'll fat it up. *(laughs)* Y'know what I mean, man.

KAALIYAH: My mom, when I was young, my mom took care of me like I didn't, my dad is nothing to me, like my dad was whatever, you know, so whatever *I* have, even if I'm in a shelter right now, whatever I have I give it to my mom, it doesn't go to me, it goes to my mom.

Beat.

OUTSIDER: Now, do you have anything else to say?

KAALIYAH: Well like, to anyone who's watching this?

OUTSIDER: Yah, kind of, like—if there were actors and you could have them say something, what would you have them say. Something that could help someone else, in trouble.

KAALIYAH: People in trouble?

OUTSIDER: Yah.

Beat. For the first time, the residents' gaze moves from the OUTSIDER to the audience.

KAALIYAH shakes her head, then punctuates each word with her head.

KAALIYAH: Cut. Your. Shit.

MALIK: Just enjoy life. But not too much.

OUTSIDER: Why do you say not too much?

MALIK: Cuz I enjoyed it too much. That's why I'm here. Too much of anything is bad.

KAALIYAH: Every action comes with a reaction, I believe that one hundred percent cuz if you decide to eat the candy and you get a stomach ache, it's because of the candy you ate. Right? Like goddamn come out that stupidness about the whole "let me sell drugs" 'n' stuff, yah it's fast money but leave it alone, work hard, go to school—*shelter* not what it *cracked* up to *be*. It's *not*, it's a place to come *do* what you have to *do*.

NEILL: I would give bad advice in this situation because, I don't know . . .

DUSTIN: The more good things you do, that you try to do, just one good thing after another, makes a huge difference . . .

NEILL: As long as you have a smile on your face, man, do whatever yo.

TRAVIS: Don't let people put you down, you shouldn't let that happen to you, you should just ignore people and keep going even, even if the whole world is against you just keep it in your head that you know you're right and keep going you're right and don't let no one ever stop you, just keep going, like, like, as if, even if you were to die, just keep going. That's my best idea.

NEILL: If there's love there, I'll fat / it up.

TRAVIS: It's more like the harder you get stressed, the more you get stressed, the more you're gonna explode, and you're—your body is just waiting for that to happen because you can only get so stressed and then you eventually will explode but when you explode, explode the right way. Don't explode the wrong way.

DUSTIN: Sometimes I, I, sometimes my thoughts go . . . *(big gesture)* way over the top when it comes to thinking about human beings it's . . . it's pretty amazing the, the things that are being accomplished right now.

PAUL begins to pop and lock.

AIDAN: At one point in your life you're always going to have to make that step to change.

KAALIYAH: Realize life . . . either way you're trying to run from it, you're gonna have to face it.

AIDAN: It's just when do you decide to do it?

NEVAEH: It's not like putting myself down by telling myself my life is not great.

KAALIYAH: *Shelter* not what it *cracked* up to *be*.

NEVAEH: I believe that there is a lot of things that make you smile in this world, right?

> *Beat. PAUL stops, looks at NEVAEH, looks at the OUTSIDER. All but NEVAEH and PAUL leave. PAUL steps forward as if to say something. He looks down. Beat. He then pulls invisible earbuds from his ears and holds them out to the OUTSIDER. We can just make out the music he's been listening to. He puts them back into his ears. He leaves NEVAEH and the OUTSIDER.*

EPILOGUE

OUTSIDER: I forget, we gave you a name in the last interview, I think it was . . .

NEVAEH: Nevaeh, remember?

OUTSIDER: It was, heaven backwards.

NEVAEH: Mm-hm.

OUTSIDER: Nevaeh, yup. How you doin'?

NEVAEH: Fine.

OUTSIDER: So this is our second interview.

NEVAEH: Did you do that with a lot of people, or no?

OUTSIDER: Uh, second interview, you're the first second interview I've ever done.

NEVAEH: Is that a good thing or a bad thing?

OUTSIDER: I think it's a great thing because I—I found our first interview so interesting and um, you have such an interesting story and I'm just, you know? And I'm like really . . . what I felt that I didn't uh, have the time to ask more about is um, like you're gonna—are you still expecting to have a kid? Is that . . .

NEVAEH: No.

OUTSIDER: No?

NEVAEH: *(scrunch face)* I did the abortion.

Beat.

OUTSIDER: Oh, okay.

NEVAEH: I didn't think that um, I can't do it.

OUTSIDER: Yah.

NEVAEH: To be honest, the kid's name was supposed to be Neveah.

OUTSIDER: Yah.

NEVAEH: Yah.

Beat.

You feel better once you say it and let it out, I just, sometimes . . . I don't know, sometimes I share my story with people and my own experiences just to like make sure they don't do like, the same mistakes. Um, I'm not saying that it always works *(laugh)* but you know?

OUTSIDER: Yah. Of course.

Beat.

AIDAN: And it's weird, cuz like you don't hear very many people—like if my kids ask me, I don't know what I'm gonna tell them, I met her in a shelter.

OUTSIDER: Well maybe that's part of relaying your experience and teaching them—

AIDAN: Mm-hm. But it's also what I'm thinking, like so Dad came from a shelter, but now he's a carpenter making forty-five bucks an hour, so if he can go from the dumps to something . . . then we're okay, you know what I mean? That might help my kids sleep better at the end of the night, okay well, so Dad was in a shelter, but now look at him. We've got a house, a big backyard, dogs and we have nothing to worry about. There's enough food in the fridge / . . .

MALIK: I don't wanna be an extra.

Beat.

I want main parts. As long as they don't make me cut my hair.

OUTSIDER: You love your hair.

MALIK: Yah.

OUTSIDER: Let's see.

MALIK *turns his head.*

It's pretty long. And is it always, um, in rows, or . . .

MALIK: No sometimes I single braid it . . . or sometimes I just let it out.

OUTSIDER: Well that's cool. It's like Antonio's hair, like he'll never cut his hair do you know what I mean, like . . .

MALIK: Yah, yah, yah. *(smiling)* Exactly.

DEE: I mean I couldn't have asked for a better childhood and more supportive parents. I'm extremely lucky. But a lot of my friends growing up, went through divorce, went through, you know, the criminal justice system, like so I've seen that, so I know, I mean, it could happen just like that *(snaps)*, absolutely it can, and thank god *(knocks on wood)* I mean I was lucky enough to have everything I could have asked for, um, but to be honest—it could happen to anybody.

The actress playing DEE goes and for the last time becomes KAALIYAH, who witnesses the following with the other residents.

OUTSIDER: Can you describe the collage in your room for me?

NEVAEH: The collage?

OUTSIDER: Yah.

Beat.

NEVAEH: There's a picture in the middle of a girl and it says "I don't follow any trends." And um, it said something um—I made it out of um, magazines, like I took just words. It said um, "we all walk in different shoes." Um, there's a cigarette that says like, it's a put-out cigarette and it said um, "I'm not ashamed to say I don't do drugs." And it said "looking forward to" that was at the time that I made it, it was to get married and have a baby, so . . . and there was a girl standing on the beach and it said um, something like "Hello Tomorrow." And on the other corner there were like pictures of a girl with a camera and behind her there like all those um, pictures of different places like Italy, like France, you know? So, yah . . .

OUTSIDER: Places you wanna see.

NEVAEH: Mm-hm.

Beat.

It was nice.

The actors look out as the white noise crescendos and then, along with the lights, cuts out.

End.

AND BY THE WAY, MISS . . .

URGE
Marie-Josée Chartier, Katherine Duncanson, Fides
Krucker (spearheading director),
and Linda Catlin Smith

with the Ensemble
Lauren Brotman, Andrea Donaldson, Amber
Godfrey, Christina Sicoli, and Diana Tso

and with dramaturgical collaboration
from Joanna McIntyre

Commissioned and produced by
Theatre Direct Canada

To the memory of Ann Southam and to every girl at that age when it is still possible to become who you are.

ACKNOWLEDGEMENTS

And by the way, Miss . . . would not have been possible without Ann Southam, who supported the commission, and the Laidlaw Foundation, which supported the early development of the work. Support for the production was provided by the Harbinger Foundation, the Canada Council for the Arts, the Ontario Arts Council, the Toronto Arts Council, and many individual donors.

Thank you to the many artists and educators who made the education program of *And by the way, Miss . . .* possible: Mary Beath Badian, Alan Moon, and Pat McCarthy of Theatre Direct; Grant Peckford of Harbourfront's School by the Water; Melanie Fernandez, Director of Harbourfront's Community and Education Department; Christine Jackson of the Toronto District School Board Arts Department and Bernadine Nelligan of the Toronto Catholic District School Board. Thank you to the consultants who contributed to the study guide: Pat McCarthy, Elaine Slavens, Carole St. Jules, Jane Marie James, Kira McCarthy, Dr. Karen Leslie, Kathleen Gallagher, and Laurel Brown, along with additional researchers Karen Levy and Pat Rivière.

Thanks to actor Michelle Polak and stage manager Tammerah Volkovskis, who were part of the initial development and workshop phase, and to Rick Sacks, who engineered all the bell cues. And thanks to Victoria Stacey for her contributions towards the publication of this script.

Ticket subsidies for schools were provided by the Toronto District School Board Arts Department and the Toronto Catholic District School Board.

URGE would like to extend deep gratitude to all the grade seven and eight girls we met with to research this project. We led them through voice and movement exercises and then they opened our eyes and hearts to their concerns as they talked and talked, and talked some more. One group even took us to the mall.

AND BY THE WAY, MISS . . . : DEVISING AS A MULTI-GENERATIONAL FEMINIST PRACTICE

Michelle MacArthur and Anne Wessels

The devised work *And by the way, Miss* . . . brought together three groups of Toronto women and girls: accomplished artists from various disciplines (URGE), young emergent theatre practitioners (Ensemble), and an audience of girls in grades seven and eight. Deirdre Heddon and Jane Milling suggest that devising is comprised of three strands of practices that include the actor and the body, the visual, and the political "impact" of the work.[1] This long-term project, developed through the collaboration of multidisciplinary and multi-generational female artists, braids together all three strands of devising. As devising is comprised of physical and embodied experimentation and exploration, it was well-suited to the creation of a play that features the body and social relations as subject matter. The play it yielded builds on a lineage of feminist collective creation in Canada, providing a space to explore multiple and differing perspectives on issues important to adolescent girls, from body image to depression to the complexities of friendship.

This introduction will begin by considering the processes that resulted in the script you read here, followed by a section discussing how *And by the way, Miss* . . ., a work created by women (with girl input), and performed for school audiences of young female spectators, fits into the context of Canadian feminist theatre. As you read this devised play "written down" in this anthology, it is worth remembering that this "script" also includes what Theatre Direct Artistic Director Lynda Hill calls "all of the artistic

---

1   Dierdre Heddon and Jane Milling, *Devising Performance: A Critical History* (New York: Palgrave MacMillan, 2006), 27.

languages,"[2] which include dance, music, and visual imagery. As well, the "script" holds both the history of its process and the intentions of its engagement with its audience. To write about this piece, we found we had to contextualize the social and aesthetic conditions under which it was created but also contextualize its political and educational intentions to both engage young women in dialogue and learn from them about the specificities of their lived lives. We suggest that what is remarkable about this devised piece is its intergenerational intentions and its methods of spectator engagement. Some of the practices of audience engagement, when the play was in its early stages, were then folded back into the devising process. The resulting devised piece created a theatre experience for audiences that included both the performance of this script and the post-performance artistic workshops and dialogue. The performance and the dialogue that followed engaged the audience as active participants at every single performance.

THE INTERGENERATIONAL CREATIVE TEAM AND NEGOTIATING THE FOCUS OF THE PLAY

Before analyzing the specifics of this devising process, we will describe the creative team and how the subject of the piece was negotiated. Lynda Hill, Artistic Director of Theatre Direct, commissioned the women's interdisciplinary collective URGE (Fides Krucker, Marie-Josée Chartier, Katherine Duncanson, Joanna McIntyre, and Linda C. Smith) to develop a play about adolescent girls. URGE then engaged younger, more emergent artists as the Ensemble that included Lauren Brotman, Andrea Donaldson, Amber Godfrey, Christina Sicoli, and Diana Tso. The two generations of adult women developed, negotiated, and honed the subject together in consultation with audiences of girls who informed the artistic team that they wanted to see a play about "friendship," one that considered who was included, excluded, and whom they could trust. When the artists tested out scenes about bullying, there was a very supportive response. The subject matter of the play was not didactically imposed on young audiences, but was negotiated with them.

---

2   From the Creative Collaborators foreword that follows this introduction. Unless otherwise noted, all quotations from the artists come from this foreword.

DEVISING

As Emma Govan, Helen Nicholson, and Katie Normington suggest, "Devising is most accurately described in the plural—as *processes* of experimentation and sets of creative *strategies*—rather than a single methodology."[3] Although each devising process is unique, there are some general features of devising that differ from staging an already scripted play.

Devising has developed as a way of working with multiple disciplines outside the confines of scripted plays, and the non-linear structure of a devised work allows for the expression of multiple points of view through multiple performance styles. Aspiring to achieve a non-hierarchical performance-creation practice that challenges the conventional authority of the playwright and director, devising a performance piece is co-created collaboratively by all the artists involved. To focus on the particular set of *And by the way, Miss*'s "creative strategies," we will consider the development of the performance text, soundscape/music, set, and acting styles, all of which were created with a high degree of attention paid to the relational dynamics of the group.

Theatre makers who want to include and express multiple perspectives on a particular topic embrace devising as a means to counter a singular narrative or point of view. According to Heddon and Milling, collaborative devising processes can produce

> a performance that has multiple perspectives, that does not promote one, authoritative, "version" or interpretation, and that may reflect the complexities of the contemporary experience and the variety of narratives that constantly intersect with, inform, and in very real ways, construct our lives.[4]

And by the way, Miss . . . presents the multiple voices of the Ensemble as they express their different views and experiences of their bodies and their social relations.

---

3 Emma Govan, Helen Nicholson, and Katie Normington, *Making a Performance: Devising Histories and Contemporary Practices* (New York: Routledge, 2007), 7.

4 Heddon and Milling, 192.

URGE was particularly interested in exploring interdisciplinary performance practices: music, movement, and song. Interdisciplinary ways of working develop according to the skills and interests of the people doing the devising and Govan, Nicholson, and Normington suggest that "this builds a language of performance that uniquely suits the actors' particular identities, strengths and abilities."[5] Lynda Hill describes this particular "language of performance" when she outlines how the girls' stories made their way into the piece:

> Every aspect of their research informed the final script: the workshops they did as research, the girls' words, their ideas—if it didn't find its way in through actual words, it could be through a gesture, a sound, a look—such an effective research process. It was not just about confirming their [the artists'] instincts, but about being truly open and receptive to this really unique constituency.

The URGE method of devising was not based on writing alone but used embodied techniques such as physical and vocal shared improvisation to generate material. One of the Ensemble actors, Andrea Donaldson, says that the "content came seamlessly out of the actual training" and as she explains it, the actor/creators were the "living document." In this sense, the Ensemble offered their embodied experiences as a crucial part of the devising process. And it is important to keep in mind as you read this script that what is found on these pages is a flattened "description" of this living and embodied performance. In other words, the embodied and performed piece was the "real" text and what you read in this collection is written, two-dimensional, and arrested-in-time approximation.

URGE artist Joanna McIntyre describes the embodied nature of the devising and its relation to the training offered to the Ensemble: "It had to come out of their bodies. That's why the training was so important, and why the non-verbal ideas had to really come out of them." As Donaldson suggests this training practice was integral to the devising. Specifically, their working day began with training in the morning, starting with a physical warm-up, followed by breath work and voice. Then they developed an extended improvisation that became part of the devised material. They

---

5   Govan, Nicholson, and Normington, 6.

used various ingenious methods to uncover and create story. Donaldson explains that they would write to each other a kind of chain letter that was to contain their secrets. They also created rituals with mundane objects used as catalysts for improvisation. Once they had collected a quantity of devised scenes, URGE and the Ensemble sequenced the materials on storyboards comprised of bristol boards and sticky notes.

In *And by the way, Miss . . .* , the finished performance did not have a linear narrative and its storytelling was fractured and multimodal. For example, vocal material ranged from schoolyard rhymes to taunts to sports cheers, beat-box chants, and even fragments of Disney songs. Linda C. Smith describes the centrality of sound and music to their devising as "our core, in varying degrees. So you can see from the script so much vocabulary is sonic and connected to emotions. That's the way we work." This script carefully describes the soundscape that includes bells that regulate the girls' lives at home and at school, whistling, and the sound of their feet as they brush against the surface of the floor.

Just as the devised performance included multiple styles of music and sound, the performance was not confined to a singular, consistent acting style. In the script, the collaborators define two performance styles: "Treated Mundane" and the "Extraordinary." The first represents the rhythms of ordinary life, while scenes performed with the "Extraordinary" treatment allow for a fuller range of emotion and offer the actor/creators the opportunity to "live large emotionally."[6]

When reading this piece, you will see that the collective has included descriptions of the visual and design elements because they were integral to the movement score and equal to the words spoken and other aspects of the aural landscape of the play. Spatially, the actor/creators moved their own mobile screens to create the playing space in which the action took place. These moving screens suggested that the actors' bodies were extensions of the places in which they lived and were schooled. These screens also allowed the characters to actively create space, suggesting a kind of agency. Doreen Massey connects the relational aspects of space with the political and says that when space is "open, multiple and relational, unfinished and always becoming, [it] is a prerequisite for history to be open and thus a

---

6   URGE, personal interview with the authors, 4 November 2014.

prerequisite, too, for the possibility of politics."[7] Spatially and visually, this mobile, actor-controlled set worked to suggest that these young women were not wholly determined by the spaces in which they found themselves but were actively shaping their space.

RELATIONAL PEDAGOGICAL EXCHANGE

Devising can interrupt the power relations of conventional theatre between writer, director, and actor—as directing becomes a collective task accomplished through shared decision-making. All participants, URGE artists and the Ensemble, took active roles in both the generation of materials/content and in the negotiation of the sequencing and shaping of the performed work.

And by the way, Miss . . . was highly pedagogical, involving several kinds of learning exchanges in this intentionally intergenerational "girl-centred" devising process. In their consultations with teenage girls, URGE and the Ensemble learned about the breadth and complexities of their social relations. Secondly, the accomplished URGE artists instructed the younger acting Ensemble in their creation methods and training practice.

Training the Ensemble and developing the material to be performed were important, but of equal importance was the attention paid to the emotional and the relational aspects of the devising process. The URGE artists describe how they began and ended their sessions with check-ins and check-outs. Donaldson suggests that in creating *And by the way, Miss . . .* there was care not just for *what* was done but *how* it was done. The URGE artists recognized the importance of the relational and how crucial the right combination of Ensemble collaborators would be to the success of the devising process and the piece they collaboratively produced. Looking to devise a piece that expressed multiple perspectives in multidisciplinary ways, they sought a multicultural cast of actors who possessed a strong second skill. The URGE artists auditioned actors by asking for a prepared monologue written specifically for this project and used improvisation as a means of seeing how particular combinations of actors would work together.

---

7   Doreen Massey, *For Space* (Washington, DC: Sage, 2005), 59.

As the relational aspects of the work were crucial, the Ensemble artists "under consideration" also needed a facility for working with youth in post-performance activities such as group discussions and workshops. To assess their abilities in this area, the URGE artists took the group of aspiring Ensemble artists to schools where the young women would try out bits they had devised for an audience of young people. This offered URGE the chance to see how these younger artists interacted with youth and each other.

TIMEFRAME

The episodic creative process took place over two years. Donaldson explains that there was time spent with the project and also time spent away from it. At various stages the work was shared with different audiences that provoked discussions regarding content and associated issues of race, gender, and sexuality. This process was so intentionally collaborative that it opened itself up to negotiations the creative team had not prepared for, especially as they encountered the school system. Accessing an audience of girls through the schools embroiled them in unexpected political discussions about what could and could not be said. Specifically, the creative team brought viewers from the Toronto District School Board and the Toronto Catholic District School Board and what followed were discussions about vocabulary referencing the body and the racial mix of the participants— even questioning whether a bi-racial actor was "black enough" for the role. Tensions arose around the use of the words "menstruation" and "vagina" in schools. This exchange produced a discomfort in the artists who were uneasy being told what they could and could not do. Attempting to be actively consultative and dialogic, at times, the artistic aspirations of the collective clashed with the interests and constraints of schools. But these restrictions were also catalysts for creativity, and the limits placed on the work, according to URGE artist Katherine Duncanson, "gave us a creative impulse to find different ways to address the material—sonically—and then it was actually better. But previously as a collective, we never had to deal with, you know, censor this, censor that." In terms of what could and could not be said, Fides Krucker suggests performing in schools differed from performing in theatres, "If we were to do the piece in the school we wouldn't be allowed to say vagina, but in the theatre, there was an agreement that you know, 'My vagina's calling,' was okay."

AUDIENCES AND THE WORKSHOP DIALOGUES

The audience was not asked to just listen and absorb the piece, but to also become active participants or co-creators of the piece, offering feedback that informed the devising process that followed. As well, the intention of the devising was never just to "present" the work to an audience, but to use it as a tool of engagement, as a catalyst for political dialogue and further artistic expression. About the play, one teacher remarks how impressed both she and her students were:

> The best performance I've seen in a long time!!! I was truly impressed. I cried, I laughed, I cringed, I was entertained. The staging was simple but ingenious the way it transformed. Excellent use of sound, music and chants. Excellent acting. Well-paced. Good mix of funny and sad. All of the girls loved it! They even thanked me for taking them. They felt like they were being treated like grown-ups because of the sensitive issues, proper vocabulary and candid views and comments were used. They looked over at me during the "masturbation" scene as if to say "Are we going to be in trouble? Are they allowed to talk about this?" They *really* connected with the characters.[8]

Following the play, the Ensemble engaged the audiences in breakout post-show discussions. Donaldson describes these "massive workshop days" as requiring a high level of orchestration—getting the groups to Harbourfront where the performances took place and then breaking up the school groups so that there could be dialogue amongst people who did not know each other. Lynda Hill describes the coordination of these sessions: "The logistics were intense. We had five break-out rooms for voice, dance,

---

8 Quoted from URGE's feedback forms, which are reprinted later in the Creative Collaborators section. All quotations from teachers and students, unless otherwise noted, come from these feedback forms.

WOCPS   oof

visual arts, music, and writing workshops that the Ensemble facilitated after the show."

Theatre Direct intended to create "girl safe" spaces in which to talk about what was of pressing importance to girls in each conversation circle. Referring to the full-day workshop feedback forms completed by the teachers, it is clear that some of the girls were "shy" to speak up in groups of people they did not know. One teacher remarks, "Girls were given a safe environment to talk about their issues, thoughts, feelings" while another suggested that "I noticed that many of the girls felt self-conscious when they had to speak out loud. My colleague and I noticed most of the girls 'of colour' did not want to speak at all in front of the group when it was their turn." The girls themselves expressed how it was challenging, especially to speak alone. The reticence observed is worth noting because it points to the complexities and challenges associated with creating and sustaining trusting and safe relations, particularly in dialogic spaces that focus on the power relations associated with gender and female friendship.

Helen Nicholson troubles the notion of safe space and the assumed importance of trust in the field of drama education and pedagogy. She suggests that trust in drama classrooms and in applied theatre environments is not a given but that it has to be renegotiated constantly. According to Nicholson, trust is not sentiment or feeling but a performed act.[9] If a space is to be considered by participants as trustworthy, it has to be negotiated "not only in individualized terms, but within the context of the range of cultural, experiential and social differences represented in any given drama group."[10] Linda C. Smith recounts that "there were some girls who would not participate in the workshop discussions, even in a room full of girls, for fear of leaving themselves open to ridicule."

Even in such sensitively orchestrated dialogue sessions, it may have been that for some of the girl participants the risk of talking was too great. On the teacher feedback forms a variety of opinions were expressed regarding the "safety" the girls felt. Perhaps this variety of response suggests that in some of the workshop/dialogue sessions, there was frank talk and that a kind of safety was established for some of the girls, while for others it was

---

9   Helen Nicholson, "The Politics of Trust: Drama Education and the Ethic of Care," *Research in Drama Education* 7.1 (2002), 84.

10   Ibid., 87.

"safer" to remain quiet. We suggest that it could be a mistake to assume that the girls who stayed quiet were disengaged. Jacques Rancière challenges the easy division between participation and being passive in *The Emancipated Spectator*. Instead, he states that even what might appear to be passive is actually active as the spectator "observes, selects, compares, interprets. She links what she sees to a host of other things that she has seen on other stages, in other kinds of place. She composes her own poem with the elements of the poem before her."[11] What he suggests is that for quiet spectators, there may be more going on than meets the eye.

There may be an additional dimension to consider. Drawing on the work of Elizabeth Ellsworth, Kathleen Gallagher, in her work using drama with urban youth in schools, suggests that "knowledges of the body, desire, and emotion are most often pedagogically marginalized."[12] Given that the girls attended the *And by the way, Miss . . .* workshops with their teachers on school trips, perhaps even away from school, the youth perceived the post-performance workshop space as an extension of school space where the body is not often considered or talked about. Matthew Reason suggests in his study on audiences that talking and reflecting on performances may be "multiple and indeed contradictory. It will certainly be impacted upon and transformed by the process of reflection and constrained by the limits and structures of our discourse."[13] Whatever the reasons for silence on the part of some of the youth, we consider this as representative of the range of audience engagement rather than evidence of youth disengagement. On the feedback forms, both the teachers and the youth praised the efforts of the *And by the way, Miss . . .* team and made enthusiastic suggestions for future work.

We would like to offer one final point about the role of the audience in the archiving of this devising process. The script you read here has the suggestions of audiences folded into it, and, as such, the audience acts as a kind of invisible part of this performance script. The script has not been annotated with the reactions of the audience specifically, as this would be impossible given that the performances took place so long ago. For future

---

11   Jacques Rancière, *The Emancipated Spectator* (New York: Verso, 2009), 13.

12   Kathleen Gallagher, *The Theatre of Urban: Youth and Schooling in Dangerous Times* (Toronto: University of Toronto Press, 2007), 81.

13   Matthew Reason, "Asking the Audience: Audience Research and the Experience of Theatre," *About Performance* 10 (2010): 32.

devising projects, however, to record the important and active role the audience plays would be a fascinating dimension to include in a devised "script" that gets "written down."

FEMINIST COLLECTIVE CREATION

And by the way, Miss's use of devising as a pedagogical tool to bring together multidisciplinary and multi-generational female artists also builds on the rich legacy of feminist collective creation in Canada.[14] Rising from Canada's alternative theatre movement of the 1960s and 1970s, which employed collective creation as a key means of developing a distinct, national body of dramatic work,[15] feminist theatre collectives of the 1970s and 1980s saw collaboration and devising as strategies to challenge the centrality and authority of the text in theatre and give voice to multiple perspectives. While these outcomes were and continue to be part of the appeal of devising for theatre practitioners more generally (as discussed above), they were particularly attractive to feminist artists. Ann Wilson, in her 1985 article "The Politics of the Script," emphasizes the historic importance of displacing the text for feminist theatre artists in Canada:

> Power, as it is constituted by logocentrism, refuses to reveal the terms of its authority and, instead, establishes itself as absolute and beyond interrogation. Given that this has effected the exclusion of

---

14 We use both "collective creation" and "devising" to refer to URGE's creative process in this piece. While theatre scholars have debated the distinctions between these two terms, Kathryn Mederos Syssoyeva and Scott Proudfit use them interchangeably, defining collective creation as "the practice of collaboratively devising works of performance" (2). They suggest that "devising" has been historically used in Britain and Australia, but that the term has come to replace "collective creation" in North America over the past decade, particularly amongst theatre scholars (10). We align ourselves with their understanding of the terms, and use them interchangeably as well. Kathryn Mederos Syssoyeva, "Towards a New History of Collective Creation," in *Collective Creation in Contemporary Performance*, ed. Mederos Syssoyeva and Scott Proudfit (New York: Palgrave Macmillan, 2013), 1–11.

15 Alan Filewod, *Collective Encounters: Documentary Theatre in English Canada* (Toronto: University of Toronto Press, 1987), viii.

women, the project of feminism should be to question, subvert, and disrupt the authority of the signifier, the word.[16]

By challenging a model of theatre based on the single-authored script, collective creation prompted experimentation with form and highlighted non-textual elements of performance such as movement, multimedia effects, and music and sound. As seen in the diverse work of companies such as Winnipeg's Nellie McClung Theatre (1968–2002), Toronto's Nightwood Theatre (1979–present) and Company of Sirens (1986–present), Montreal's Théâtre Expérimental des Femmes (1979–1987), and Calgary's Maenad (1987–2001), collective creation yields theatre that is non-linear, imagistic, and polyvocal.

The URGE collective's *And by the way, Miss . . .* shares many similarities with the feminist work that preceded it. We have discussed how the group's devising process distributed the power amongst the creators, ensemble, and even the audience of young people, who were consulted as the piece was workshopped at school and community performances. The play that we see as a result is episodic and features stories told from multiple perspectives, suggesting that there is no single "truth." For example, in Scene Three, the characters bounce around the stage like "emotional atoms" recounting their differing takes on an interaction with a cute boy. Heavier issues are also examined from multiple points of view, like when speculation about Lauren's sexual history in Scene Twelve is followed by her revelations of abuse in Scene Sixteen:

> See, you think that because I'm fourteen I must be out of control, right? Yeah, well, how about this. One night I was going up to my room and I accidentally knocked over this vase that was like a hundred and fifty years old. You want to talk out of control? Yeah, well, why don't we talk about what happened when my dad came up the stairs.

No single perspective is positioned as more legitimate than others— the audience never learns the "truth" of Lauren's sexual experience, but

---

16   Ann Wilson, "The Politics of the Script," *Canadian Theatre Review* 43 (1985): 175.

rather gains insight into her complex reality. These multiple perspectives are enforced by the play's *mise en scène*, which often features separate but concurrent action, providing the audience with "simultaneous POVs of each girl."

Moreover, like much of the feminist theatre that came before it, *And by the way, Miss . . .* displaces the power of the text by using sound, movement, and image as integral storytelling components. For example, in Scene Two, the "rhythmic and pitched vocal score" and the "onomatopoeic text," which builds and overlaps, combined with the "playful, synchronized gestural choreography" facilitate an exploration of beauty ideology, female competition, and friendship that establishes the tone of the play and some of its central themes. The preening in which the girls engage in this scene becomes a trope throughout the play, shifting between humour and seriousness. In Scene Seven, the characters playfully examine their changing bodies; in Scene Eight, the spotlight is on Christina, who delivers a monologue about her eating disorder as the other characters "form a vocal and physical chorus" in the background. This interspersing of monologue with group scenes and powerful, collectively performed songs also draws on a legacy of feminist performance work. In productions like Nightwood's *This Is For You, Anna*, a collective creation about gendered violence that began development in 1983, monologues are used to give voice to women's individual struggles, while collective moments demonstrate their shared struggle to overcome discrimination and oppression. Scene Eight provides a window into the pressures experienced by one character to stay thin, but its placement directly after Scene Seven shows that Christina is not alone as she grapples with body image issues.

What distinguishes *And by the way, Miss . . .* from feminist collective creation in the 1970s and 1980s, however, is how it adapts the practice for a new generation of artists and audiences by celebrating differences between women.[17] Collective creation reached its peak of popularity amongst feminist artists in the early 1980s; after this point, many companies including Nightwood and Théâtre Expérimental des Femmes began to move to single-authored work. This change happened for different reasons, but

---

17 "A new generation" is key here, as unlike many of the feminist collective creations from the 1970s and 1980s, the URGE collective made *And by the way, Miss . . .* for—and in collaboration with—teen girls.

particularly because the collective process's drawn-out development period was time-consuming and costly, and involved constant negotiation and compromise that proved straining to many company members. Moreover, the broader feminist movement began to shift at this time, as women questioned assumptions about their shared experiences and the notion of a universal sisterhood. How could theatre account for the differences amongst women? While collectives tried to preserve difference by resisting a traditional, fixed, and authoritative script, power dynamics within groups meant that equitable representation in performance was sometimes an ideal rather than a reality. Connectedly, the importance, at the time, of giving voice to women's experiences in a socio-political climate that silenced them led some groups to subsume individual needs and identities under those of the collective in order to present a "unified" front.

Developed during the third wave of feminism, which is often characterized by its "comfort with contradiction and pluralism," *And by the way, Miss . . .* shows careful attention to difference.[18] Just as there is no single "truth" inherent in the narrative, the play avoids making essentialist generalizations about all women or privileging one young woman's experience over others. Lauren, Diana, Christina, Amber, and Andrea, in their cultural backgrounds, life experiences, and sexualities, represent a diversity of identities that would have mirrored its Toronto audience. Moreover, in their contradictions they reflect the complex realities of young women's lives, where friendship coexists with jealousy and competition, where confidence hides insecurities, and where "you're nowhere / And ev'rywhere at the same time." Like many feminist collective creations, the play does not offer narrative closure. Though in its penultimate scene the friends save Andrea from a potential suicide attempt, the play resists resolving the characters' personal problems that it has exposed. In the closing scene of the play, the girls sing a song about friendship that underscores the tumultuousness and uncertainty of their relationships:

---

18   Shelley Scott discusses the difficulty of defining Third Wave feminism, but offers this description of it: "Third Wave feminism is most often associated with a younger generation of feminist activism, an interest in popular culture and sexual agency, and an acceptance of pluralism and contradiction." Shelley Scott, *Nightwood Theatre: A Woman's Work is Always Done* (Edmonton: AU Press, 2010), 219, 13.

DIANA: What is a friend?

CHRISTINA: Could it be that it's just a word.

LAUREN: Something you've always wanted

AMBER: From a song you heard.

ANDREA: Or just another one of those

ALL: Big fat lies
'Cause many nights this word has made me cry
So hard my stomach hurts
Deep down inside.

As a Third Wave collective creation, the play troubles the notion of unity. It does not promote an ideal of feminist sisterhood, but instead underscores the importance of respecting difference. The girls sing the final verse of their song together:

She'll never tell you what to do
And you know all that she's been through
You've seen her scars and she's seen you

She'll let you be yourself
So let her be herself
I want to be . . .

The accompanying image, of the five young women standing beside their screens and "signing off," perhaps suggests a new form of solidarity, one borne out of difference and struggle.

CREATIVE COLLABORATORS
Commissioning Voice, Creators' Voices, Performers' Voices, Audience Voices, Compiled with Notes by Heather Fitzsimmons Frey

Theatre Direct commissioned URGE, a music-driven all-female collective based in Toronto, to make an interdisciplinary piece for grade seven and eight girls (aged eleven to fourteen) that was about their lives. Over the course of two years, they did workshops with girls in schools to get material and learn about what girls cared about. A few subjects—birth control, menstruation, masturbation—were taboo because they were working with schools, but when Theatre Direct decided the performances would take place outside of schools, and there would be only girls (no boys) in the audiences, the options for what they could create and the topics they could address expanded. The URGE collective decided they were too old to play the parts themselves, so they went through a complicated audition process in order to find an ensemble of multi-skilled and multicultural young actors who had the instincts to work the way they did and who were willing to learn the URGE process. Every rehearsal, the women cast as the Ensemble did three hours of warm-up and training in the URGE core skill areas: breath, embodied voice, movement, and music. Improvisations and exercises in the afternoon led to the creation of storyboards, and finally a show that was tested with five different schools before it was actually a full production, with all-day workshops for girls, that took place at Toronto's Harbourfront Centre.

In an effort to emphasize the multi-vocal nature of the devised process, what follows are comments made by many of the creative collaborators who built the show: leaders, writers, performers, and audience. Ten years after the piece was staged, Heather Fitzsimmons Frey interviewed Lynda Hill, Artistic Director of Theatre Direct (25 November 2014); conducted a focus group with URGE (25 August 2014); and spoke to one audience member about what she remembered (25 August 2014). Lynda Hill requested email commentary from several members of the Ensemble (August 2014). Besides these reflections from a temporal distance, the Audience Voices section includes comments drawn from audience feedback forms that Theatre Direct gave to girls and their teachers immediately following performances in 2004.

Commissioning Voice—Lynda Hill, Artistic Director, Theatre Direct

HEATHER: Why did Theatre Direct commission this work and why is it special?

LYNDA: I wanted a piece of theatre for young audiences unlike any that had ever been on Toronto's stages. I wanted a work that wasn't text-driven, that was interdisciplinary, and that incorporated all of the artistic languages that I really love to see in theatre aimed at young audiences—dance/movement, music, visual imagery . . . And, finally, I wanted a piece that was provocative and political and that spoke to our audience in a way that wasn't finger-wagging or predictable in its subject matter. At that time there wasn't a lot of theatre specifically for this age; twelve-to-fourteen-year-olds or grade sevens and eights. This audience was often tacked on to work aimed at children or included in performances for high schools, so the material was often above or below their level. There was an absence of theatre that engaged young people at the height of a profound, dynamic period of social, emotional, and physical development.

But I also knew that the experiences of young men and women of this age were so distinct. I wanted to really challenge our understanding of this audience and to explore the idea of speaking just to girls. I felt there was a lot of judgment and bias about girls of this age and assumptions about how they would behave if faced with a theatre piece of this nature and subject matter . . . ultimately, I wanted to stand up for them and show the adults in their lives how incredibly sophisticated they were and how capable they were of engaging with complex work.

I began to think that if we wanted to come at intimacy, sexuality, the nature of friendship during this terrifying threshold period of adolescence, it would be better to just perform for girls and remove the boy element altogether. There were a bunch of news reports at the time about girl-to-girl bullying, and a whole bunch of material depicting girls as evil, covert, undermining, divisive beings who would smile and then stab you in the back. As a woman, I know the nature of bullying among girls is very different than with boys, but I felt that girls were not being given a fair shake.

And then I thought who better to tackle this subject matter than URGE, who were, at the time, considered to be one of the most progressive interdisciplinary collectives. And as professionals and artists of great integrity they took this on with such respect, attention to detail, and spent so much time on their front to develop a really effective process that involved training an entire young ensemble. They are such professionals that it was impossible for them to compromise in quality, in detail, and that's the way it should be with Theatre for Young Audiences.

Every aspect of their research informed the final script: the workshops they did as research, the girls' words, their ideas—if it didn't find its way in through actual words, it could be through a gesture, a sound, a look—such an effective research process. It was not just about confirming their [the artists'] instincts, but about being truly open and receptive to this really unique constituency.

It's a process of translating, in a way—at an early workshop the audience sat with their arms folded, slumped in their chairs, heads down. And the performers were terrified because they thought the audience hated it, but actually the girls were just intensely engaged—that's the way they showed it! They had a lot of feedback afterwards. So those girls weren't checking out—they were actually deeply involved.

Another challenge of doing work for adolescents is to avoid mimicking teen behaviour. The actor needs to find the essence of that character, the truth of that character. URGE and the Ensemble negotiated that so beautifully.

HEATHER: What about the show was special?

LYNDA: Well, it was the audiences of girls and teachers and how much they loved it. I don't remember schools really questioning or worrying about bringing only the girls. Instead, they embraced this really positive girl-focused event. The production and audiences basically took over Harbourfront Centre, thanks to their generosity. The logistics were intense. We had five break-out rooms for voice, dance, visual arts, music, and writing workshops that the Ensemble facilitated after the show. The head of the arts at the Toronto District School Board at that time and at the Toronto Catholic School Board were extremely supportive, both in terms of facilitating our outreach to schools, and also financially.

The scale was big—but I was new at Theatre Direct, I was eager to take on challenges—I knew I had the freedom to be radical! We created this piece when arts and education sectors were starting to experience the true impact of the Mike Harris Ontario government. However, along with the investment in a commission, and a full research and development process, Theatre Direct engaged over thirty professional women in the creation and production of this piece. Quite audacious, really, for the times, and for the size of our company!

Creators' Voices—URGE (Fides Krucker, Marie-Josée Chartier, Katherine Duncanson, Joanna McIntyre, and Linda C. Smith)

HEATHER: How did you decide to do a piece for teenage girls?

FIDES: Lynda Hill of Theatre Direct had the spark. She commissioned URGE to do this piece about teenage girls. She thought telling the story in an interdisciplinary fashion—to tell the story of grade seven and eight girls—would be more effective than just using a script. She approached *us* about it.

LINDA: . . . It was about that age, you know, where it is still possible to become who you are . . .

KATHERINE: Even before casting the piece we—we didn't even have a piece—we were doing workshops in schools in the fall, and we brought in girls as animators who could potentially have been cast, who did the exercises along with us, and—and as a result we kind of had a sense of the themes in the show before we even had a cast.

MARIE-JOSÉE: I remember trying to figure out what this show would be about. And we came to the place where we asked the girls [who came to the initial workshops], "If you went to see a show, what would you like to see on stage?" There were some thematic things that kept coming back, but friendship was the thing that everything was orbiting around. It came up with all of them.

LINDA: It was just before the whole bullying thing got super public, but it was clearly in our piece. And things about betrayal . . . there were some girls who would not participate in the workshop discussions, even in a room full of girls, for fear of leaving themselves open to ridicule.

MARIE-JOSÉE: You said teenagers but we were really creating for tweens. There was a lot of discussion around "one second you're a little girl and the next second you're an adult." And that fine line that a lot of them are navigating. Culturally some of those tweens are way more precocious than others. Even in different schools. That was a huge gap.

LINDA: Friendship and body image were the big themes that emerged. But there were a lot of topics that we just didn't have time for.

KATHERINE: There was some discussion about including sexuality in terms of "same sex" but that wasn't in the show either.

JOANNA: Well, Christina stood for that, in a way. She was pretty androgynous.

KATHERINE: In 2002 in that age group, it wasn't a part of the conversation—but now it would make sense to do that. But it wasn't really there. In those workshops that started in 2002—a lot has happened since then. Because I think the show still translates, but . . . But now that it's being published, it's interesting to think that if someone were to do it, could there be room, say in Christina's character, to go there. You know, somewhere within the improvisation of the piece. Otherwise they have to update the text and do their own process. But even in our own group, one of the actors hadn't come out yet. She has now. But it was a different time.

HEATHER: Could you talk about the *And by the way, Miss . . .* creation process?

LINDA: We work collectively, and interdisciplinarily to learn from each other. Music was our core, in varying degrees. So you can see from the script so much vocabulary is sonic and connected to emotions. That's the way we work.

JOANNA: I came to this multidisciplinary work through the theatre and text and I found . . . You can say so much with an object, like the Slinky, or stamping feet, or collective vocalization that you can't express in words. It doesn't really shout out in the video document, as when you're in the space. The penetrating sound, the collectiveness of this work, the multidisciplinary nature—it really got *right in here*.

SEVERAL WOMEN AT ONCE: So much can be expressed through just the rubbing of the feet. And the humorous parts. Like the hair—the pubic hair—the monkey. Without text it can be over the top and it helps.

FIDES: We always look for irreverence in the way we work.

MARIE-JOSÉE: The warm-ups were creating material and warm-ups and training all at once.

JOANNA: When the Ensemble girls came in I became a kind of dramaturgical voice.

LINDA: You took us through a dramaturgy workshop!

JOANNA: *(laughing)* That's right! I did! We did a lot of storyboard stuff at Fides's place, with tons of Post-its. We had a meeting to try and uncover that dramaturgical process and approach.

MARIE-JOSÉE: When you came in, you had to learn to be a facilitator and not a director. And then we had to learn how to direct the Ensemble as a group.

FIDES: This all came from Joanna recognizing that we were really too old to play this particular age group, and it took us all to the next level in our co-creative skills.

LINDA: It also gave us a window into our process that we may not have had. When you have to put it on somebody else and *explain* it to somebody else, it crystalizes what it is.

JOANNA: It had to come out of their bodies. That's why the training was so important, and why the non-verbal ideas had to really come out of them.

FIDES: I want to say one thing about a decision I made very early on when writing the script from the video. I decided to try not to use the word "awkward" in any of the stage directions. Whenever Victoria [Theatre Direct Associate] and I were talking about the story in the beginning, the word "awkward" came up, like, thirty times. So I said, let's see if we can do this without using the word "awkward." "They moved awkwardly"; "They spoke awkwardly." It stopped having meaning when we used it too much. It's a cliché. We needed something that could be more expressive and more specific. It *is* so true of that age group—in a way, they are like insects, trying to find all their little bits—but it isn't enough. I just had to share that. The urge to use it was incredible.

KATHERINE: It kind of summed up how I felt at that age, too. I felt so exposed. As if people would *notice* me. Everything about me felt so enormous.

HEATHER: How did you develop your process as a company?

FIDES: I had a desire to work in a non-hierarchical fashion. I didn't know these women, but I went to them to see if they wanted to work together in a way that—since we could all use our voices we could all do sound; since we could all walk we could all do movement—I never thought about text—because I had never really used text before in performance. But I *really didn't want any guys in the room* and I didn't know why. I just wanted to try it. I'd worked well with guys. Some women do work in a patriarchal way too—but here we were. And I wanted to start from scratch. We didn't know what we were doing, but we were artists . . .

KATHERINE: And being all women is different—it gives us a rawness, a willingness to fail. For me anyway. Just to feel that the real truth could come out and it would be safe. We could cry; we could be exhausted.

MARIE-JOSÉE: It was really very intense.

HEATHER: What aspects of the show were controversial or challenging?

KATHERINE: The feedback we got from the girls in that workshop when the boys were there was that they couldn't watch it. The boys were making comments. They were saying things. Girls wanted to say things because they loved it, but they couldn't because of the boys. They wanted to talk about these taboo things but they just couldn't because of the boys.

MARIE-JOSÉE: They're twelve-year-old boys!

FIDES: And they often go through puberty a little later so they seem younger. At that age in particular girls are becoming more nurturing, but they are becoming super covert about their natural aggression. That scene where they are working with their feet, and it seems sort of like gossip, and gossip spreading like wildfire . . . it seems like that.

MARIE-JOSÉE: The bullying scenes got a really strong response. That seemed really radical to their age group to be able to show that thing. They would cheer, as I recall it. That it could happen between girls. After working that scene with Diana—people—the cast—we all felt really yucky.

JOANNA: Sometimes there were interesting mixes about why people were laughing in certain sections. Like Christina and the chocolate. They were like, "Why are people laughing? They don't know what it's like." Sometimes they couldn't laugh because it was too close to the bone. One person said the bullying scene did not go far enough, although it was hard to get it that far.

KATHERINE: We couldn't say "menstruation" in a school. So, it gave us a creative impulse to find different ways to address the material—sonically—and then it was actually better. But previously as a collective, we never had to deal with, you know, censor this, censor that.

FIDES: If we were to do the piece in the school we wouldn't be allowed to say vagina, but in the theatre, there was an agreement that you know, "My vagina's calling," was okay.

MARIE-JOSÉE: After one early showing we broke into groups and I was in a corner with three black women from the board of education and I found out that they thought Amber wasn't black enough, and that she was too skinny. I'll never forget that. This kind of friction within that community.

HEATHER: What is a moment you loved?

FIDES: I think what impressed me most is how much is going on in any one moment and how the Ensemble tracked each other. They were processing on so many different levels as they were performing. And then as an audience member, you can't really separate it out. It's coming to you as a whole, not just visual or . . . and you get to receive as a whole person. And the scene for me that is really emblematic of that is the sleepover scene.

LINDA: Yeah—how did they become mermaids? And suddenly they're boys. And it's audacious without really whacking people over the head with it.

FIDES: And it's irreverent.

MARIE-JOSÉE: The over-the-top scene with Andrea. The hair—the monkeys, the pubic hair—the release in the house. You could feel them think, "This is so ridiculous." But then they let themselves go and then they would lose it. The joy in taking that to ridiculousness. It was joyful, that recognition.

KATHERINE: I loved that "Hi, Benjamin," the exaggerated quality they got . . . that cartoon feeling, the humour. They really did a wonderful thing with that. The humour came through with the zits one—they all went EWWW, but the audience all went there.

JOANNA: And then everyone jumped in . . . Andrea's monologue at the end is, for me, very powerful. That song was so powerful. It was so Andrea. The message—it came so close to the end of the show. And so unexpected that *she* was the one going through that. I think it's always like that that you don't see any signs—any warning signs—before. And that the friends are really *there*.

HEATHER: How is it different to create work for a young audience compared to work for a general or adult audience?

KATHERINE: I don't think we thought about it. We just tried to be truthful.

MARIE-JOSÉE: In fact it's a more demanding audience. A younger audience—you feel their reaction right away.

LINDA: We had all these areas of expertise and virtuosity, but we were using mundane objects, everyday objects to inspire us. We didn't work differently for a younger audience because those things really translate beautifully across ages. We wouldn't have known how to leave that behind. It took us a while to develop our style, but once we had the values related to collective, interdisciplinary creation, these were always always there—it just took us a decade to become half decent at it!

FIDES: Joanna gave good advice: don't let them act like thirteen-year-olds, just let them channel that energy. I think that's perfect advice for the work that we do. Through sound, music, you can channel that energy. It felt like that was a really excellent interface. And the girls were always surprised to find out the age of the performers. Diana was thirty-six in this show! I think the screens that Shawn Kerwin suggested and designed opened us up imaginatively and concretely to the public and private spaces of girls in that age group. I remember panicking at first because of all the logistics we would be faced with . . . but you embraced them, Josée! It was brilliant that the actors got to move them—a subtle way to let girls have agency. And then Bonnie Beecher's lighting illuminating their extraordinary emotional lives.

LINDA: After we performed in the schools, we did some movement work, and then we broke up into groups to talk (with food) and we told them that we were making a play for their age group, for girls, and we wanted their advice about what it should be about. Just when we were talking to them—it was really interesting—different things came up, little stories came it, it was like, being included or not being included, who you could trust. We had a remarkable discussion at Jane and Finch. It was predominantly a black school, but there was a white girl in that group and she said, "I can't wait till I learn how to drive. Because I know exactly where I'm going to go. And I know the *way*." Ottawa or something because that's where her aunt lives. The group kind of got quiet. You [Katherine] said, "Do you have someone you can talk to or do you keep a diary for what's going on?" You know, because it was clear that something was going on. And she said, "She's my diary," pointing to her friend. And for me it was such an illustration of friendship. She couldn't tell anybody. But she could tell *that* person, and that person could listen and that person kind of had her back. It made me feel how deep thirteen-year-olds are. How extraordinarily complex their lives are and how deep their feelings are.

Performers' Voices—The Ensemble (Lauren Brotman, Amber Godfrey, Diana Tso, Andrea Donaldson)

LAUREN: *And by the way, Miss . . .* was a tremendous time for me, for all of us, artistically speaking. We had the rare privilege of creating a new work over a two-year period and, at the same time, being trained in interdisciplinary performance by the stunning URGE collective. Lynda Hill and Theatre Direct were brave enough to commission this work that was sophisticated in form and content, challenging all of us to dig deeply into subject matter and theatrical styles that were unfamiliar to most. And at the same time we were asked to collaborate with the young women in high schools for which this piece was being created, leading workshops throughout the process as well as post-performance. We were given incredible tools that we could use for the rest of our careers, as performers, theatre-makers and artist–educators. And for all of us to be honoured with two Dora Awards and the Jessica Fraser Award for Outstanding Contribution to Theatre for Young Audiences was equally rewarding. It was a time of immense growth, one where we developed immense trust in and respect for one another and the work . . . It is one that will stay with us for the rest of our careers and lives.

AMBER: In terms of impact . . . working on *ABTWM* was easily the highlight of my four years in Toronto. From the first audition—we had to bring in three minutes of original work to perform and I had never in my life performed my own material. I remember we had to call in to a voicemail service to find out if we'd been called back. The anticipation—the excitement!

And then of course the ladies. All the amazing, beautiful, inspiring women who I got to be around and learn from. The URGE collective, Lynda Hill and Marie Beath Badian and of course our strong Ensemble. I learned so much about collaboration, about trust and mistrust, how ego and insecurity can get in the way but how anything can be overcome when you feel supported.

DIANA: The impact of this project on me as a theatre artist continues to be the journey and joy of collaboration, ensemble creation, on a playground experimenting as an actor and a writer. My work continues to be creations balancing text, sound/music, and movement in collaboration with other artists in bringing to life a story. As I write this reflection in August 2014, I am working on the second draft of my new play, a love story during war, in preparation for its development next month. As part of the development of this play, Fides Krucker will guide our collective in her evolving pedagogy for voice and music creation, creating and recreating scenes and characters. We'll also explore "Chorus," which as an ensemble in *And by the way, Miss . . .* was instrumental and continues to be so in the way I create theatre, as the heartbeat of a story that carries characters on their journey.

ANDREA: . . . so stirring to rethink about it. It is a major artistic highlight and (of course) career-launcher for me.

I got a bit tearful thinking about how much Theatre Direct invested in it—how much care was taken. It felt like the most important project in the world at the time—partially because of my youth/innocence and partially because we wanted to give everything that we could (expose ourselves, live the experience really honestly)—somehow that came from the top down. From Lynda Hill.

Audience Voices—Audience survey comments from girls and teachers, 2004

GIRL: I liked that it was funny and the singing was good.

GIRL: I liked that they used foul language because it made it more realistic and you could relate to it.

GIRL: I disliked: When Christina was talking about killing a cat & when Diana was made fun of because of her height.

Theatre Direct saved many more audience surveys, but these three comments highlight several notable things. First, sometimes the comments are not what might be considered sophisticated analysis ("it was funny and the singing was good," for example) but we should not assume that means spectators had a simple experience—rather that they may have lacked the words to put it onto paper. The second comment affirms that URGE found effective ways to connect to girls where they were at in their own time—the piece felt fresh to contemporary audiences, and at least one audience member felt the text-devising choices made the piece seem "real." I suspect when the girl wrote that foul language made it seem more realistic that she also felt respected, rather than "talked down to" because of a more honest portrayal of young people's conversations. This use of the word "real" is also particularly interesting in relation to the ideas about "real" life discussed by Alan Dilworth and Andrew Kushnir regarding *The Middle Place*. Finally, young audience members sometimes indicate "dislikes" that might, at first glance, seem to suggest that the spectator would have preferred the play to be different in some way. However, it is possible to read these "dislikes" as reactions to the character and content—that the "killing a cat" moment and the bullying moments were upsetting and disturbing, but not necessarily "bad" theatre. After all, a play can be appreciated and thought-provoking even if it makes a person feel uncomfortable. That this audience member did not like Diana's bullying scene actually affirms URGE's claim that the scene was very powerful for many girl spectators.

TEACHER: The preparatory work was some of the most memorable work done in 2004. Girls were given a safe environment to talk about their issues, thoughts, feelings.

TEACHER: Regarding the workshops, I noticed that many of the girls felt self-conscious when they had to speak out loud. My colleague and I noticed most of the girls "of colour" did not want to speak at all in front of the group when it was their turn.

These above two comments attest to the complexities of finding a safe space, even in an all-girl environment, and the ways that social constructions such as race could influence a girl's interest in or willingness to participate.

TEACHER: They thoroughly enjoyed it, found it relevant, well acted. Liked that just girls were there. Liked the humour.

TEACHER: On a number of occasions throughout the performance I heard one or two of the girls exclaiming about something that they particularly related to. When I asked the girls what they liked best some of them would tell me, but most were still too self-conscious to say.

TEACHER: They could relate to the issues surrounding feeling left out and feeling not pretty enough.

All three of the above teachers commented that they felt their students could "relate" to the work, and that they found it relevant—just like the girls did in their own comments. But, just as some spaces did not feel safe enough for some girls to talk about their feelings, some girls did not feel comfortable discussing their spectatorship experience with their teachers.

TEACHER: The best performance I've seen in a long time!!! I was truly impressed. I cried, I laughed, I cringed, I was entertained. The staging was simple but ingenious the way it transformed. Excellent use of sound, music and chants. Excellent acting. Well-paced. Good mix of funny and sad. All of the girls loved it! They even thanked me for taking them. They felt like they were being treated like grown-ups because of the sensitive issues, proper vocabulary and candid views and comments were used. They looked over at me during the "masturbation" scene as if to say "Are we going to be in trouble? Are they allowed to talk about this?" They *really* connected with the characters.

This comment is significant because the teacher notes the complexity of the multidisciplinary performance style, the contemporary, honest, and connected nature of the script, and the way that the language and the content made the girls feel respected. The teacher also seems to suggest that in a show like this, "really connecting with the characters" rather than being introduced to someone unexpected or unfamiliar is part of the goal—the characters should be a mirror of the spectators' own lives and seem to be someone they might know. The research and development phase of creating this script was absolutely essential for getting to that point.

LAURA DUNCANSON: (grade eight student in 2004, reflecting on the play ten years later) . . . I was coming to Toronto from a small town in Nova Scotia. Not a lot of exposure to music or dance or theatre.

My first experiences with the style of the piece were at first sort of "whoa"—but in the end really loving it, thinking it was cool. But initially feeling a bit weird, I guess, because I hadn't been exposed to that kind of interdisciplinary work.

I totally connected with Christina's focus on wanting to be thin and hiding under baggy clothes. And also, girls at that time can be really *mean* and I myself had only one really good girl friend. We both understood each other. We were a bit older for our age and because we found each other those years were happy years for us, but you know, we would see other girls in grade eight and grade nine—these girls would be talking about each other and saying mean things and—we knew could be a part of their group but it wouldn't be very fun.

I was surprised about the real age of the performers. They really captured the struggles one goes through at the age, and the awkwardness. The obsession with being really thin—I was really struck by Christina's performance. And also with Lauren, she was sort of— she didn't strike me as the promiscuous one, but the one who was a lot more developed, and I remember at that age in grade eight, I had boobs and I had a butt, and not many girls at that age did, and I received a lot of attention. And you know, at first it was flattering it was like, "Oh, kind of nice," but then it wasn't nice because then you feel fat. To be curvy—it was like, the back and forth. Yeah it was so cool to come up and see the play. I really liked it.

CREATIVE JOURNEY

And by the way, Miss . . . was developed over two years through research and workshops. A production workshop took place at Young People's Theatre in May of 2004.

Students participating in the initial research and development phase came from St. Matthew Catholic School, St. Francis de Sales Catholic School, Bowmore Road Junior and Senior Public School, King Edward Junior and Senior Public School, and Central Technical School, all in Toronto. URGE also met with an ad hoc group of Toronto Island tweens and went to the mall with Fides's niece Naomi Krucker and her friends to get less urban perspectives.

And by the way, Miss . . . was presented in a daylong theatre and education program designed exclusively for girls. Students watched the performance in the morning and then participated in music, movement, visual-arts, and spoken-word workshops inspired by the themes and issues in the production. The visual-arts workshops were designed and coordinated by the Harbourfront Centre's School by the Water and led by Golnar Rastar, Anne Devitt, Liliana De Irisarri, and Carol Shelly. Many thanks to Melanie Fernandez, Toronto Arts Council Director of Community and Education, and Grant Peckford, School by the Water Coordinator.

The published script was reconstructed and fleshed-out by Fides Krucker with preliminary assistance from Victoria Stacey.

And by the way, Miss . . . was commissioned, developed, and produced by Theatre Direct Canada. It premiered at the Studio Theatre, Harbourfront Centre, Toronto, on November 21, 2004. It featured the following cast and creative team:

The Ensemble:

Lauren Brotman
Andrea Donaldson
Amber Godfrey
Christina Sicoli
Diana Tso

Direction: URGE collective, spearheaded by Fides Krucker
Stage management: Annie McWhinnie
Set and costume design: Shawn Kerwin
Lighting design: Bonnie Beecher
Bell cues: Rick Sacks
Production management: Peter Debrecini
Scenic painting: Mattea Kennedy
Dramaturgy: Joanna McIntyre

NOTES ON THE SCRIPT

Improvisation: 1) This piece was created through improvisatory structures that were gradually refined to make a fixed script with a clear and repeatable text, sound, and movement score. 2) A few scenes in the piece still lend themselves to improv within performance, as long as the dramaturgical architecture stays intact. Christina's stand-up routine in "Skinny Cat" is an example of this, as well as Andrea's growing-up speech in "Eternal Slumber Party." 3) Many of the sung vocal sections use some improvisation, asking the performers to have an immediate and flexible engagement with the musical structures, and a heightened sensitivity to one anothers' impulses. 4) The text in this script reflects the archival video taken at the dress rehearsal.

Screens: There are five movable screens, one for each girl, that roll freely to set each scene. To keep transitions simple each screen moves within a fixed corridor running from upstage to downstage. These screen corridors are assigned, from stage right to stage left, to Andrea, Christina, Diana, Amber, and Lauren. The screens are two-sided and each one is a slightly different size. The side indicating institutional/public life is flat and grey like a hallway locker. The bedroom/private side is brightly coloured (according to character) and has a low platform where each girl can sit or stand as well as a curtain. Their props and clothing are stored here. The screens are used as musical instruments to add to the layered soundscape of the show.

Screen formations: The screens' various onstage formations create location. Private Side (colourful side to the audience): a) screens on a slight diagonal within each girl's corridor, spaced for maximum privacy, denotes each girl in her bedroom, b) a slight curve created by the screens upstage means the girls are in a shared private space, Amber then Andrea's bedroom. Institutional Side (always with the grey side flat to the audience): a) lined up across the back to create the schoolyard, b) random spacing of the screens within the corridors allows the girls to chart an imaginary hallway.

Alarm bells, school bells, and transitions: There are two types of bells used to mark changes in scenes/location as well as time moving forward or into a fantasy realm . . . alarm bells and school bells. Like the screens they indicate private or public space. To encourage flow through the piece we used the bells musically, stretching and/or layering their sound, at times using radical dynamics or reverb, reflecting the occasionally fevered pitch of the girls' emotional states. Transitions should be enjoyed as a legitimate part of the storytelling.

Performance style: This is an interdisciplinary piece and relies on movement and sound to tell the story. To make clear how far each scene should go into extended storytelling form we called our two main styles Treated Mundane and Extraordinary Space. Treated Mundane lives a little closer to the everyday while employing text, sound, and movement, and Extraordinary Space extends into the surreal with vocal sound and physical movement leading the way even more vigorously. This aesthetic helped our teenaged girls live as large as their lives feel.

Stage directions: Vocal, movement, and sonic elements within the stage directions are considered to be a part of the piece's "score" and need to be fully inhabited. An example of this is Amber's vocal work. In several scenes she uses her voice as a guitar, in place of text, as her main means of expression and communication.

CAST

Five Grade Eight Students

Lauren—Hot Pink: The most experienced with regards to dating and pop culture. She is generous with what she knows. Her home life is rough. Best friends with Andrea. Wears the latest jeans, and wears them well.

Andrea—Bright Yellow: Seems to be the most together and mature, developing very fast physically. But she is feeling quite different inside—lonely and afraid of growing up. She uses clothes to dress up in a variety of personas.

Diana—Royal Blue: Probably skipped a year—really smart but still feels she must pressure herself to do better at school and in her extra-curricular activities. Best friends with Amber. She dresses in a conservative and sporty fashion. Still small enough to wear kids' clothes.

Amber—Rich Red: An independent original, comfortable in her body, loves edgy rock music. Has the most developed sense of social fairness and asks questions. Will always stand up for a friend. Her look is groovy and cool.

Christina—Kelly Green: The new girl, a natural comic. A bit young and a bit physically outside of her body. She is struggling with an eating disorder and hoping to fit into the new school and find friends. She wears baggy clothes and puts her baseball cap on backwards.

It is important that the actors never try to act younger than they are, but rather channel a sense of play, and the energy and volatility of the grade seven and eight age group; find the part of themselves that allows for the intense, giddy, dark, up and down, and frequently uncertain world of a twelve-to-fourteen-year-old girl to pour forth.

PROLOGUE

Five grade eight girls are dressed for the first day of school, personalities shining through their choice of clothes and accessories. They move down the aisle and onto the stage singing a heartfelt R & B anthem, taking in the audience. As they sing the group's dynamics and their friendships emerge through movement and staging. AMBER and DIANA are best friends, as are LAUREN and ANDREA. LAUREN and ANDREA are a little more "grown up" than the other two, but they are all good friends and comfortable with each other. CHRISTINA is the new girl, who they have yet to meet.

ALL: What is a friend?
Could it be that it's just a word.
Something you've always wanted
From a song you heard.
Or just another one of those
Big fat lies,
'Cause many nights this word has made me cry
So hard my stomach hurts
Deep down inside.

There goes that word again,
I thought you were my friend,
Forever—till the end.

You want to hide.
She's still the one who gets inside,
Too close at times 'cause you

Need room to cry.
Can she hear your hurt when nothing's said at all?
Will she sit with you when you're feeling small?
When she's heard the worst, will she like you at all?

Scared to tell you. I
Won't dare to tell you. Why?
Might trust you, should I try?

> *While singing the girls go to the screens, lined up along the back of
> the stage, Institutional Side showing. Each girl turns her own screen
> to reveal its brightly coloured Private Side and moves it downstage;
> all screens end up in a variety of diagonal facings and depths within
> their assigned corridor. The lighting takes us into night, each girl now
> alone in her bedroom.*

When you're nowhere
And ev'rywhere at the same time.
A friend will find your song, she'll hear your rhyme.
She'll never tell you what to do,
And you know all that she's been through.
You've seen her scars and she's seen you.

She'll let you be yourself,
So let her be herself,
I want to be myself.

SCENE ONE: DEAR DIARY ONE

> *Treated Mundane; Private Side screens.*

> *The night before the first day of school.* ANDREA *is trying on clothes
> in front of her screen.* CHRISTINA *is behind the curtain, inside her
> screen, playing with chocolate-bar wrappers; this sound is one of the
> musical elements in the scene.* DIANA *lies on the floor, centre stage, in
> front of her screen; she is tossing and turning in bed.* AMBER *sits on her*

screen's platform, silent, still, thinking hard. LAUREN is brushing her hair furiously beside her screen. These sounds and actions take time, establishing the girls' individual worlds before the text begins, continuing through the scene as movement and sonic elements, weaving in and out of the language, creating the scene's integrated holistic flow.

LAUREN: Dear Diary . . . I can't believe tomorrow / is the first day of school.

DIANA: / . . . I can't believe tomorrow / is the first day of school!

CHRISTINA: I can't believe tomorrow is the first day of school!

AMBER begins by singing a few bluesy riffs on the vowel "Oh," tumbling her non-verbal, vocal music into words:

AMBER: I changed a lot this summer. In a good way.

ALL: Dear Diary.

ANDREA: I'm going into grade eight and like nothing fffits—

AMBER uses her vocal riff to cut off ANDREA and continues under LAUREN's next line.

LAUREN: I'm going out with a guy in high school . . .

DIANA: Pencils . . .

DIANA rolls forward quickly, an extension of her sleepless night.

. . . don't forget pencils . . . pencils!

LAUREN: . . . and he's got his licence!

ANDREA: Dear Diary . . . I wonder if Lauren . . .

DIANA: Amber . . .

AMBER: Diana . . .

LAUREN: Andrea . . .

ALL: . . . got her period?

> *AMBER's riffing continues on the sounds ow . . . ow . . . ow . . . ow . . . ow!*

> *ALL layer giggles, expressing the newness/embarrassment/surprise of getting menstrual cramps.*

> *CHRISTINA slides oddly and uncomfortably face first out of her screen and onto the floor.*

CHRISTINA: I wonder if they'll like me?

ANDREA: This really weird girl moved in next door.

CHRISTINA: *(getting up and stepping forward as she straightens her clothes)* I hope they'll like me.

LAUREN: Who's the new girl?

ANDREA, AMBER, & DIANA: I don't know!

> *They start a schoolyard rhyme with rhythmic foot stomps and clapping.*

"New girl's out of step, doesn't know the rules" . . .

CHRISTINA: . . . yet.

> *CHRISTINA's word and accompanying single foot stomp completes the other girls' rhythmic rhyme.*

They'll never like me . . .

> *AMBER sings another bluesy line, her song's notes now big and sensual. She then signs off . . .*

AMBER: Amber.

ANDREA: Andy.

DIANA: Diana.

LAUREN: Lauren.

CHRISTINA: *(slipping out in a disappointed sigh)* Christina.

The lighting takes us deeper into night as the girls settle.

TRANSITION

Five recorded alarm clocks ring, each with a different pitch and tonal quality, overlapping one another. It is morning, the first day of school. ANDREA, DIANA, AMBER, and LAUREN turn their screens to the Institutional Side, spacing them within their assigned corridors in what appears to be a random pattern but will give the most play in creating the school's hallways. CHRISTINA remains in front of her screen, which is still on the Private Side. She seems uncomfortable. After putting on a second oversized boy's sports shirt she carefully sorts her chocolate bar wrappers. This ritual lasts through the following scene.

SCENE TWO: GIRL GROUP B.C. (BEFORE CHRISTINA)

Treated Mundane; the screens face Institutional Side, with hallway/washroom spacing.

Morning of the first day of school. The girls arrive at school, jumping up and down, hugging one another, excited to start grade eight.

The order and pairing of the "heys" denote the existing "best friend" dynamics and group power structures.

LAUREN & ANDREA: "HEY" "HEY."

DIANA & AMBER: "HEY" "HEY."

ALL FOUR: "HEY."

The girls circle around each other, acknowledging what has changed over the summer. In order, AMBER's hair extensions get "wows," LAUREN's hips provoke "ows" and whistles, ANDREA's large breasts earn "woahs," and DIANA's petiteness prompts a group "ooooh" that rises right up to the high peep range of their voices. These sounds create a musical chorus of appreciation and discovery.

Anticipating each other's every move, the group surges downstage left, like a school of fish, into the lighting for the girls' washroom. They line up in a row in front of an imagined mirror, facing out to the audience.

A rhythmic and pitched vocal score makes up the scene's soundscape. Language is not used naturalistically, instead the onomatopoeic text is exaggerated, building and overlapping, accompanied by a playful, synchronized gestural choreography. The four girls start by wiping their eyes of sleep and checking their mascara. These gestures begin naturally and build to cartoon-sized, launching the girls into the following sections.

GROOMING

The following text happens simultaneously with each girl looping her words.

AMBER: pluck, pluck, pluck . . .

AMBER's elbows and heels jut out painfully as she exaggerates eyebrow plucking.

DIANA: squeeze, squeeze, squeeze, pop . . .

DIANA's whole face is a pimple that she is trying to pop.

LAUREN: swish, swish, swish, swish . . .

LAUREN's putting on mascara, shifting her weight from hip to hip, practising being "flirty."

ANDREA: slime, slick, slick, slick . . .

ANDREA wipes her right hand across her face, releasing her arm in a heavy downward swing, flicking pubescent grease from her hands.

EYELASHES

Each "bat" is sung as a complex and pleasing chord as the girls bat their eyelashes. As the pitches rise, we imagine that the girls could lift themselves up by their eyelashes.

ALL: *(slowly)* Bat . . . . bat . . . . bat . . . . *(more quickly)* Bat . . bat . . bat . . bat . . . *(increasing tempo and gradually raising the pitch of the chord up, up, and further up!)* bat, bat, bat, bat, bat, bat, bat, bat, bat, bat, bat, bat, bat, bat, bat!

A beat as the girls look more intently into the mirror.

ZITS

ALL: Zit!

Each girl sees the zit on her face.

Ziiiiiiit!

Each one points out and zones in on her zit, body contorting as she begins to squeeze, with exaggerated effort. This ends as ANDREA turns and accidentally pops her zit onto LAUREN.

ANDREA: Oh . . .

LAUREN: Ew . . .

LIPS/LIPSTICK

Returning to face the washroom mirror they bend forward, their hands on their knees, in mildly provocative movie-star poses. ALL, in unison, make three long slightly ascending oooooos, tracing extremely large idealized lips in the air with their own puckered, ooooing lips. An ooooo for the right upper lip, another for the left upper lip, and the last one for the lower lip. The final ooooo is the longest, leading the girls into low, rapid, excited arm flutters. The flutter is interrupted by loud lip pops as they try to spread and perfect the lipstick they just applied.

PERSONAL STYLE

Each of the following words is accompanied by a brief flashy pose as the girls announce their personal style.

LAUREN: hot

AMBER: cool

DIANA: sporty

ANDREA: unique

DIANA: comfortable

ANDREA: original

LAUREN: grown-up

AMBER: casual

ANDREA: *(gesturing to her own clothes and to LAUREN's)* Parasuco?

LAUREN: *(confirming)* Parasuco!

ANDREA & LAUREN: *(turning excitedly to the other two girls)* PARASUCO!

AMBER: Value Village.

DIANA: The Bay.

ANDREA & LAUREN: Cool . . . Cool . . .

ALL: *(remembering and resigned)* Dress code . . .

DRESS YOUR AGE/DRESSAGE

They each alter the one thing that has marked them as unique for the first day of school. ANDREA takes off her hat, DIANA tries to look taller, LAUREN pulls her tube top straps back up onto her shoulders, and AMBER tones down her hair. These gestures gradually transform them into young fillies, flicking their imaginary manes and tails, nickering and snorting until they are almost chomping at the bit.

TRANSITION

A very loud school bell. Girls charge out into the hall with pent-up mustang energy, bumping into CHRISTINA, who turned her screen to the Institutional Side before leaving home for school.

SCENE THREE: THE NEW GIRL

Treated Mundane into Extraordinary Space; the screens remain on the Institutional Side.

Flowing from the transition, this begins as a naturalistic scene that takes place before first class on the first day of school.

CHRISTINA: *(with a crack in her voice)* Watch it!

LAUREN: *(genuinely not hearing CHRISTINA)* 'Scuse me? Sorry, what did you just say?

CHRISTINA: I said, "Where's math class?"

AMBER: Grade seven or grade eight?

DIANA: General? Collegiate? Academy?

CHRISTINA: Grade eight. *(mumbles)* I am in grade eight.

LAUREN: . . . Oh, it's just down the hallway to the right. Then you walk through the front foyer where we hang out Monday, Wednesday, Friday. We can't Tuesday or Thursday because we have soccer practice. Then you go through the tech wing, which has this really great spot if you and your friends want some privacy to talk about something important. Oh wait . . . but then you'll want to miss the girls' locker room, so you double back, go through the cafeteria so you can avoid passing the principal's office, then turn to your left, go back upstairs, past the blue lockers, and then you're right there. *(lip pop for punctuation)*

CHRISTINA: Okeedokee . . .

DIANA: So you're the new girl?

LAUREN: Where do you live?

ANDREA: She moved in next door.

AMBER: Where'd you come from?

CHRISTINA: My mom.

> *CHRISTINA laughs while trying for a laugh from the others, who respond with awkward laughs.*

LAUREN: Hey, I'm Lauren.

DIANA: I'm Diana.

AMBER: Amber.

ANDREA: Andy.

CHRISTINA: I'm Christina.

LAUREN: Actually we're going there now—if you want, you can come along.

CHRISTINA: Yeah.

LAUREN: Cool.

CHRISTINA: *(voice cracking)* Cool.

ANDREA & AMBER: *(echoing under their breath)* Cool . . . cool . . .

HALLS AND CORRIDORS

The positioning of the screens leaves a pathway of halls and corridors with many twists and turns which the girls know well. The others talk and walk exuberantly, changing friendship formations behind each screen. CHRISTINA tags along, using the walk to practise how she should have said cool. The activity crescendoes into a Boy Sighting.

The following movement section is in Extraordinary Space and is precise and highly choreographed. It begins with a slow sharp intake of breath in unison that should read as a gasp of pleasure/fear.

All of their bodies pull far, far back except for CHRISTINA's.

CHRISTINA: *(caught practising a last "cool")* . . . Who's that guy?

ANDREA: *(very slowly waving her hand, arm extended way, way up, voice high-pitched and airy to match)* Hi, Benjamin!

LAUREN: *(singsongy, slightly teasing)* Andy really likes you!

All the girls sing a musical chord on "likes."

AMBER: *(slow and low-pitched, a little gritty)* He's so hot!

The group collapses forward onto the floor.

DIANA: *(loudly at normal speed)* He looked at Christina!

The other girls roll up slowly and snap their heads to look at CHRISTINA.

AMBER, ANDREA, DIANA, & LAUREN: *(their voices sliding up a good octave, in unison with the previous movement)* Whaaaaat??!!

MATH/AFTERMATH

Treated Mundane. The girls are like emotional atoms trying to repair themselves. They move about the stage, changing formations by taking each other by the hand or huffing off, grouping and regrouping. This all happens quite rapidly. The crosses are bold and deliberate, illustrating the emotional math with each new placement on stage.

LAUREN taking CHRISTINA downstage right.

LAUREN: So then I say: "Christina, we've got to talk."

ANDREA heading upstage right to one of the screens.

ANDREA: And I say: "Thanks, Diana."

AMBER: So I say: "This is causing tension." *(taking a step towards ANDREA)* And she says:

DIANA: *(looking back at AMBER, shrugging)* "It's what I saw."

Beat.

AMBER, ANDREA, DIANA, & LAUREN: *(holding their places)* And then the new girl goes:

Everyone looks at CHRISTINA.

CHRISTINA: "I didn't do anything."

LAUREN: So I tell her: "He's out of bounds!"

AMBER: *(circling up to ANDREA)* And I'm like: "I've got to fix this," and she's like:

DIANA peeking from the front of her screen to watch ANDREA and AMBER.

DIANA: "I better check this out."

ANDREA taking AMBER's hand and crossing down to DIANA.

ANDREA: So I go: "I'll try."

LAUREN grabbing ANDREA and heading upstage left.

LAUREN: And I'm all like: "We've got to talk."

Beat.

AMBER, ANDREA, DIANA, & LAUREN: And then the new girl goes:

They all look at CHRISTINA, even if they are in motion. CHRISTINA looks back at all of them.

CHRISTINA: Great first day.

AMBER: *(looking at DIANA)* So we say:

DIANA & AMBER: *(looking at CHRISTINA)* "It's not your fault."

LAUREN: *(holding both of ANDREA's hand)* So we hug and say:

LAUREN & ANDREA: *(hugging)* "Okay."

ANDREA: *(holding LAUREN's hand)* Then we go to the new girl:

BOTH crossing down to CHRISTINA.

LAUREN & ANDREA: "Everything's fine."

AMBER slapping her hands on her thighs once and crossing to upstage left with DIANA.

AMBER: And I'm all like: "Great, now we're left out."

LAUREN rushing after AMBER and DIANA.

LAUREN: But then I'm like: "Guys, wait!"

Everyone faces front.

Great.

They all sigh loudly in unison, collapsing into one hip, arms folded across their chests.

ALL: Now nobody's talking . . .

They all stand in a ragged line across the stage.

FINGERING

Extraordinary Space. This is the first moment when all five girls sink into a shared emotional space. The mood darkens. The girls perform a very slow and thoughtful demi rond de jambe par terre approximately eight times on the same foot in the same direction. The audience can hear the quiet and continuous hiss of their feet sweeping on the floor throughout the scene. It is the sound of bad things happening and gossip spreading, neither of which can be controlled.

ANDREA: *(softly, so that we can still hear the foot sweeps)* Did you hear about that girl who went to that party?

Long pause.

AMBER: Some guys got her really drunk so she could barely move . . .

Pause.

LAUREN: They took her to the bathroom and this guy just started fingering her . . .

Long pause.

DIANA: Her friends didn't help her?

The foot movements stop. All of the girls are caught in an ungainly stance. Each girl makes two extremely long, mid-range whistles, without rushing the inhales. Each pitch is without vibrato, and randomly chosen. These hollow tones overlap to create a soft, sparse, dissonant, and eerie soundscape. Once the whistles have stopped CHRISTINA speaks.

CHRISTINA: She'll have to change schools . . . I would change schools if some . . .

TRANSITION

The heavy mood is interrupted by the school bell, which launches the girls into the next scene. They push the screens upstage and into a straight line. Their feelings of anger explode into the hyped-up sports play of the next scene.

SCENE FOUR: SOCCERBULLY

Treated Mundane into Extraordinary Space; the screens face the Institutional Side, flat to the audience, far upstage, making room for a game of soccer in the schoolyard.

Noon on the first day. Unsupervised time. As the screens arrive upstage at the end of the transition, the girls burst into cheers and turn to face the audience, jumping, clapping, and running after an imagined ball. The audience gets simultaneous POVs of all of the girls as they each move within a defined corridor that runs downstage from each of their personal screens. They always face out. ANDREA takes on the role of a cheerleader.

ALL: We can do it! Let's go team! Okay, let's do it, guys! We can really do it!

ANDREA: *(taking over with a cheerleading song)* Go fight win tonight, boogie all down all right, all right . . .

ANDREA continues chanting/singing this song throughout the scene.

LAUREN: Hey, new girl!

CHRISTINA: It's Christina!

LAUREN: Christina!

CHRISTINA: Debbie!

DIANA: It's Diana!

DIANA kicks the ball high and far.

CHRISTINA & LAUREN: *(disappointed complaint)* Out of bounds . . .

All retreat upstage then perform a combination of quick shallow runs towards the audience in a wide-legged stance, dribbling the ball between their feet and passing it back and forth between all the girls. Soccer drill.

AMBER: Come on, Andy, okay let's go . . .

ANDREA: I'm not open! I'm not open!

CHRISTINA: I got it!

CHRISTINA dribbles the ball between both feet and then kicks it to LAUREN.

Lauren!

LAUREN: *(scores)* Score!

CHRISTINA, DIANA, and LAUREN run up and down their individual corridors three times, touching the ground with their fingers each time they finish a lap. All cheer loudly, jumping up and down with excitement.

ANDREA is overlapping the others' cheers with some fun and fabulous rhyming.

ANDREA: . . . some are tall and some are small!! Hit the wall, catch the ball, don't let it fall, what's with the ball?!

LAUREN: *(bumping into ANDREA)* Dammit, get out of my way!

ANDREA: Sorry, Lauren . . .

The tone of the scene begins to change; the girls' physicality becomes focused and they each take a defensive stance near the front of the stage.

ALL: . . . defend, look, look, defend . . .

An out of sync beat-box rhythm starts to develop as the girls loop these words.

LAUREN: *(interrupting)* Look, guys, it's coming, it's coming—

ALL: Whoa!!

They extend the word while leaning back and following the ball with their eyes.

DIANA: I got it I got it I got it!

DIANA backpeddles upstage, tries to kick the ball, but falls on her bum.

LAUREN & CHRISTINA: *(furious)* Diana!

DIANA: I'm trying my best!

AMBER: Okay, I got it; we're still a team!

AMBER has the ball now and she throws it back into play.

CHRISTINA and LAUREN pass the ball back and forth three times, gradually moving downstage while monopolizing the play.

LAUREN: Christina!

CHRISTINA: Lauren!

LAUREN: Christina!

CHRISTINA: Lauren!

LAUREN: Christina!

CHRISTINA: Lauren!

LAUREN jumps, heading the ball over to DIANA.

LAUREN: *(screaming)* Diana!!!!

DIANA is confused and accidentally catches it in her hands.

ALL: PENALTY?!

AMBER: *(this time AMBER does not save the moment)* Thanks Diana . . .

ANDREA: Tiger Lilies don't be mad—some are good and some are bad . . .

LAUREN and CHRISTINA mutter back and forth under ANDREA's rhyme, eventually taking over with a dark, taunting jeer.

LAUREN: She's a neat girl,

CHRISTINA: sweet girl . . .

LAUREN leads the girls to form a circle around DIANA.

ANDREA, CHRISTINA, & LAUREN: straight-A perfect petite girl. Honour roll, hallway patrol, never has time to meet girl!

ALL: *(even AMBER)* Tries her best, lets down the rest, can't stay up on two feet girl!

(They skip around DIANA.) She's a neat girl, sweet girl, straight-A perfect petite girl. Honour roll, hallway patrol, never has time to meet girl. Tries her best, lets down the rest, can't stay up on two feet girl.

DIANA: Stop it!

> *They circle her twice. The movement slows down and the girls close in on DIANA, bullying. When the movement stops the taunting becomes even more deliberate and nasty.*

LAUREN: She's a neat girl

CHRISTINA: sweet girl

LAUREN: straight-A perfect petite . . . girl.

ANDREA: Honour roll

AMBER: *(joins)* hallway patrol

ALL: never has time to meet girl!

> *AMBER, changing her mind, starts to retreat from the meanness.*

LAUREN & ANDREA: Tries her best, lets down the rest, can't stay up on two feet girl!!!!

AMBER: Cut it out!

Pause.

> *LAUREN, CHRISTINA, and ANDREA respond with the earlier beat-box chant, "Look, look, defend." They use this chorus as if protecting*

themselves. Little squeals and scratching sounds are added. A musical loop is created by everyone but DIANA. *AMBER uses the words "Cut it out!" as her hook in the rhythm.*

DIANA crosses downstage centre and sits down, now in her bedroom, angry and hurt. She takes off her shoes and starts to toss and turn, lying on the floor, trying to get comfortable in bed. The rest of the performers back away and then turn the screens (including DIANA's*) to the private, individual bedroom side. They continue the beat-boxing while resetting the stage, gradually thinning out the musical texture by the end of the scene. We are left with a final taunt.*

ANDREA: look . . . look . . .

SCENE FIVE: DEAR DIARY TWO

Treated Mundane; the screens face Private Side.

The lighting changes indicating bedtime after the first day of school. Each girl is sitting on the platform inside her screen, or standing in the shadow of her screen, in a dark, self-hating space. CHRISTINA crinkles her chocolate-bar wrappers and LAUREN runs the bristles of a hairbrush against her screen, adding a prickly quality to the uncomfortable texture of personalized sighs that the girls are making, all of this creating the musical score of the scene. Each performer has one of her shoes at the ready to drum on her screen.

DIANA is on the floor, still in bed tossing and turning, further developing her movement phrase from "Dear Diary One."

DIANA: Sleep . . . sleep . . . can't sleep . . . sleep.

Her movements become more extended as she suspends at the end of each rolling sequence.

LAUREN: Dear Diary.

DIANA: Tuesday, five p.m.—piano lessons—Minuet in G—chromatic scale—twenty times . . .

CHRISTINA: I'm not hungry.

> *AMBER suppresses her words and allows her feelings to come out musically. She uses her shoe to bang four or five times loudly, unevenly, and angrily on her screen.*

ANDREA: I wonder if what happened today was . . .

LAUREN: *(as if her dad were speaking it to her)* What are you . . . stupid?

> *LAUREN rubs her hairbrush on the screen.*

> *AMBER crescendoes and accelerates through eight or nine shoe bangs, making it a musical build.*

(scraping her brush against the screen) I hate my dad . . .

> *She throws her brush down onto the platform.*

CHRISTINA: I'm so hungry.

DIANA: Saturday, ten a.m. Chinese school; three p.m. fan dancing; six p.m. dinner.

> *AMBER builds into a second crescendo and then back into a quiet, insistent rhythm.*

LAUREN: I know I was mean today but . . .

ANDREA: *(taking over)* I hope it didn't "seem" like I was mean.

> *AMBER lays down a slow, Kodo-like drum rhythm in 4/4 time (accenting the one and every odd four: 1 2 3 4, 1 2 3 4, 1 2 3 4, 1 2 3 4) that is borne out of the girls shared emotional state. LAUREN, then*

ANDREA, then CHRISTINA join in, shoe to screen, weaving in and out of the main rhythm. Each screen sounds a slightly different pitch by virtue of the varying sizes and weights of the screens.

DIANA intensifies her earlier movement patterns from slow and sustained to fast and angular. This build is enough to lift her off the ground to standing. She puts both her shoes on her hands; they now serve as fans, and she performs a version of the "Iron Fan Dance" to the rhythm of the drums. The inner strength she discovers through the dance leads her to drum on her screen with both shoes. Her drumming complements and counterpoints the other girls' solid rhythm. She eventually takes over the powerful accented 4 and 1 beats of the primary pattern. The feeling is slow and deliberate, relentless and menacing. Her shoes suspend in the air one final time, iron fans raised above her head. She arches her back and for a moment resembles a stylized dragon.

TRANSITION

Five alarm clocks launch the girls into the morning of the second day of school. The first alarm clock rings for a very long time and the others layer in with lots of reverb. The alarm clocks decrescendo slowly as the girls turn their screens back to the Institutional Side, hallway formation.

SCENE SIX: PENCIL CHECK-IN

Treated Mundane; the screens facing Institutional Side, creating a school hallway, leaving room for the downstage left washroom.

The girls are at school after a sleepless night. Each one stands in isolation, facing her screen/locker. AMBER emerges from between the screens singing a soulful, introspective torch song.

AMBER: I'm so mad at myself . . . today

The four other girls start a very soft 4/4 beat, fists to screen, backs to audience. This continues through the whole song. They become a backup chorus echoing key words from the song, sometimes in call and response, and sometimes harmonizing on a final word. AMBER is vocalizing the internal monologue of the group, anchoring the feeling of being angry at oneself.

Why did I . . . get so carried away? *(backup chorus echoes "away")*
It's so easy to start *(chorus echoes "start!")*
and so hard to stop. *(chorus whispers "stop")*
It's so easy to start *(chorus echoes "start!")*
and so hard to stop. *(silence)*

I want to play fair *(chorus glissés "fair")*
but we're all afraid. *(One voice responds with a fragile, descending "I am afraid.")*

(building) If it happened to her it could happen to me . . . wo-oh-oh oh . . .

I get how she feels.
I should have known better than to label her by what is on the cover. *(chorus harmonizes on "cover")*
I want them to see what's deep inside me,
so please don't label me by what is on the cover. *(chorus harmonizes on "cover")*

Don't pin me down.
Don't pin me down.
I want to feel free.

(quasi-spoken) To just be me.

At the conclusion of the song there is a clear lighting change to indicate the school bathroom.

LAUREN and ANDREA enter the washroom and greet each other—"Hey," "Hey"—downcast.

CHRISTINA and AMBER enter the washroom greeted by a low-key flurry of "heys." After the girls have all trickled in DIANA enters and takes her place in the centre of the group. They subtly clear away from her on both left and right. This lineup is the same as the mirror lineup from Scene Two.

Each girl stares into the mirror trying to get her hair "right."

LAUREN: *(breaking the silence)* "If anybody wants I could do their hair."

CHRISTINA: *(rushing in)* "You can do my hair . . . "

LAUREN moves to CHRISTINA; ANDREA counters left.

Pause.

AMBER: You know, my parents almost didn't let me get these extensions. Remember how big my hair was last year? Remember how the guys used to stick pencils in it? Sometimes I'd be walking around with like five pencils in my hair and I wouldn't even know it! If that happens this year . . .

LAUREN: That's okay, Amber! We'll just do a pencil check . . .

A tense and uncomfortable pause.

ANDREA: Or we could all come to school with pencils already in our hair.

DIANA: *(still upset)* Pencils!! Pencils don't stay in my hair!

AMBER: Sure they will. I could help you.

AMBER moves towards DIANA as if to help and then hesitates and pulls back. ANDREA takes over and moves behind DIANA to help her with her hair; their difference in height means she towers over DIANA.

ANDREA: Oh my god, today on the way to school I bumped into a midget. It like totally freaked me out . . . *(sensing everyone's discomfort)* Um, I'm sorry . . . is that racist?

AMBER: No, but actually, it's prejudiced.

Pause.

ANDREA: Well he was kinda cute . . .

Pause. DIANA reacts with irritation. ANDREA pulls away, crossing back to the end of the mirror lineup.

I'm sorry. I'm sorry.

AMBER: *(to DIANA)* By the way, I don't think you're too short. I think I'm way too tall. I'd much rather be short like you.

DIANA: *(brightening)* Really?!

TRANSITION

A very loud school bell. All exit the washroom towards centre stage, ANDREA following behind.

ANDREA: *(under bell but still loudly)* What am I, a giant? What am I, a giant with ginormous boobs? What am I, a giant? What am I, a giant with ginormous boobs? What am I, a giant? What am I, a giant with ginormous boobs?

Boy Sighting reprise. CHRISTINA is now a part of their surreal world. All of the language and movement is in an exaggerated slow motion.

CHRISTINA: *(low voice)* Oooh . . . there he is!

ANDREA: *(high and floaty)* Hi, Benjamin!

LAUREN: *(mid voice, a bit carnal)* Andy really REALLY likes you!

The other girls join on her "likes," making a bawdy chord by choosing a wide spread of horny, hormonal harmonies.

AMBER: He's so . . .

ALL: *(roaring)* HOT!

They all collapse onto the floor in laughter.

A second loud bell ends this transition.

SCENE SEVEN: GOING PUBIC (BODY IMAGE ONE)

Extraordinary Space; the screens remain facing the Institutional Side.

The lunch bell has spilled the girls into the schoolyard, which quickly becomes full of goofy, over-the-top play as their bodies change right under their noses.

BREAST BOUNCE

Each girl examines her body via the shadow it casts on her screen, discovering her shape/profile and sharing her unique/individual breast "ahas" with us. The action is simultaneous. From stage left to stage right, AMBER shakes and twists her whole body side to side, making her hips and breasts practically dance; LAUREN twists relentlessly, exploring all of her curves a bit manically; DIANA eventually turns her small breasts into little pistols that go "piewpiewpiew"; CHRISTINA squeezes and honks her breasts, "bababababe, bababababe, meep . . . meep," trying to figure out what they can do; and ANDREA jumps up and down, feels the weight of her large breasts in her hands. She takes the weight of her breast bounce into running, circling the stage in front of the screens, prompting all the girls to start shooting at one another with their breasts . . . a flurry of varied gunfire sounds. This transitions quickly into LAUREN hollering "five, six, seven, eight." They all shout in a proud and rhythmic chant from their stage left to stage right lineup across the back of the stage.

ALL: We know the order of whose are bigger!

As they march forward, they lift their arms, right for the bra band width and left for the cup size, one girl after the other, staying in rhythm, as they each announce their size.

ANDREA: 36D.

CHRISTINA: 34B.

DIANA: 34A.

LAUREN: 32A . . .

ALL: Five, six, seven, eight . . . hers are coming along. Fffffttt!

All arms sweep stage left to DIANA with the sound "fffffttt."

ARMPIT HAIR

DIANA lifts her centre stage arm and discovers an armpit hair: "Ew." In quick succession from stage left to stage right they each lift an arm, each discovering and plucking a single armpit hair: "Ew . . . Ew . . . Ew . . . Ew . . . "

PUBIC HAIR

Each girl's lifted arm drops quickly to her vagina. She looks down and immediately uses both hands to cover this area. The girls display a range of emotions, from discomfort to excitement, in response to the advent of pubic hair. They rise onto tiptoe, still hiding their private parts, moving in erratic circles about the stage, bumping into each other as they revolve. There is general undecipherable genital chit-chat and hubbub. DIANA bumps into ANDREA with a loud "whoah," pushing ANDREA to stage right.

TARZAN JUNGLE BUSH

ANDREA calls loudly, using Tarzan's iconic cry while beating her chest. LAUREN, DIANA, and AMBER make loud monkey sounds and massive ape movements as they leap across to her. From behind her they strategically place their head hair under ANDREA's arms and between her legs—this is how copious the new hair feels, how extreme puberty can be for some girls. The girls collapse to the floor, having made themselves laugh once again.

CHRISTINA has split off from the group through the Tarzan scene and goes into the washroom.

SCENE EIGHT: SKINNY CAT

Extraordinary Space; the screens still upstage, facing Institutional Side.

CHRISTINA has entered the washroom after lunch. She is alone and she has not eaten. The others are upstage right, their laughter taking them into a tight stage left to right lineup, all facing the audience; they are not lit. They form a vocal and physical chorus throughout this scene.

CHRISTINA, alone in the washroom, stage left, cautiously approaches the mirror. The following text is like stand-up comedy, an improvisation with tight parameters so that the chorus work fits in easily. CHRISTINA is fixing her baseball cap in the mirror.

CHRISTINA: . . . it's cool *(voice cracking)* . . . it's cool . . . *(deep breath)* just be yourself. "So, what's your name?" *(high-pitched)* Christina . . . *(heavy sigh)* just breathe . . . *(deep and brutish)* Christina . . . no, you're not a man! Christina *(normal and relieved)* . . . "So, where you from?" My mom *(laughter from the other girls, who we don't yet see)* . . . my dad *(more laughter)* . . . the womb *(more laughter, CHRISTINA now milking it)* womb, womb, womb! . . . Barrie . . . *(silence)* Barrie *(more silence)* . . . Ontario? *(losing her confidence, apologetically)* . . . It's just north from here.

Pause.

(looking into the bathroom mirror, pulling her tummy in tight) Mirror, Mirror on the wall, who's the skinniest of them all?

> CHRISTINA *holds this odd held-breath posture for far too long, then exhales. A dim light cuts across the other girls' bellies and they start to explore their own hips with their hands.*

"So, why did you come here?" Because my school didn't accept aliens!

> *Laughter from the chorus continues through the next few lines.*

Because my dog ate everyone's homework . . . 'Cause I ate everyone's lunch . . . 'Cause I killed a cat.

> *The laughing chorus is abruptly silent, then blurts "ew, gross," etc.*

I'm not a freak . . . it's true. You don't believe me? There was this one time when I was in the girls' washroom and there was this cat, just watching me, as if I was doing something wrong. Like eating one square of chocolate in the bathroom stall is a crime.

> *One girl mews a twisted meow.*

So I lured it in.

> *She reaches into her pocket for a piece of chocolate.*

Here, kitty kitty kitty.

> *All the girls begin to purr and make happy, cute kitten sounds.* CHRISTINA *begins a gentle treading of her feet, like a cat kneading a carpet.*

Here, kitty kitty kitty. Until we were face to face. And then the cat said, *(hissing)* "Eat it . . . Swallow it . . . It's just one piece of chocolate . . . Fatso . . . "

(responding as herself) NO! . . .

(as the cat) "Eat it, it's just one piece of chocolate . . . "

I SAID NO . . .

"Eat it. Swallow it. Fatso."

GET IT AWAY FROM ME . . .

"Eat it. Fatso. Fatso . . . "

I SAID GET AWAY FROM ME!

> *CHRISTINA's foot-treading turns into running.*

I go running!

> *The girls bend forward, heads dangling to the ground.*

I do sit-ups!

> *The girls use their forward bend to initiate a series of staccato sit-ups, coming up to standing each time, ending in a forward bend.*

I work out.

> *The girls come back up to standing with soft bellies, and explore them with their hands during the following line.*

So I grabbed the cat by the neck and I killed it.

> *The girls emit a soft, disgusted "ew."*

It's not true. I didn't really . . . I didn't really kill a cat.

Pause.

The real reason I came here was because my friends called me Skeletor . . . and I liked it.

> *The girls are still in the belly light. They raise their arms into gaunt skeletor bodies. Their voices rise to long, high, peep sounds, a tight cluster of shrill pitches. On tiptoe they stumble around the stage, a grotesque cross between models and zombies.*

> *The lighting brightens to daytime. The girls return to normal and head down the hall, babbling inanely—"I'm a model," "I only eat celery," etc.—experimenting with these cultural identities/obsessions.*

> CHRISTINA *is calming herself in front of the mirror as they enter the washroom.*

LAUREN: Hey!

AMBER: Hey!

DIANA: Hey Christina!

ANDREA: Where did you go?

AMBER: Where were you? We were looking for you!

LAUREN: We're going back to Amber's house.

AMBER: You want to come?

CHRISTINA: Cool!

LAUREN: Cool!

AMBER: Cool!

> ANDREA *is not so sure . . .*

TRANSITION

Under a long end-of-the-day school bell the girls move the screens into a shallow upstage semicircle, private sides exposed. We are in AMBER's *bedroom.*

SCENE NINE: CLOTHES PILE

Treated Mundane; the screens face Private Side, the shallow upstage semicircle holding AMBER's *bedroom.*

It's early evening, after the second day of school. The girls are grabbing clothes from their own screens and tossing them over their shoulders out into the middle of the stage. They chat with each other, CHRISTINA *trying unsuccessfully to be friendly with* ANDREA, AMBER *and* LAUREN *bonding, and* DIANA *commenting periodically above the burble: "Too cute. Too big."* CHRISTINA *is looking for the baggiest clothes possible.*

In the middle of this mayhem, LAUREN *and* ANDREA *dive for the same dress. They are both holding onto it.*

LAUREN: *(simultaneously)* Oh!

ANDREA: *(simultaneously)* Oh my . . .

LAUREN: *(pushing the dress towards* ANDREA*)* Go ahead.

ANDREA: *(pushing the dress towards* LAUREN*)* No, you go ahead.

LAUREN: *(pushing it back a little harder)* No, forget it, I don't really care.

ANDREA: *(pushing it back, her anger building)* No, Lauren, I think you do care.

LAUREN: *(aggressively throwing the dress at* ANDREA*)* Take the dress.

ANDREA: *(throwing it back, matching* LAUREN'S *aggression)* You take the dress.

LAUREN: *(with one last violent toss to* ANDREA*)* No, you take the dress.

ANDREA: You know, this is the most we've talked all year.

Voicing a simultaneous, disgusted, exasperated, under-the-breath, yet loud, "Oh!"

ANDREA throws the dress to the floor and stomps back to her screen. LAUREN leaves her and goes over to CHRISTINA. CHRISTINA, already in many layers, continues dressing, eventually putting on a big vest and babushka scarf. LAUREN finds a tiny tube top that CHRISTINA tries to help her get into.

The focus shifts to DIANA and AMBER. AMBER is putting on some very groovy seventies garb.

DIANA: You look great! *(a little desperately, first to LAUREN and then to AMBER)* You look great! I don't know what to wear!

AMBER: Well—what's your favourite colour?

DIANA: I want gold sparkly shoes—high ones.

AMBER: I have some!

DIANA: You do?

AMBER: *(handing DIANA the shoes)* Beads! Oh, yeeesss!! Yes!

DIANA: Oh! Look at that jacket!

AMBER: *(stroking an incredible, fluffy, pink fur jacket)* It's fake.

DIANA: No kidding.

ANDREA: It's ugly.

AMBER: It's mine.

ANDREA has accessorized herself with a head kerchief and shoulder bag.

ANDREA: I guess I'll just rollerblade by myself . . .

She circles behind the screens, repeating a high and airy "Hi boys!"
each time we see her in the gaps . . . this continues under the follow-
ing dialogue.

AMBER: *(as ANDREA leaves)* Okay, cowhead . . .

CHRISTINA is still trying to help LAUREN into her tube top.

CHRISTINA: I think that it's a little too small for you . . .

LAUREN: No, it fits me perfectly!

CHRISTINA: It doesn't really cover . . .

LAUREN: *(all of a sudden noticing CHRISTINA's layers)* You look just like my nonna!

CHRISTINA: I have a nonna too!

CHRISTINA impersonates her nonna, pinching LAUREN's cheek.

She always says, "You look too skinny . . . *mangia*! *mangia*!"

LAUREN laughs so much during her own nonna story that we can't
make out all the improvised words.

ANDREA, still really out of sorts, arrives back in AMBER's bedroom and
yells over LAUREN's story, shutting everyone up.

ANDREA: That's my vest!

Pause.

CHRISTINA: Can I wear it?

ANDREA: No!

LAUREN: *(crossing aggressively to ANDREA)* Guys, relax!

DIANA: Peace Patrol!

A verbal fight starts to break out between ANDREA and LAUREN: "Watch your step!" etc.

Peace Patrol!

DIANA strikes a Charlie's Angels *pose, down on one knee, making a gun with her hands.*

As the argument continues CHRISTINA and AMBER cross to ANDREA and LAUREN to try and stop the fight and DIANA rolls, imaginary gun still in hand, towards the fighting girls.

CHRISTINA points towards AMBER and yells in a deep and large, sloweddown voice, initiating the slow-motion physicality of the ensuing fight.

CHRISTINA: DIE!

The following sequence is an overblown action scene that everyone participates in. Kung fu mixed with Charlie's Angels *with a dose of Saturday morning cartoons. We can't make out the words but there are barbs exchanged along with the faux blows. DIANA uses her little breast gun sounds (piewpiewpiew) throughout. This play lasts several surreal minutes.*

AMBER initiates the clean-up, causing the fight to peter out. Martial arts moves morph into domestic art chores.

AMBER: Guys, help me clean up.

LAUREN: Whatever, Amber . . .

DIANA: It's Amber's house!

ANDREA: Yeah and it sucks!

All the girls start to clean up the clothes.

AMBER: Well, why don't you leave?

LAUREN: Well maybe we'll leave when we want to leave.

DIANA: It's up to her.

LAUREN: Shut up, nerd!

AMBER: She's not a nerd!

DIANA: *(into spoken-word delivery)* Got to be heard.

AMBER: Yes.

The group has assembled stage left, leaving DIANA centre stage.

DIANA: Disturb the majority.

AMBER: Yah!

DIANA: Who rule with oppressive authority . . . Who are indifferent to my voice.

AMBER: My skin.

DIANA: My belief in . . . You . . . Me

AMBER & DIANA: Who d'you wanna be?

DIANA: Be seen, be heard.
Disturb the "in" mentality.
Break down the black-and-white reality.
Break out of limitation.
Escape their temptation to silence you into annihilation.

AMBER: Can't box me up!

DIANA: Can't shut me up!

AMBER: Won't give up.

DIANA: Don't give a fffffff!

Touch my nerve, I feel the pain!
Can't stand the shi . . .
It makes my insides scream, not to be seen for who I am.

I'm not a mathematic, scientific Japanimation machine.
I paint walls with my poetry.
I'll take my oriental fan and shove it up your . . .
If you're bawlin' or a stranger or a friend
I'll defend the underdog to the end.

AMBER: Yeah!

DIANA: Yeah!

CHRISTINA: Cool!

> *AMBER starts an insistent celebratory vocal guitar riff. A low note followed by a high squeal. The rest join in to make a crazy exuberant beat section while dancing around the stage.*

> *DIANA's lines weave through the beats.*

DIANA: Can't box me up! Can't shut me up! Won't give up. Don't give a fffffff!

> *As their vocal beat-boxing and dancing continue they put away any stray clothes and each one discretely takes a colourful plastic Slinky from inside her screen and hides it on her person. They make their way to centre stage, collapsing to the floor in a loose mound of friendship, exhausted from both the fight and the play. Their music winds down through a final downward vocal glissando. The girls roll onto their backs, one after the other, saying "Dear Diary . . . "*

TRANSITION

> *The girls' five alarm clocks ring in cannon, the reverb on the bells increases, extending the soundscape. A mid-range drone and some high chimes add to the surreal moment. All the girls start singing long, magical "ooos," harmonizing with the bells. Each girl appears to be pulled to seated by an external force that draws her up by the sternum . . . each one turns slowly towards the audience, wide-eyed and*

in an altered state. They continue to stand while turning, mesmerized and in awe of something important. They seem to be transforming before our eyes. They end by facing the audience in an upstage row, from stage left to stage right: LAUREN, DIANA, ANDREA, CHRISTINA, *and* AMBER.

SCENE TEN: QUEEN OF MENSTRUATION

Extraordinary Space; the screens remain on their Private Sides, still in AMBER's *bedroom.*

All the girls except CHRISTINA *are holding plastic rainbow Slinkys.* ANDREA *is in the centre and leads a slow advance towards the audience. The girls' goddess-like long tones, which began under the alarm bells, now include airy, individual "ows" that punctuate the texture. These are the magical sounds of menstruation. With each girl's "ow" she stretches out her slinky, feeling her cramps.*

They stop and ANDREA, *our Queen of Menstruation, blows imaginary dust at the audience.*

ALL: *(sung in a gentle musical chord, nobly inflected)* Good morning.

ANDREA: I am the Queen of Menegen—

LAUREN: —strunugu—

DIANA: —anaga—

AMBER: —shanagun.

ANDREA: And today is your special day. It's time to celebrate!

ALL: We've got our periods!!

The girls make make a ta-da gesture, expanding their Slinky in the process.

The rhythm of the following text is quick and needy, each line practically overlapping the previous. Over-the-top, melodramatic gestures amplify each thought.

ANDREA: Don't touch me!

CHRISTINA: Give me chocolate!

CHRISTINA still does not have a Slinky, nor does she seem in the know.

ANDREA: Don't you listen?

LAUREN: I said . . .

DIANA & AMBER: Give me chocolate!

ANDREA: Rub my back . . . bring me chocolate . . . rub my back . . . bring me chocolate . . .

The girls enjoy the chocolate and the back rubs, continuing these sounds of appreciation under ANDREA's words.

ALL: Mmmm . . . Oooh . . .

Within ANDREA's looping text the word "bring" of "bring me chocolate" eventually transforms into the BRRRRING of a phone ringing.

ANDREA: Brrrring . . . Excuse me . . . hellooo?! Yes . . .

VAGINA HOTLINE PHONE SEQUENCE

Each brrring comes in before the previous line is finished so there is a constant flow of chatter . . . the girls open their Slinkys and place one end to their vagina and stretch the other end to their ear. Voila, a phone.

ANDREA: *(regally, to audience)* Excuse me, my vagina is calling! Hello!

AMBER: Brrring! Hotline! It's totally cool to be scared.

DIANA: Brrring! Just let it flow.

LAUREN: Brrring! Hotline! No, actually, I wouldn't wear white.

ANDREA: Brrring! Buy your tampons. Buy your pads. Tell your moms and tell your dads!

AMBER: Brrring! But don't leave it in overnight.

DIANA: Brrring! Yes, you can play soccer. I use wings.

LAUREN: Brrring! Hotline. Congratulations! That is super!

ANDREA: Brrring! Some girls don't get it until they're sixteen . . . oh! *(turning to CHRISTINA)* . . . it's for you.

> *ANDREA passes CHRISTINA the ear end of the Slinky, which CHRISTINA brings to her own ear.*

CHRISTINA: Hello?

> *ANDREA lets go of the Slinky, which bounces chaotically over to CHRISTINA.*

TRANSITION

> *A loud school bell interrupts the scene. All the girls launch into an immediate flurry of vagina gossip and first period stories as they head to their screens. They turn their screens from the Private Side to the Public Side, into the schoolyard formation. CHRISTINA is battling with her Slinky. It's a hot potato and she doesn't know what to do with it.*

SCENE ELEVEN: CODE RED

Extraordinary Space; the screens face the Institutional Side, a flat line across the back.

It's morning, some time in the past. ANDREA is left alone down centre, her voice cutting through the girls' chatter.

ANDREA: Oh my god! I have blood running down my legs. Oh my god! I have blood running down my legs. In my new white shorts. They're not even mine. They're my sister's. Oh my god, cover me, cover me!

The girls rush over to ANDREA and form a snaking conga line behind her, winding their way through the old hallway path. DIANA is at the back of the line facing backwards, making a gun with her two hands, "covering" ANDREA.

AMBER: *(yelling over their urgent chatter)* We need backup.

DIANA: Code Red!

They each make a distinct siren sound, overlapping to create a quintet of vocal panic while continuing through the halls. Their line comes to an abrupt halt. They freeze.

ANDREA: *(waving, looking upstage at an imaginary teacher)* Um . . . Hi, Mr. Como.

ALL: *(facing the audience to share the bad news)* Mr. Como?!

They sidestep downstage in a tight lineup then shuffle backwards into the washroom lighting, talking fast and furious about nothing to Mr. Como. In the safety of the washroom they all partially squat back onto each other's laps as if onto a toilet seat.

ANDREA: *(at the front of the seated lineup)* Does anyone have an extra rolo?

All the girls use their upstage hand to reach back to the girl behind, one after the other, hoping for a tampon.

DIANA: *(at the back of the line, using her cop's voice)* It's my last one!

The girls pass an imaginary tampon back up the line with their downstage hand and ANDREA mimes inserting the tampon. They all immediately stand and orient themselves to the washroom mirror, instantly dropping the previous play, looking at their reflections and checking out their figures. An abrupt shift to butt talk.

LAUREN: Guys, do you think my butt's too big?

AMBER: No, mine's way bigger!

CHRISTINA: I don't even have a butt!

DIANA: Move your butt!

TRANSITION

A loud and long school bell. DIANA repeats her text, trying to top trying to top the bell's volume, pushing all the girls out the washroom door by thrusting her pelvis into them while jumping forward on both feet. The butt talk continues, each girl still obsessed with her own behind.

SCENE TWELVE: THE 3 Bs—BIG BUTOH BUTT/ BUBBLING TAG/BLOW JOBS (BODY IMAGE TWO)

Treated Mundane into Extraordinary Space into Treated Mundane.

Midday in the schoolyard at the end of the second week of school.

The girls burst out of the washroom and straight into the schoolyard yelling . . .

ALL: Butt, Butt, Butt . . .

*Each girl has unique and flamboyant hip and butt moves that take
her through the space . . . football type runs, shaking, bumping hips
with one another, sexy walks, jumping, large sidesteps, etc.*

Big bootie, big bootie, big bootie.
Big bootie, big bootie, big bootie!
Big bootie number one,
big bootie number two.
Oooooh yaaaah!! You got a big bootie!!!
Big bootie, big bootie, big bootie . . .

*The movements from the first section are maintained and exagger-
ated. Eventually they stand facing upstage shaking their butts at the
audience.*

*A sudden silence. The lights darken, taking us into Extraordinary
Space.*

BIG BUTOH BUTT . . .

*All the girls begin to adopt large sidesteps while breathing in loudly
through their noses. Their butts appear to inflate, their hands spreading out behind them to communicate just how large their bums have
gotten. Throughout this sequence the girls revolve in a constant group
formation, bodies bent forward, legs low and wide. As they turn to
the audience we see that their faces and cheeks are now puffed out as
large as possible. Their proportions no longer make sense to them . . .
they feel like they could explode. They let their feet fall heavily with
each unison step.*

BUBBLING TAG . . .

A spanking truth-or-dare game begins. LAUREN slaps ANDREA's butt.

ANDREA: *(slapping LAUREN on the butt)* Would you do it?

LAUREN: I'm not telling . . . *(slapping AMBER)* Would you do it?

AMBER: I don't know! *(running to tap DIANA's butt)* Would you do it?

DIANA: No! . . . *(keeping the tag going)* Would you do it?

CHRISTINA: Do what?

AMBER, ANDREA, DIANA, & LAUREN: *(in unison)* IT!

BLOW JOBS

This becomes a standoff between ANDREA and LAUREN at centre stage. CHRISTINA, DIANA, and AMBER are joking around about "it," goofing around physically, circling the stage. "It's just kissing," "Everyone does it," "It's no big deal," etc.

ANDREA: You said you'd do it!

LAUREN: No, I said, I'm not telling you!

ANDREA: No, you said you'd do it!

LAUREN: No, I said I'm not telling.

ANDREA: Well did you do it?

LAUREN: What's your problem?

ANDREA: You totally did it, didn't you?

LAUREN: Why are you acting like this?

ANDREA: You totally did it!

LAUREN: Why are you being such a bitch? *(walking away)* Fine . . .

AMBER: (*breaking away from* CHRISTINA *and* DIANA) You're the bitch.

Both ANDREA *and* LAUREN *look at her.*

LAUREN: 'Scuse me?

CHRISTINA and DIANA cross down to witness this bit of nastiness. Pressure builds.

ANDREA: (*under her breath*) Slut . . .

Pause.

LAUREN: What did you say to me?

LAUREN crosses to centre stage.

ANDREA: Slut?

The three girls join in the taunting, smelling blood sport.

AMBER: Bitch.

DIANA: Stupid.

CHRISTINA: Fat.

By now they are all surrounding LAUREN.

ANDREA: Slut.

AMBER: Bitch.

DIANA: Stupid.

CHRISTINA: Fat . . .

ANDREA: Slut!

LAUREN: (*shoving* ANDREA) No, you're the slut.

AMBER: *(pushing LAUREN back)* Lauren! Chill!

> *LAUREN is thrown down centre by CHRISTINA. She lands on her knees facing out. The other girls are upstage, backs to the audience, hissing "dumb bitch, stupid slut, lost control," etc. This "girl gang" creates a backdrop of whispers that accompany the beginning of LAUREN's monologue. These whispers turn into a mosquito score that the girls perform, underpinning LAUREN's discomfort.*

SCENE THIRTEEN: AND BY THE WAY, MISS

> *Extraordinary Space; the screens remain on the Institutional Side, inside the principal's office.*

> *Friday, after school.*

LAUREN: Oh, and by the way, miss . . . that's not what happened . . . they started with me. I just stood there, okay. *(One mosquito starts on a single pitch.)* I didn't do anything.

> *The other girls add their voices gradually through LAUREN's next paragraph, mosquito thread by mosquito thread. They turn downstage and move to her, surrounding her, still and contained.*

But then that hot and cold feeling started building up inside of me . . . I don't know. Okay, I can't explain it. See, you think that because I'm fourteen I must be out of control, right? Yeah, well, how about this. One night I was going up to my room and I accidentally knocked over this vase that was like a hundred and fifty years old. You want to talk out of control? Yeah, well, why don't we talk about what happened when my dad came up the stairs.

> *The mosquito sound becomes more insistent and annoying in a tight cluster of pitches.*

All that yelling . . . *(mosquito sound intensifies)* . . . it was echoing inside my head . . . and my ears were ringing and I just wanted to punch it out of me.

(as her father) "What are you? Stupid?"

A sharp intake of breath from all of the girls, their heads snapping up in unison, faces forward. The mosquito sounds have stopped.

No, Dad, it was an accident . . .

(as her father) "Shut up. You are going to pay for this, little girl!"

The mosquitoes resume.

Ow. Ow. Dad, you're hurting me, please . . . Dad, please, you're hurting me . . .

Each girl begins a full body twist, starting from her shoulder and ending up on one knee, at LAUREN's *feet.*

I just dove on her. I couldn't help it.

The mosquito sounds escalate as the group smoothly lifts LAUREN *up onto their shoulders.*

It was like four hundred pounds of pressure building up inside me and I kept telling myself, "Walk away! Please just walk away!" But I couldn't stop hitting her. My fists . . . I swear to god. I don't know. Okay. I couldn't stop.

The mosquitoes stop abruptly.

Everyone was staring at me.

The ensemble gradually lowers LAUREN *to standing throughout the following three lines.*

And all of a sudden I felt ashamed and guilty and I just wanted to take it all back. I'm not a hateful person, all right? It's not who I am.

All the girls look like they are at choir practice. They softly hum "My Favourite Things" while slowly retreating back to their screens. They watch LAUREN from the shadows.

LAUREN continues her monologue to this choral accompaniment, joining in with the occasional half-sung word, trying to hold on to two very different activities: explaining her extreme behaviour and simply being a grade eight girl.

I just feel like whenever I want to let something out, I hold it in, and every time I want to hold something in, I let it out. It's like I have two stomachs. There's the one that I can touch with my hand, and then there's that other one . . . it's like it's really far down, underneath my skin . . . it's always hurting and tight and it makes me feel anxious and nervous. I just want that pit in my stomach out of me, okay? I just wanted it to spread out a little bit. Just a bit, okay? *(crossing her arms)* And that is all I have to say, miss.

TRANSITION

The school bell starts realistically and has a very long and reverberant fade-out. LAUREN waits, looking out at the audience, staring down the principal as the bell fades. In the decay of the reverb she goes back to the screens, thudding her screen once with her fist, as if slamming a door. All the girls turn their screens to the Private Side in unison, setting them in a slightly curved semicircle.

SCENE FOURTEEN: ETERNAL SLUMBER PARTY

Treated Mundane into Extraordinary Space; the screens are turned to the Private Side, creating ANDREA's bedroom.

It's a Friday night sleepover after the second week of school. All the girls pull sleeping bags out from their screens and step into them, pulling them up to their chests while standing in front of their screens. They start to hop up and down on the spot during ANDREA's opening text. Their sleeping bags look a bit like potato sacks. They are excited to be at a sleepover and throughout this scene each tries to tell the best/worst story, or share a secret.

ANDREA: Oh my god . . . this summer I was at this party, and um . . . Jamie Oakley was there and we were totally making out. And I asked him, "Jamie, how much do you like me?" and he said, "I like you *(pause)* sixty percent."

The other girls make small sounds of disapproval, "ew," "oh," etc. LAUREN hops over to ANDREA and forces her to hop backwards around the stage.

LAUREN: Yeah, well one day I was going to the movies with my best friend and my best friend called me up and she was like, "Guess what?" and I was like, "Guess what, what?" And she said, "I'm going to the movies with my new best friend!"

ANDREA: I wouldn't say that!

DIANA: Well Bobby walked up to Monique and said, "You want to dance?" And she said, "Yes, yes, yes!" And he said, "Go ahead."

The girls make even louder sounds of disapproval, "Jerk off," "Masturbator," etc. The energy of the name-calling causes an increase in the exuberance of their hopping.

CHRISTINA: *(her jumps cutting into the fray)* What exactly is masturbation?

AMBER enthusiastically makes large sideways hops from stage right to stage left, facing the audience.

AMBER: It's something you do by yourself, that's private, that feels good.

DIANA: That must be right because you're in control, that's probably where the Master *(drops her sleeping bag to the floor and picks it back up)* comes from.

AMBER: Well then what's the "bation" part?

DIANA: The action word.

AMBER: Oh, the verb.

LAUREN: Guys! You touch yourself!

The sleeping bag jumping continues, everyone fully committed to it.

DIANA: Yeah, you're "bationing." You're the master of your "bation."

CHRISTINA: Where do you do it then?

LAUREN: You do it whenever you want!

DIANA: I could be doing it right now!

In their bags DIANA, CHRISTINA, and AMBER drop to the floor and roll onto their backs, curling into little balls. CHRISTINA and DIANA are at LAUREN's feet, testicles to LAUREN's sleeping-bag penis. AMBER, lifting her legs up in the air, still in the sleeping bag, becomes a "hard-on."

AMBER: I'm doing it right now! AAAAAAHHHH!!!

LAUREN: I'm penis erectus!

LAUREN pulls her sleeping bag up over her head.

Hey guys.

DIANA and CHRISTINA bounce their feet in the air and roll away.

Well . . . where are you going? Hey guys, my balls are separating!

ANDREA: *(pointing an imaginary gun at DIANA)* Freeze, little ball!

They all make general genital talk as they leap up and form a flat line stage left, their backs to the audience. They are standing at urinals, the same location and lighting as the girls' bathroom. Their voices deepen and thicken, overlapping in the following text.

Dude, where's my ball?

DIANA: How about those Jays?

AMBER: How about the Leafs?

LAUREN: How about that lockout?

ALL: AARRGGOOSSSSSSSS.

The SSS makes the sound of pee; when done, they shake their imaginary penises off and zip up. DIANA turns around first and sees "a girl."

DIANA: Hey guys, heads up . . . two o'clock . . .

A sequence of helpless, slack-jawed "uhs" as they turn to see her. They are gently stunned guys lining the school hall, their bro mentality allowing them to compete for the girl as one.

CHRISTINA: Bethany?

ANDREA: Bethany, what's your middle name?

AMBER: Yo, Bethany, what's your number?

DIANA: Bethany, I'll do your homework!

ANDREA: Bethany, what's your dog's name?

LAUREN: Uh Bethany, what's your first name?

Cracking voices and nervous laughs as they rib LAUREN *for her stupid question. These boy laughs turn into seal laughs as they jump up and down hysterically in their bags. They drop to the floor, rolling stage right as a group into the unknown.* ANDREA *is the first to sit up and discover her tail. She is perched on her right hip, on a slight diagonal, her sleeping bag now a mermaid tail.*

ANDREA: Oh my god . . . *(her voice changing to that of a fantastical creature)* . . . I'm a mermaid.

All the other girls sit up and become mermaids too!

Oh my god . . . look!

ANDREA *points out into the audience.*

AMBER: A boat is coming!

DIANA: A boat of beautiful boys!

ANDREA: *(waving her arm to get their attention)* Helloo-oo!

ALL: *(all alluringly waving their arms)* Helloo-ooooo!

This hello becomes a juicy musical chord.

ANDREA: *(with a flip of her tail, shifting over to sit on her left hip)* We'll save you!

AMBER: *(tail flip and hip shift)* We'll feed you fruits!

DIANA: *(tail flip and hip shift)* We'll feed you sushi!

LAUREN: *(tail flip and hip shift)* We'll brush your hair!

CHRISTINA: *(a clumsy, unsuccessful tail flip and hip shift)* I've got clams!

CHRISTINA *falls onto her back, her tail up in the air.*

LAUREN begins singing Ariel's song from Disney's The Little Mermaid, *"Ah-ah-ah, Ah-ah-ah," and the others join, fluttering their hands under their chins like gills.*

ALL: *(interrupting their own singing in the middle of the high note)* TIDAL WAVE!!!

A tidal wave washes over them, interrupting the song and pushing them into chaotic, erratic shoulder rolls upstage. DIANA, LAUREN, and CHRISTINA are now out of their sleeping bags, standing on them like surfers. AMBER is rolling back and forth in her sleeping bag, waving at their feet. She invisibly sneaks the flashlights from a screen and surreptitiously passes them out to all the girls but ANDREA.

ANDREA is now standing, still in her sleeping bag, leaving the world of roughhouse play, as the bag becomes a couture gown. She puts on appropriate airs.

ANDREA: I can walk and I don't even have legs!

The girls train their flashlights on ANDREA, providing follow spots for her walk down the red carpet. They are on their knees in adoration.

I can put on an evening gown, French perfume, and watch my breasts grow.

Yes! Yes! Walk out of being a girl and into a woman.

She smells her armpit.

Apply deodorant, shave my legs, search for my soulmate, *(a little jump of joy)* "Oh where are you? Where are you? You're late!"

Prepare to dump and be dumped.

She starts to feel the pressure of having to grow up and, beginning to overheat, fans herself with her hands. The other girls begin to share in her anxiety, echoing key words.

Put on my platforms, powder my nose, excel in art, math, physics, French, friends, family, photography, feeling a little warm?

Pausing, she looks like she could faint.

I need a Slurpee . . .

She bends over to pick up a glass.

ANDREA sucks back an enormous Slurpee as the rest of the girls create a chorus of sucking sounds.

She tosses her glass over her shoulder, making the sound of glass breaking. The girls follow suit, echoing the KKSSSSHHHHH and falling to the ground.

A lighting change takes us into Extraordinary Space, intensifying ANDREA's anxiety and fear. She steps out of her sleeping bag and pauses.

I don't want to grow up . . . I don't want to grow up . . .

She reaches out her arm and drops her sleeping bag as far away from her as she can. The other girls all sit up to look at her, unnerved.

DIANA, CHRISTINA, and LAUREN make the sound of whispering leaves while AMBER sings a very deep, sustained breathy tone.

ANDREA sings her true self. The words are spaced out, somewhat halting. Her voice does not have a lot of tone, and is as hollow as she is feeling. The melody is stilted and eerie, a slightly improvised feeling of discovering the truth.

(all on one note, mid/low-range) I . . . don't . . . want . . . to . . . grow . . . up . . .

ANDREA turns upstage and starts to walk slowly, circling behind the screens. The girls now use the flashlights as headlights on a highway, catching her in between the screens. They are still seated on the floor.

(two descending laments) I want to walk . . . into the highway.

(ending with repeated notes) This is my last . . . day . . . here.

(two downward detuned intervals) Don't cry . . . I'm not.

(repeated notes till the last one falls) I know I seem hap . . . py.

(in a high, disembodied voice) Wouldn't it be romantic if I left early.

(two descending laments) Walk down the grass . . . into the highway.

As she disappears behind the second to last screen at stage right, the girls stand and shine their flashlights on the floor and move to stage left. A search party. Their rustling leaf sound is transformed into dark breath from low in the chest, sounding a bit like cars passing in the distance.

(two downward detuned intervals) Don't cry . . . I'm not.

(high, disembodied voice, last syllable falling in pitch) I'm hap . . . py.

(detuned interval descending into speaking range) Don't . . . cry.

ANDREA appears between the two stage right screens, gingerly stepping in front of her own screen and then moving straight towards the audience. She steps cautiously, balancing precariously on tiptoe, her arms extended forward.

(all on a single speaking-range tone) I don't want to grow . . . up . . . I . . .

She moves right to edge of the stage. The girls walk forward in their soccer ball corridors, shining their flashlights straight ahead, still searching for the missing girl. When they get to edge of the stage ANDREA carefully lowers onto her heels.

ALL: *(long, breathy inhale, which is held through* ANDREA's *next line)* HHAAAHH . . .

ANDREA: *(speaking)* You found me.

ALL: *(their unison exhale turns into bossy words of relief)* I don't care if it's three in the morning. The next time you feel this way, you better call me.

Pause.

ANDREA: *(turning to face the girls)* I'm right here.

Flashlights are turned to ANDREA *as they move towards her.*

Let's go home.

They walk upstage in the dark, dropping each friend off one at a time at her screen. When they are all home they turn their screens to the Institutional Side.

SCENE FIFTEEN: SHE'S MY DIARY

Treated Mundane; the screens are presented in a new pattern: Magic Bedroom Space.

It's early dawn, the sun just rising. The girls turn their screens onto a shallow diagonal so that we can see the Institutional Side and the Private Side at the same time. Using chalk to write on the flat grey Institutional Side, each girl starts a diary entry about friendship. When they are finished writing they repeat, one after the other, "Dear Diary . . . " and then begin to sing the opening song.

DIANA: What is a friend?

CHRISTINA: Could it be that it's just a word.

LAUREN: Something you've always wanted

AMBER: From a song you heard.

ANDREA: Or just another one of those

ALL: Big fat lies
'Cause many nights this word has made me cry
So hard my stomach hurts
Deep down inside.

> *They pick up the sleeping bags and shake them out.*

You want to hide
She's still the one who gets inside
Too close at times 'cause you
Need room to cry.

> *The sleeping bags are laid out on the floor, and then rolled up; each girl is in front of her own screen.*

Can she hear you're hurt when nothing's said at all?
Will she sit with you when you're feeling small?
When she's heard the worst, will she like you at all?

> *They take each other in, hugging their sleeping bags.*

Scared to tell you. I
Won't dare to tell you. Why?
Might trust you, should I try?

> *They place their sleeping bags into their screens. The song expands musically, incorporating subtle harmonies.*

When you're nowhere
And ev'rywhere at the same time.
A friend will find your song; she'll hear your rhyme.

> *Each girl revolves her screen while wheeling it downstage to present the Institutional Side to the audience. We can now easily read their diary entries.*

She'll never tell you what to do
And you know all that she's been through
You've seen her scars and she's seen you

She'll let you be yourself
So let her be herself
I want to be . . .

Each is girl standing beside her screen; one after the other they sign off: ANDREA, CHRISTINA, DIANA, LAUREN, AMBER.

Blackout.

BENEATH THE ICE

Eva Colmers

To Bill, Isabelle, and Phillip Colmers, whose love and encouragement kept me going

and

to the people of Kangiqsujuaq, whose fascinating land, community, and traditions inspired my play.

ACKNOWLEDGEMENTS

First, I would like to thank Jan Andrews and Ian Wallace, whose picture book *Very Last First Time* was my children's favourite bedtime story and inspired me to write *Beneath the Ice*. Thank you also to the Canada Council for the Arts and the Alberta Playwrights' Network; without their generous support the play would not have achieved the same authenticity and accuracy. Thanks to my spirited travel companion, dramaturg and director Tracy Carroll. A heartfelt thanks to the many kind people in Kangiqsujuaq who opened their doors to us and allowed us to experience their life: Brian Urquhart, Economic Development and Tourism Coordinator from the Nunaturlik Landholding Corporation of Kangiqsujuaq; Father Jules Dion and reader Paasa; Principal Shona McCusker; the librarian, teachers, and students at the Arsaniq School who worked with me during the shadow puppet workshop; and many more.

Thanks also for the encouragement and advice from Vern Thiessen, Joyce Doolittle, Gin May, Marissa Kochanski, Coleen Young Schneider, Scott Shpeley, Ava Jane Markus, Alison Wells, and Devon Dubnyk.

Thank you very much to the passionate directors and actors of previous productions of *Beneath the Ice*. They all added nuances to the characters and action that triggered small revisions here and there: Tracy Carroll, Nikki

Loach, Alison Wells, Lisa Truong, Brendan Meyer, Zina Lee, Eric Wigston, Chantal Quintal, Devon Dubnyk, Darlene Auger, Dakota Hebert, and Scott Roberts.

I much appreciated the comments on my script by Ulaayu Pilurtuut, Sylvie Côté Chew, and Pauyungie Avataq. A big thank you to teachers and students who watched the DVD recording of the Quest Theatre production and provided helpful feedback: teacher Christina Garrett and her students at the Arsaniq School in Kangiqsujuaq, teachers Bill Akerly and Alison Corbett, and their classes at the Netsilik School in Taloyoak.

Much gratitude goes to editor Heather Fitzsimmons Frey for her continuous support and encouragement and to Blake Sproule and Bruce Barton for their guidance during the final revision and publishing process.

And thank you to my husband Bill and children Isabelle and Phillip, who never doubted that this would be a beautiful and meaningful play, one day.

Enjoy and *nakurmiik*!

LOCATION-SPECIFIC, CROSS-CULTURAL PLAY DEVELOPMENT RESEARCH, COLLABORATION, AND LISTENING TO FEEDBACK
Heather Fitzsimmons Frey[1]

Naammagijarpit ungataanut pitsanak.

Do not take more than you need.

—Sedna, *Beneath the Ice*

Working with Eva Colmers to include *Beneath the Ice* in this anthology has been full of challenges, incredible learning opportunities, introductions to generous artists and Northern community members, and, I suspect, many mistakes on my part. My hope, despite my lack of expertise about Inuit culture, is to contextualize Eva Colmers's play within the Canadian theatre landscape, to discuss and problematize her creation process, and to begin to analyze the complex community feedback. It is telling that, after recognizing the importance of insight into Inuit culture in examining this play's journey to publication, my efforts to find a more qualified scholar to write this introduction were unsuccessful. The hesitance of scholars to wade into this pool foreground how fraught this process has been, and what you read here contains highlights of a conflicted relationship I have had with the potential and promise contained in *Beneath the Ice.*

1   I would like to thank Manon van de Water, Geesche Wartemann, and ITYARN, who heard about this project in the early stages; *Youth Theatre Journal,* where portions of this writing originally appeared; the guests of One Theatre World (OTW) Chicago who discussed the project with me as it developed; and Antje Budde, Christine Sokaymoh Frederick, Kathleen Gallagher, Tanya Lukin-Linklater, Christopher Morris, and Zoe Todd, who gave me advice and encouragement regarding the feedback process for this project. Thanks to Skye Perry for project insights and Pamela Anthony for helping me make connections. Thanks to Tiffany Ayalik, Nyla Carpentier, and Tracy

For a young, Southern audience, the content and themes of *Beneath the Ice* are thought-provoking: Colmers's script is deceptively simple and is based on the familiar journey motif. David, a Southern Canadian teenager, has convinced his mother, who is conducting research on climate change, to bring him with her when she goes to Kangiqsujuaq[2] in Nunavik, Northern Quebec. David does lots of advance research on the community, so he is convinced that he will impress his mother with his knowledge and be a big help to her. However, when he arrives, David's mother has to go to a more remote research station, and he is left in the care of a grandmother (Aanak) and her young granddaughter (Paasa). David's prior Internet research proves

---

Carroll, who agreed to discuss their experiences concerning artistic collaboration between North and South, and between Indigenous and non-Indigenous people. Very important for my written work, Keavy Martin generously read an early draft of this piece and gave advice on ways to write about and think about these issues. Thanks to Heather Davis-Fisch who helped me clarify and deepen some ideas. Thanks to Nikki Loach of Quest Theatre, Calgary, and the cast of their production of *Beneath the Ice* for sharing their archival DVD. As for the research participants, I want to thank Brian Urquhart for helping me to connect with people in Kangiqsujuaq, for answering many of my questions, and for connecting me with Ulaayu Pilurtuut, Lucasi Pilurtuut, and Avataq Cultural Institute, Quebec (Sylvie Côté Chew and Pauyungie Nutaraaluk—who I would also like to thank for the way they offered cultural and language advice). Thanks to Teacher Claude Pike and the Family Care Office at the University of Toronto for connecting me to Netsilik School, Taloyoak, in Nunavut. Special thanks to teachers Bill Akerly and Alison Corbett and their generous students for taking the time to respond so thoughtfully to Eva's play. Akerly's students were: Annie Kanayuq Aklah, Maggie Aqqaq, Andrea Iqilliq, Raymond Manniliq, Christopher Sarasin, Hayley Totalik, and Holly Tulurialik. Corbett's students were: Lonnie Alookee, Wendy Alookee, Sandra Aqqaq, Barney Igutsak Jr., Jonathan Jayko, Kole Keenainak, Jerome Kripanik, Wilson Mannilaq, Aupila Neeveacheak, Phoebe Niviatsiaq, Tammy Pauloosie, Suzanne Qavavau, Peter Qayutinuaq, Jr., Ian Qilluniq, Duncan Totalik, Mimi Tucktoo, Edmond Ugyuk, and Anna Wolki. Thanks to the Arsaniq School Centre, Kativik School Board, Kangiqsujuaq, to Teacher Christina Garrett and Principal Thomas Colter, and especially to the Kangiqsujuaq students, who have asked to remain anonymous here. Finally, thanks to Eva Colmers for her enthusiastic and thoughtful participation in this rather unconventional road to publishing a play.

2   According to Brian Urquhart, Colmers's government contact in the town, while "Kangiqsujuaq" is the official government spelling of the community, most local people do not consider it to be phonetically correct. The municipal council uses Kangirsujuaq. Other spellings exist as well. Similarly, there are multiple possible spellings of other community names. One reason for these discrepancies is that the written form of Inuktitut uses syllabics rather than the Latin alphabet used in written English and French. Brian Urquhart, email correspondence with the author, 12 August 2013.

completely inadequate for understanding and appreciating his new surroundings and the people who care for him, but when Paasa goes under
the ice to collect mussels, he is intrigued. Aanak tells him he is not ready
yet, and in a fit of jealous frustration, he does the very thing Aanak warns
him against: he sneaks off and goes under the ice to take pictures. While
he is on the ocean floor, he gets disoriented, loses his camera, parka, and
mittens, and has to be rescued by Paasa because the tide is rushing in.
As a result of his near-death experience and rescue, and an under-the-ice
spiritual experience with Sedna, David realizes that Aanak and Paasa do
have something to teach him, and he promises to be more respectful in the
future. Although *Beneath the Ice* uses Inuit characters, the play is told from
David's (the Southern outsider's) perspective, in an echo of the playwright's
own position as a white Southern Canadian.

In the context of the straightforward narrative, the play invites young
audiences to discuss globalization, climate change, and ways of knowing.
It stages North–South relations, foregrounding Southern ignorance about
the North, and it features aspects of traditional Inuit culture and a modern
Inuk girl who respects her grandmother and the old ways of doing things.
Just as she did in the research and feedback processes, within the text of
Beneath the Ice Colmers grapples with issues concerned with how listening
can be difficult, even when the listener is trying to hear.

Beneath the Ice offers the promise of stimulating content, but what really
appealed to me in terms of this anthology was the promise inherent in the
idea of constructing a play using location-specific cross-cultural research.
Eva Colmers approached the project as an artist, not as a scholar, and with
an effort to be as respectful of the people of Kangiqsujuaq as she could
imagine. As I will explain, the promise of cross-cultural, location-specific
research did not result in a straightforward journey. The script published
here is different than the one that was originally staged because Colmers
honoured the community feedback she received by making some changes.

SITUATING THE JOURNEY: CONTEXTUALIZING WITHIN THE CANADIAN THEATRE LANDSCAPE

Like the other plays in this volume, *Beneath the Ice* features an unusual creation journey. In this case, the journey began with specific inspiration: when Colmers's children were very young their favourite picture book was Jan Andrews and Ian Wallace's *Very Last First Time*, a story set in Kangiqsujuaq. Her journey became one of epic physical proportions because Colmers and her dramaturg, Tracy Carroll—recognizing the issues surrounding white, Southern Canadians writing a play about the North— decided to travel to Kangiqsujuaq to conduct creation research. They learned they would have to fly from Edmonton to Montreal to Kuujjuaq, "about 21 ½ hours from Montreal and quite the hub of Nunavik . . . From there we hop onto a Dart 8 prop plane and fly to Kangiqsujuaq stopping in two communities along the way."[3]

When Colmers applied to the Canada Council for the Arts for funding for the trip, she knew that after spending a week in that Northern community she could not pretend to *know* the North or to truly understand Inuit culture, but she hoped to be able develop a more respectful and complex representation of the North in her play than exists in the often unreflective Canadian imagination. Canadian theatre scholar Ric Knowles writes, "Ever since the mid- to late 1980s, it has been impossible for non-Native playwrights to simply or unproblematically appropriate Native stories or perform Native characters," just as it has been impossible for non-Native scholars (like myself) to discuss Native work or work with Native subject matter without careful positioning.[4] Indigenous people, especially women, have asked non-Native people to stop telling Indigenous stories because non-Natives are usually trapped by clichés and prone to

---

3   Tracy Carroll, "My Kangiqsujuaq Journal," 9 January 2009, http://www.thecookie. ca/My_Kangiqsujuaq_Journal_html.

4   Ric Knowles, "Marlon Brando, Pocahontas, and Me," *Essays on Canadian Writing* 71 (2000): 48–60. In the context of debates about appropriation of voice, Knowles also reflects on how to view "Native" theatre productions. He refers to non-Native academic Alan Filewod's 1992 essay "Averting the Colonizing Gaze: Notes on Watching Native Theatre," which begins with the assertion that "I can't write about native theater; all I can write about is my response to it."

essentializing characters as "Indigenous other[s]."⁵ Instead, Native women ask that writers give Indigenous people space to "define their own reality."⁶ Carroll immediately acknowledges that two white women creating the play was inherently problematic, saying, "We felt very white . . . There were so many things we just didn't understand."⁷ Colmers agrees that they were aware that they were writing outside of their own culture, saying, "I cannot change my culture, but I wanted to show the greatest respect for their culture by going there at least."⁸ Colmers hoped to surround herself with the community and have an opportunity to watch and learn, and to use the experience to avoid clichés—ultimately a more complicated and ambitious goal than she initially imagined.

Those clichés and essentialized, reductive imaginings that Colmers hoped to combat are indeed ingrained in much of the Canadian South's concept of the North. The Arctic landscape is far from invisible in Canadian identity: the Arctic and Inuit are significant parts of the Canadian imagination. Northrop Frye explains that Canadians have constructed a shared "social mythology" based on Indigenous symbols and stories. Northern examples include *Ookpik* the owl,⁹ the symbol for the 1967 World Fair in Montreal,¹⁰ and the inuksuk symbol for the 2010 Vancouver Winter Olympics. Sherrill Grace's *Canada and the Idea of North* offers thoughtful analysis and numerous other examples. Embodying ideas of survival and ruggedness in a harsh wilderness, as well as a kind of cartoon "cute" image, bundled-up and giving "Eskimo kisses," the "imaginary Inuk"

---

5   Laura Smyth Groening, *Listening To Old Woman Speak: Natives and alterNatives in Canadian Literature* (Montreal: McGill-Queen's UP, 2005), 178.

6   Ibid., 5.

7   Tracy Carroll, personal interview with the author, 3 March 2013.

8   Eva Colmers, personal interview with the author, 3 March 2013.

9   In another neo-colonial move, Ookpik was first introduced at an economic fair in Philadelphia, 1964. The organizers discussed their search on CBC television but neglected to name the artist who created Ookpik. She was Jeannie Snowball of Kuujjuaq, the "big community" near Kangiqsujuaq. Carroll learned that making Ookpiks for Expo 67 became a significant source of revenue for Kuujjuaq.

10   L.S. Pupchek, "True North: Inuit Art and the Canadian Imagination," *The American Review of Canadian Studies* 31.1–2 (2001): 204.

exists alongside or is sometimes conflated with the "imaginary Indian."[11] The Imaginary Inuk also influences the way the Inuit are constructed in children's stories: until very recently they were primarily portrayed in an exclusively historical timespace, conducting life in a "traditional" way, associated with "the past." In these narratives, this way of life is declining and ultimately doomed because of environmental destruction and/or the assimilating pressures of globalization or modernity. Meanwhile Euro-Canadian culture is implicitly associated with the future.[12]

The North and Inuit cultures also exist, often in problematic ways, on Canadian stages, both for general and young audiences. In Sherrill Grace's introduction to *Staging the North* she describes ways that Herman Voaden argued the North was essential to Canadian theatre in the 1930s, the "strikingly inept" ways Inuit were staged by Southerners in the 1950s and 60s, and pieces like *Changes* in which Inuit playwrights chose to create performances for their own audiences. Since Grace published her anthology, Canadian artists have strived for better and more complex depictions of the North, even as they continued to reimagine and stage Northern people. Two recent projects that involved a significant number of Inuit actor-creators include a performance of the Inuit story of "Kautyayuk" created with Avataq's Theatre for Youth in Nunavik initiative, which offered theatre workshops in Puvirnituq for Hudson Coast participants, and in Kuujjuaq[13] for young people from the Ungava Coast; and *Night* by Christopher Morris, Artistic Director of Human Cargo, devised in connection with communities in Pond Inlet, Nunavut, and with Southern Canadian, Inuit, and Icelandic actors. *Beneath the Ice* was not co-created by Inuit, but unlike much early Canadian work, Colmers made it a priority to involve Inuit in research and feedback stages of her creative process in an effort to avoid

---

11   Inuit and First Nations peoples are often "collapsed into a monolithic original indigenous population" (the way they are represented in non-Native cultural expression is what Daniel Francis calls the "Imaginary Indian.") Daniel Francis, *The Imaginary Indian: The Image of the Indian in Canadian Culture* (Vancouver: Arsenal Pulp, 1992).

12   Groening, 20.

13   Kuujjuaq is the "big" community closest to Kangiqsujuaq, and when Eva Colmers visited Kangiqsujuaq, she changed planes in Kuujjuaq. Avataq's website explains that the workshop resulted in a play concerning the story of Kautyayuk. https://uqavvik. wordpress.com.

problematic staged representations of modern Inuit life and culture, even though the work was outsider-created.

However, as alluded to earlier and as we learned from community feedback, aspects of *Beneath the Ice* elicited a variety of positive and negative responses. One of the difficulties that only emerged in retrospect stemmed from the heterogeneity of Northern culture. In *Staging the North* Grace aptly points out that "Canada is certainly a northern nation, but it contains many norths."[14] To say that a play "represents" the North, or that certain characters are "typically" Northern, is simply not possible. Colmers wanted her story to include the practice of collecting mussels beneath the ice in the wintertime, but that activity is only conducted in Kangiqsujuaq, where the tides are extreme enough to make it possible. A "generic Canadian North" could not contain her story. As a result, *locating* the piece in Kangiqsujuaq in a way that seemed recognizable to residents, to create characters that were not reductive but allowed for complex performances of identity, and to create character relationships that resonated with Northerners were especially important. Colmers needed to write about the North she briefly experienced and to create characters and relationships that exist in communities she barely encountered.

This challenge, although formidable, is neither definitively undesirable nor insurmountable. As I will explore, there is value in staging respectful Indigenous identities and relationships for young audiences, just as there is value in openly acknowledging ignorance about the North—a vast part of the country Southern Canadians claim. As Sam McKegney argues, one important strategy for non-Native scholars dealing with Native literature is to admit ignorance—but that has very little value if the writer does not work hard to change that.[15] Artists and scholars need to operate as engaged allies, acknowledging the vitality of Indigenous communities. Another very important tactic is *listening*, which I also explore below.

Although they still need to create their work with care, Indigenous performers who produce specifically Indigenous work navigate issues of

---

14   Sherrill Grace, introduction to *Staging the North: Twelve Canadian Plays* (Toronto: Playwrights Canada, 1999), xxi.

15   Sam McKegney, "Strategies for Ethical Engagement: An Open Letter Concerning Non-Native Scholars of Native Literatures Studies," *American Indian Literatures* 20.4 (2008): 56–67.

cultural visibility and staging Indigenous identities with confidence. Santee Smith, of the Mohawk nation Six Nations Reserve (Haudenosaunee), who is the artistic director and choreographer for Kaha:wi Dance Theatre, argues that Indigenous work is systemically marginalized in Canada, it "lacks public attention and honour," and is "too easily made invisible."[16] She believes favourable visibility made possible through staging Indigenous stories and Indigenous identities can counter negative news that perpetuates stereotypical notions regarding Indigenous cultures and peoples. But when she was workshopping *A Story Before Time*, a performance for young audiences, getting the story "right" became important for her too. Initially a wordless, exclusively dance performance, she decided that for the sake of clarity she would augment the dance with text, and found that was more satisfying for her and for spectators. In workshops for the wordless performance she found even audiences from the Six Nations Reserve were confused, and it was important to her that the story be clearly understood, especially since she anticipated some audience members would be encountering Haudenosaunee (Iroquois) culture for the first time. As Smith explains, there are potential positive meanings produced when effectively staging Indigenous identities and stories—and, similarly, Colmers hoped to stage positive Inuit characters.

For artists staging Northern identities and issues in the context of TYA, the stakes are especially high. In Alberta and Saskatchewan, where *Beneath the Ice* first toured to schools, the Grade 2 Social Studies curriculum includes studying Inuit communities in comparison to their own community.[17] Since teachers are short of effective instructional resources, the play's link to the curriculum is one reason why *Beneath the Ice* was popular with schools, but it also meant the content of the play would have a distinct effect on the educational message of that part of the curriculum. Like children encountering Haudenosaunee culture through *A Story Before Time*, young audiences may encounter Inuit culture for the first time through a performance of *Beneath the Ice*, increasing a need to be responsible in the way that cultural identity and difference is portrayed.

---

16   Santee Smith, personal interview with the author, 26 September 2014.

17   At the moment, the Grade 2 Social Studies curriculum in Alberta demands students study a Prairie community, an Acadian community, and an Inuit community in comparison with their own.

Some other Canadian artists believe that a non-Inuit can effectively write and stage Northern identities, but the key is effective listening. When I asked Inuit actor Tiffany Ayalik (who has performed as an Inuk woman on stage several times, including her very recent performances in *Night*) to share some of her ideas about portraying Inuit characters on stage, she remarked in conversation with me, "You can't speak on behalf of a whole people. I'm only an expert in my own experience . . . admitting that you [a non-Inuk] don't know everything is really important . . . and I'm saying proceed with caution, NOT don't do it . . . you should have a deep deep sense of very active listening and respect."[18] Through a multi-site workshopping process, Christopher Morris and Human Cargo embraced the need for active listening and respect as they created *Night*. Besides the earlier play development workshops, to date the piece has been performed in seven different Arctic communities. The script contains material that is very painful to see on stage, perhaps especially because it includes sensitive topics many Northern spectators are living through. Morris says that theatre creation work is "challenging, and must be approached with as much sensitivity as possible. In the end, factors may dictate that it's not appropriate to be trying to do what you're doing, that your 'set' process you want to implement has to change, be given up on, or that the project should end. And as a creator, you have to accept that and respond accordingly."[19] Whether the piece is presented to general or young audiences, there are post-show discussions after every performance of *Night*, so Morris has a strong sense of the variety of ways Inuit spectators see *Night* and some of the kinds of issues it raises for them. As an outsider, really listening is an essential element in creating located and culturally specific work.

Unlike *Night*, *Beneath the Ice* could not be workshopped in an Inuit community: without the resources to bring a production of her play north, Colmers relied on her process of visiting Kangiqsujuaq and consulting community members about her story, her characters, their community, and Inuktitut. Moments of that visit were indirectly transposed into moments in the script.

For example, although *Beneath the Ice* uses Inuit characters, the play is told from David's perspective, in an echo of the playwright's own position

18   Tiffany Ayalik, personal interview with the author, 15 May 2015.

19   Christopher Morris, personal interview with the author, 21 May 2015.

as a Southern Canadian. Furthermore, the significant character journey is for the Southern David rather than the Inuit characters of Aanak and Paasa, who remain relatively constant, although they are not written as historicized, static people living in a frozen mythical place. I suspect many writers from the South shrink from including Inuit stories and characters in their work because they are concerned about misrepresenting and misunderstanding the North and the Inuit. Writing a Southerner–Inuit encounter can also be problematic: in an interview with Keavy Martin, Taqralik Partridge describes her frustration with narratives that imply that a particular story can only be told because a white person is there to interpret it, and because of "the world's appetite for stories that are framed by whiteness."[20] By positioning the story from the point of view of an outsider from the South, Colmers privileges white perspective, but she also places her own uncertainties and assumptions on stage in the form of David— who is not necessarily a *white* character, but is definitely a *Southern* child.[21] Rather than presuming to write a meaningful and believable journey for Aanak or Paasa, she focuses on David and demonstrates that David has to learn how to *unknow* not just through South-dominated book-and-Internet research, but through experience, through listening and respect, and through a willingness to accept that there are things that exist well beyond his past experiences and the way he knows how to know. In the process, David echoes the way that learning how to *know* and *unknow* became a part of Colmers's Kangiqsujuaq journey, leaving spectators with the impression that David (and Colmers) has not yet learned everything he needs to, or digested everything he learned. Written with a Southern school-child audience in mind, in some ways *Beneath the Ice* problematically follows in the footsteps of non-Indigenous stories of discovery and exploration set against an Inuit, Northern landscape, but Colmers's narrative decision gives Southern children a "way in" to the North through

---

20   Keavy Martin and Taqralik Partridge, "What Inuit May Think: Taqralik Partridge and Keavy Martin Talk Inuit Literature," in *Oxford Handbook of Canadian Literature*, ed. Cynthia Sugars (Oxford: Oxford UP, forthcoming).

21   Canadian TYA companies strive to include non-white actors in their casts and there is nothing in Eva's script to suggest that he has to be *white*, only that he has to be from the South.

David, and her attentive creation process made a thought-provoking and complex final script possible.

PLANNING THE JOURNEY: CROSS-CULTURAL LOCATION-SPECIFIC RESEARCH

When Colmers and Carroll arrived in Kangiqsujuaq, they were open to any and all experiences. Carroll says, "We did everything anyone suggested we do, even if we couldn't see a connection; we knew that it would serve the play."[22] Since developing fictional characters about a real place in an unromantic way that did not reinscribe notions of a futureless Inuit were priorities for Colmers, activities that helped her to gain a sense of life in Kangiqsujuaq meant any community activities were welcome. Although, as she explains in her introduction, the ice was not thick enough for her and Carroll to go under it the way David does, they did try to experience other aspects of local culture. A throat singer named Elisapi and her student performed for them; they went to a sewing circle where women fined each other if they did not speak Inuktitut, and where Carroll and Colmers attempted to soften sealskin by chewing it and stomping on it; they attended one of the three Christian churches and met with the priest from another church; they worked with one of the employees at the newly opened hotel to translate and record numerous phrases into Inuktitut that they hoped might be used in the final script; and they visited local buildings like the co-op, the museum, the school, and the school library. Even though there are no roads in and out of Kangiqsujuaq, Carroll was struck by the way the South impacts the lives of people in the community, not only through climate change, but also through Internet and satellite television, the availability of relatively cheap products like Coca-Cola, the high cost of other products like oranges or milk, the existence of cars and trucks (not to mention snowmobiles), and the pressure to make decisions about what Southern language to learn at the age of nine (French or English), and whether or not to go and take employment at the nearby nickel mine. Contemporary globalized reality is reflected in the play. When Aanak tells David that the reason they have

---

22   Carroll, personal interview.

different lives than her ancestors is not climate change but "people change," she is not bemoaning a lost heritage or an irretrievable utopian landscape; rather, Colmers is using Aanak's voice to acknowledge the experiences she had when she visited Kangiqsujuaq and to incorporate the global tensions that pull and tug on the lives of Kangiqsujuaq's 430 inhabitants.

EVALUATING THE SCRIPT AS PART OF THE JOURNEY: LISTENING TO INUIT YOUNG PEOPLE

For the most part the themes, subjects, and ideas in *Beneath the Ice*, like patience, climate change, globalization, North–South relations, respect for other people, and ways of knowing, can speak for themselves in the pages of Colmers's script—but as editor of this anthology, I believed it was also crucial for Inuit community members to share their reactions to the play. Inuit performer Tiffany Ayalik cautions that when artists create theatre concerning Northern people,

> It's really important to work with the community that you are potentially representing. It's one thing for us to push our own boundaries within our community, but it's different than someone coming in and pushing us around. It's especially important if a character could be perceived as expressing an authentic version of events . . . whose voice is it? . . . if you aren't in the community you don't understand the "fullness" of the community.[23]

I was intrigued by Colmers's creative risks and efforts to have a mean-ingful research encounter with Kangiqsujuaq, and approached her about including the script in this anthology. But initially I was not aware that her efforts to connect with the Kangiqsujuaq Inuit community to consult them as she wrote the final script or to share the finished product had stalled. Much as I appreciated Colmers's script, its potential, and the jour-ney to make the piece, I was not comfortable publishing the script without community feedback, so I offered to spearhead an effort to connect some Kangiqsujuaq residents with *Beneath the Ice*. Both Colmers and I wanted

---

23   Ayalik, personal interview.

to listen to the opinions and ideas of the children of Kangiqsujuaq and, ultimately, Colmers incorporated Northern feedback. However, getting their reactions, as I outline at the beginning of the Creative Collaborators section, proved to be difficult. My kind contacts in Kangiqsujuaq would agree to help, but later would find that they were too busy, or would sometimes stop replying to my emails. Numerous scholars and artists more familiar with Indigenous communities offered advice on how to get the feedback I felt the play needed, and also suggested potential reasons why my communication with specific people in Kangiqsujuaq frequently faltered. I pondered what the silence could mean: could it indicate a lack of time, a lack of interest in the project, a desire for financial compensation to participate, or even a resistance to the project? Silence as resistance is a topic that reverberates through academic discourses at the moment. If it was, in fact, resistance, were my contacts resisting the playscript itself or were they resisting the way that I was requesting feedback, the way that I invited them to communicate answers in English (which would be a second language), the way that I suggested correspondence by email (which could be difficult to write or just inconvenient) or by phone but in English, or the types of questions I asked? Could it be a lack of confidence or could they be hesitating to become a "research subject"—something with which they may or may not have experience—either positive or negative? Perhaps silence could indicate uncertainty about what their participation could mean for the project and for their community. I tried to address these imagined potential reasons for silence, but my efforts to engage Kangiqsujuaq community members with giving feedback to *Beneath the Ice* kept failing.[24]

One Kangiqsujuaq teacher eventually told me that the script was difficult to read and imagine on stage because she had never seen a play before, so I decided that we could try to get beyond the printed word—especially important in a community where English and French are almost always the

---

24   Some scholars who discuss issues concerning and meanings around silence include Jo-ann Archibald in *Indigenous Storywork*, especially chapter three, in which she discusses ways she conducted research with elders, and chapter six, in which she discusses possible meanings of silence in reaction to Indigenous stories; Paulette Regan, who in *Unsettling the Settler Within* discusses decolonizing struggles, truth-telling, and reconciliation. Jo-Ann Archibald (Q'um Q'um Xiiem), *Indigenous Storywork: Educating the Heart, Mind, Body, and Spirit* (Vancouver: UBC Press, 2008). Paulette Regan, Paulette, *Unsettling the Settler Within* (Vancouver: UBC Press, 2011).

second language following Inuktitut. While Cookie Theatre could not provide a DVD of their performance, Nikki Loach at Quest Theatre, Calgary, contacted all the performers in that company's production and, with permission from the Canadian Actors' Equity Association, they unanimously agreed to send an archival DVD of their performance to the community that inspired the script.[25] At one point I was so worried that we would never get community feedback related to the play that I also contacted teachers in the community of Taloyoak, Nunavut; while certainly a different community and subject to Sherrill Grace's caution about "many Norths," I reasoned that their perspective was an improvement on no Northern feedback at all. Two teachers in Nunavut were enthusiastic about the project: Alison Corbett (grades eight and nine) and Bill Akerly (grades ten through twelve). Their students also answered several spectatorship and dramaturgical questions about the piece and sent their responses to Colmers and me.

The Quest Theatre DVD did eventually elicit feedback from some Kangiqsujuaq students in Christina Garrett's grade three-four-five class at Arsaniq School. According to Garrett, the students refused to put their names to the feedback (although Garrett summarized their answers to my questions). In Taloyoak, on the other hand, grade eight through twelve students strongly liked the play—although they also had some criticisms. Determining when students were responding to Eva Colmers's words, when they were reacting to the performance, and when they were reacting to the poor quality archival DVD would have been helpful, but it was impossible. Furthermore, the tenor of the student discussions, the influence of the teachers on their students' opinions, and the approach teachers took to transcribe or summarize student comments were impossible to ascertain: we were grateful that the conversations about *Beneath the Ice* happened, but we knew much less about them than we would have liked. In some ways the Northern student responses affirmed that the piece was intended for a Southern audience. In early versions of the play, Colmers intended David to seem rude, naive, and arrogant because she wanted to show how much the experience in the North taught him and helped him to grow as a person.

---

25 In 2010 Tracy Carroll had sent the script to Kangiqsujuaq and had let them know about the Alberta and Saskatchewan tours, and while there was a short article in the community online newspaper, it was not clear that anyone actually read the play. Quest Theatre's production may have been the first contact all but a handful of Kangiqsujuaq residents had with *Beneath the Ice*.

Kangiqsujuaq and Taloyoak students certainly perceived him that way, but they also found his character *offensive* to *Northerners*. Some of their comments are collected in the Community Feedback section, but Taloyoak students included things like, "I did not like the boy's attitude. I think it was too much to take for a grandmother and granddaughter"; "I didn't like the boy yelling at Aanak and thinking that he knew it all"; "I feel like David is too much for old lady Aanak. He shouldn't be treating them like that, just cause he wants to know about the north." When David was trying to say the name Kangiqsujuaq and then said, "Oh . . . somewhere up North," the elementary school students in Kangiqsujuaq were personally offended. It is notable that Colmers was writing for an audience outside the Inuit community. However, the students' comments demonstrated that staging an ignorant, rude Southern boy can actually reinforce the impression of disrespect between the two communities, even if the intention is to demonstrate the need for the opposite. Colmers took this feedback seriously, and the version that you see here has been modified so that David is initially still ignorant but hopefully less offensive.

In spite of Colmers's efforts, students in Kangiqsujuaq were also concerned that some of the performances of cultural identity promoted stereotypes, such as a "too childish" Inuit girl character, the lack of availability of electricity in remote hunting shacks, and the elder's poor English and lack of knowledge about the South. At the same time, they really appreciated the addition of specific indications of Inuit culture, such as throat singing in the soundtrack, the two female actors speaking a bit of Inuktitut, how certain traditional skills like softening sealskin were featured and treated with respect, and how aspects of modern Inuit life such as many family members living in one house were treated with gentle humour. Children in Kangiqsujuaq were offended when they saw two actors rub noses affectionately, but in Taloyoak, a student said that she liked that moment because she also does "kunik" with her grandmother. When I talked with Tiffany Ayalik about performing Inuit identities, she told me that in addition to collaborating with communities to make work, one of the important things to avoid is staging "token characters like the noble, stoic savage and the childlike Eskimo, or the reverse, the alcoholic, broken human being."[26] It's hard to know whether or not the students who

---

26 Ayalik, personal interview.

thought Paasa was too childish to be Inuit were reacting to the script or the actor's exuberant performance, but as Eva and I looked at the feedback, it highlighted how complex it can be to create characters that are perceived as "representative" of another culture, even if they are intended simply to be believable. When I interviewed Indigenous performer Nyla Carpentier about a different project in which she participated, she bemoaned the fact that in Canada, "Indigenous performers are often hired, but rarely listened to."[27] In the case of *Beneath the Ice*, initially it was difficult to get feedback to listen to, and then it was challenging to know how to listen and to decide how to respond ethically and artistically to what was heard.

One of the most ethically complicated decisions Colmers made was to employ the Inuit Sedna story to underscore the play's theme of taking no more than you need.[28] The decision resonated in Taloyoak: one student, Maggie Aqqaq, wrote, "My favourite part of the play is when David wakes up after dreaming of Sedna because he learns his lesson of respecting the land and the culture of the Inuit." Other students in Taloyoak also said they loved the addition of Sedna, and that they knew the story from their childhood, although they noted that in their community the story is a little different and they call her Nuliayuk.[29] However, in Kangiqsujuaq, where the story is set, an Inuit teacher informed me that Sedna was not an Inuit story, but might be Cree, while the grade three-four-five teacher transcribed her post-show discussion with the students and wrote, "The

---

27   Nyla Carpentier is from the Tahltan and Kaska nations of Northern British Columbia, but she grew up with Ojibway and Algonkian culture in Ontario. Nyla Carpentier, personal interview with the author, 10 April 2015.

28   Keavy Martin analyzes multiple ways Sedna's story is told and suggests many powerful meanings of the story; Colmers's understanding is one interpretation. Martin cautions against the desire to reduce complex stories like Sedna's to a moral. "Trouble that occurs when the moral of the story threatens to become definitive, and when writers and editors are intimidated, or frustrated, into excising the text's more provocative moments. When the ideology of a text becomes an impenetrable glaze, when it smoothes over every bump and crevice, then it is no longer doing its work." Keavy Martin, "Rescuing Sedna: Doorslamming, Fingerslicing, and the Moral of the Story," *Canadian Review of Comparative Literature / Revue Canadienne de Littérature Comparée* 38.2 (2011), 196.

29   Martin suggests that Nuliayuk or Uinigumasuittuq are more common names for Sedna in Nunavut. Keavy Martin, personal correspondence with the author, 29 May 2015.

myth of Sedna is not believed here anymore. Inuit are Christians. The myth is not even taught as a teaching method. There is religion class and church that teaches morality and life lessons."

When Eva Colmers went to Kangiqsujuaq she offered the gift of her skills as a shadow puppeteer and provided workshops to the school children. Given the planned role in her script, Colmers centred the shadow puppet workshop around Sedna, starting by inviting children to retell the story, which she assumed they knew. After the workshop, Carroll and Colmers did not agree about whether or not the children were previously familiar with Sedna. In fact, Colmers and Carroll did not remember several aspects of their trip the same way (which emphasizes how personal and open to question experience and memory can be, and how efforts to listen well are complicated not only by cultural background, but by the individual's perspective). Colmers believed students were familiar with Sedna's image, but only some teachers and a few students knew her story. If Colmers ignored Sedna in her script, she felt she would be avoiding a significant Inuit myth and an important kind of spiritual, non-Eurocentric knowledge, further contributing to a process of forgetting and cultural shift. But by including the myth, Colmers could be perceived as deciding what it means to be Inuit, potentially redefining a spiritual outlook, and reimagining Inuit knowledge from a Euro-Canadian, Southern perspective. "We did not want to be in the position of teaching the children their own culture," mused Colmers.

But is employing Sedna actually an inappropriate or even offensive choice? There are several potential reasons why the myth seemed unfamiliar to Kangiqsujuaq children when Colmers gave her shadow puppetry workshop. The workshop was mediated through language and cultural translation, with some Inuit teachers and some Southern teachers. Carroll also points out that although the myth is known throughout the North, Sedna sometimes goes by different names, and oral retellings vary, so perhaps the children knew the story differently. Certainly children in Taloyoak called her Nuliayuk (although they readily recognized the myth despite the name change). Given that there are only 430 people living in Kangiqsujuaq today and there are three Christian churches, it is entirely possible that the story had been suppressed, forgotten, or even, as Martin suggests, "in hiding"—after all, Nuliayuk is regularly depicted in art. According to anthropologist Louis-Jacques Dorais, today's Inuit see abiding by Christian morality as continuing traditional values and as fundamental to "genuine Inuk" identity.[30] But when I mentioned to Ayalik the way Christina Garrett transcribed her students' response to Sedna in the script, Ayalik said,

> I am not a cultural expert, but—that almost breaks my heart that a grade three kid would say that. To have no context for that part of your culture is so sad. I'm almost crying. Life in the Arctic is hard. It always has been. If religion is what helps you get through it, that's your prerogative. But where's the balance? The loss of culture and the damage to culture cannot be ignored. All the traditional values—what helped people survive for thousands of years . . .

She trailed off speaking and I asked if she thought it was possible that children really did not know or identify with Sedna, because it is a concern that they said they found the association of the story with their community inappropriate. Ayalik pointed out that every Northern community is different, and shifted the discussion to talk about Sedna as a powerful mythological figure throughout the North.

Colmers wanted to respect and listen to the Northern community and, simultaneously, to be true to her own artistic impulses and the needs of *Beneath the Ice*. In an email she declared, "I believe in the timeless message and relevance of *Beneath the Ice*, I treasure the overwhelmingly strong feedback from students and teachers."[31] She concluded that Sedna was still the best Inuit story to carry her play's message "do not take more than you need," and she was encouraged to retain that aspect of her original script by supportive comments from Taloyoak children regarding Sedna, even if Kangiqsujuaq children did not seem to know the story. Furthermore, our Nunavik contacts Sylvie Côté Chew and Pauyungie Nutaraaluk assured me and Colmers that "the story is very good, it makes sense and it brings a good message . . . [Our] comments do not put in question the interest and soundness of the play, it is very good on the whole." Significantly, although Aanak and Paasa talk about Sedna, David is the character who imagines he hears Sedna's voice, and the audience "witnesses" Sedna through him. His

---

30   Louis-Jacques Dorais, "Comparing Academic and Aboriginal Definitions of Arctic Identities," *Polar Record* 41 (2005): 4.

31   Eva Colmers, personal email interview with author, 8 April 2015.

experience might be seen as offering a spiritual privilege to a Southerner, but hopefully it emphasizes the idea that Sedna is being reimagined by a Southern writer. David even tells Paasa, "Call me crazy but the voice I heard . . . it sounded just like my mom's." The decision to incorporate Sedna is not simple, but Colmers's approach to addressing belief in her play text strives to avoid oversimplifying Inuit perceptions and beliefs about Sedna, and even aims to complicate perceptions about belief and the significance of story, without drawing conclusions.

CREATION JOURNEY MOVING FORWARD

Among other things, the experience of getting feedback from Taloyoak and Kangiqsujuaq students demonstrates how Indigenous cultures are not monolithic, and how very difficult it can be to "get it right," despite the best of intentions. Not only is travelling to places distant from Southern centres difficult and expensive, but once the trip is made, collaboration, communication, and listening *well* are not necessarily easy. As Ric Knowles argues, it's inherently problematic for non-Indigenous people to tell Indigenous stories. Yet there is a long history of relationships between Inuit and Southerners, and systemically ignoring contemporary Inuit cultures on stage is a kind of erasure. Furthermore, as Ric Knowles and Ingrid Mündel suggest, whether or not a production accurately *reflects* a particular community may be less important than the meanings about cultural identities *produced* through a performance.[32] I thank the young people of Kangiqsujuaq and Taloyoak, whose contributions helped shape the play you read here. I hope that the meanings produced through *Beneath the Ice* promote respect and are thought-provoking to young audiences.

---

32   Ric Knowles and Ingrid Mündel, introduction to *"Ethnic," Multicultural, and Intercultural Theatre*, ed. Knowles and Mündel (Toronto: Playwrights Canada, 2009), vii–xvii.

CREATIVE COLLABORATORS
Community Voices, Compiled with Notes by
Heather Fitzsimmons Frey

In May 2013 I started the process of getting feedback for *Beneath the Ice* from the community of Kangiqsujuaq. My first contact was with Brian Urquhart, with whom playwright Eva Colmers and dramaturg Tracy Carroll met in 2009 when they visited Kangiqsujuaq.

Urquhart connected me with Sylvie Côté Chew at the Avataq Cultural Institute, Quebec, and she tried to find an Inuk to look at the play. Eventually she and Pauyungie Nutaraaluk (who is originally from Inukjuak, Nunavik, and has also performed with Avataq's Inuktitut theatre and Netsilik Youth Theatre) read and discussed Colmers's script, and while they highlighted issues, both women said they liked it. Meanwhile, Urquhart also connected me with Ulaayu Pilurtuut, a teacher and artist born and living in Kangiqsujuaq, who only had time to read the first part of the play and give short comments.

In March 2014, I attended a Skype conversation with elementary students at Netsilik School in Taloyoak, Nunavut, facilitated by the Family Care Office at the University of Toronto. Teacher Claude Pike, who was in Netsilik at that event, switched to another Northern school but eventually connected me with other teachers at Netsilik, who were interested in looking at the play in the following school year. Although it is far from Kangiqsujuaq, I thought the feedback could be valuable. In January and February 2015 two teachers (Alison Corbett and Bill Akerly) discussed the play in their senior high and junior high classrooms.

In the fall of 2014 I discussed the *Beneath the Ice* project with Thomas Colter, the new principal at Arsaniq School in Kangiqsujuaq, and he connected me with teacher Christina Garrett. Meanwhile, Nikki Loach, Artistic Director of Quest Theatre, Calgary, which performed the third professional production of *Beneath the Ice*, generously worked with the performers to get permission to send the DVD of the performance to Kangiqsujuaq to help students give feedback on the play. Ulaayu Pilurtuut had said that it was hard to read and imagine the play, and Loach said the artists unanimously supported the idea of sending the DVD to the North. Garrett's grade three-four-five class had time to watch it and provide feedback in late January 2015.

NORTHERN POPULATION VOICES: REACTIONS TO THE SCRIPT AND TO THE QUEST THEATRE ARCHIVAL DVD

Included in this section are words written by Northern community members who read and/or watched *Beneath the Ice*—not as it is published here, because their feedback influenced this publication—but as it was performed to Alberta and Saskatchewan young people. The gloss is intended to help readers to connect the significance of these comments to the larger project, but unless comments were common among respondents, I resisted paraphrasing them.

Interpreting these words is not straightforward for numerous reasons. Some feedback came from adults and some from students. The students offered their responses to the archival video and their experiences reading Eva Colmers's script, but their comments were influenced by their relationship with their teachers and how their teachers framed the feedback process—and we have no way of knowing how that worked. We received all of this feedback via email. Alison Corbett scanned her students' worksheets for us, but Bill Akerly and Christina Garrett both sent their students' answers in emails to me. In some cases, the teacher made an effort to transcribe student words verbatim. In other instances it is not clear how much influence the teachers had on their students' words. Corbett's students wanted their names to be included in this publication, but not associated with specific comments; Akerly's students enthusiastically wanted their names associated with the work they put into their feedback process; Garrett wrote that her students said, "Before we put our name to it, we would like to know if any changes will be made?" I assured Garrett that some changes would be made and that all feedback would be shared here, but she did not indicate that her students wanted to share their names, so they are not included here. Besides their relationship to the research process, it is important to consider how young people might choose to answer questions about their own community for a Southern audience. Most young people also want to construct a particular self-image for others to see. Here they were sharing feedback with Southerners who they didn't know, and also with a teacher and classmates who they did. Furthermore, their words about themselves and their community could be very true in a particular moment, but people change their minds, or decide issues or ideas are more or less or differently significant. When Colmers was in Kangiqsujuaq she worked in classrooms, but not with the same students who read and watched *Beneath the Ice*. Colmers needed to consider the Taloyoak and Kangiqsujuaq young people's words in comparison to her own experiences and observations in Kangiqsujuaq, some of which seem to contradict some student comments. "Listening" if you will, and particularly listening well, was and is very complicated.

Eva and I were grateful to Quest Theatre for letting us send their archival DVD to the North so that Kangiqsujuaq's young people could see the play located in their community—even though it meant their comments were filtered through the Quest Theatre lens. It was impossible to know whether those comments were a response to Eva's words, to Quest Theatre's interpretation, to the poor archival video, a combination of those, or something else entirely. Clearly the production influenced how Northern young people approached the work. Grade eight student Holly Tulurialik wrote, "This play was so awesome because of the sound effects and the shadows."

Locating Inuit and Stereotypes

Eva Colmers's research trip to Kangiqsujuaq was intended to help her effectively situate *Beneath the Ice* in the North—grounding the script in a less "imaginary" North than would have otherwise been possible for her. In spite of the trip, Sylvie Côté Chew and Pauyungie Nutaraaluk wrote that they assumed the play was for "a young southern public." So, indeed, the play comes across as for and by a Southerner. In fact, Bill Akerly's only criticism of the play "is that it's kind of a White person's story in that the central character is David, and he is the only character that goes through a change because of what happens in the story. There isn't really a lesson for Paasa or Aanak." Story structure aside, Colmers hoped the details regarding contemporary Inuit life she included would resonate with Northerners. Reactions were sometimes positive, sometimes critical, sometimes supportive, and sometimes offended.

I asked students to consider whether or not the play seemed believable. In Nunavut, on March 4, Akerly facilitated a classroom discussion regarding the play and afterwards wrote:

> I don't have any direct quotes as I did the first time . . . I can tell you from our discussion that they all did recognise the traditional Inuit content in the play—things such as seal skins, hand sewing, inuksuks, and hunting for mussels. They didn't understand why anyone would think the play would not seem real—there was nothing unrealistic about the story to them.

However, via Garrett, the grade three-four-five class from Kangiqsujuaq wrote:

> The biggest issue that my students have, is that the play seems to act on past stereotypes of the Inuit rather than reality.

Colmers made changes based on the Northern feedback and the comments below are based on earlier drafts of the play, rather than the one published here. For example, Kangiqsujuaq students said "No kids plays cat's cradle anymore" because that was in the original script, but she removed the reference to honour their words. Although she saw children playing cat's cradle, and although there are photos of Kangiqsujuaq young people playing string games on the Internet, for a wide range of possible reasons the Arsaniq school students did not identify with that part of the script. Below are comments Colmers grappled with when revising, some of which also demonstrate that the lived experiences of young people of such different ages in geographically distant parts of the Canadian Arctic are, not surprisingly, very different.

SENIOR HIGH SCHOOL STUDENT, TALOYOAK: I liked when Paasa said that Aanak liked living the old ways; when Aanak said too many things more worries.

SENIOR HIGH SCHOOL STUDENT, TALOYOAK: I like the part where David is learning how to soften the sealskin.

SENIOR HIGH SCHOOL STUDENT, TALOYOAK: [It was funny when] David said [he] lives in a big house with two people and Paasa said she lived in a small house with two grandparents, 2 parents, an uncle, etc. It was funny because it is common in most Inuit communities.

SENIOR HIGH SCHOOL STUDENT, TALOYOAK: There was the part Paasa named all the people living in one house that made me laugh. Because I can relate to that.

SYLVIE CÔTÉ CHEW AND PAUYUNGIE NUTARAALUK, AVATAQ CULTURAL INSTITUTE: Inuit do not rub their noses.

HIGH SCHOOL STUDENT, TALOYOAK: I do kunik my grandmother.[1]

CHRISTINA GARRETT, ON BEHALF OF HER GRADE THREE-FOUR-FIVE STUDENTS, KANGIQSUJUAQ: We liked that you included throat singing and the two female actors speaking a bit of Inuktitut.

CHRISTINA GARRETT, ON BEHALF OF HER GRADE THREE-FOUR-FIVE STUDENTS, KANGIQSUJUAQ: The young girl is far too childish even for a young girl. The Inuit grow up very quickly because of the challenges they face.

CHRISTINA GARRETT, ON BEHALF OF HER GRADE THREE-FOUR-FIVE STUDENTS, KANGIQSUJUAQ: No kids play cats cradle anymore.

---

1   Kunik is the affectionate gesture of pressing one's face close to a loved one. It has been misinterpreted and Westernized as an "Eskimo kiss."

CHRISTINA GARRETT, ON BEHALF OF HER GRADE THREE-FOUR-FIVE STUDENTS, KANGIQSUJUAQ: All homes and most shacks now have electricity.

CHRISTINA GARRETT, ON BEHALF OF HER GRADE THREE-FOUR-FIVE STUDENTS, KANGIQSUJUAQ: We were wondering how they walked to their camp without their skidoo? It is not done . . . all the camps are too far for that.

BILL AKERLY, ON BEHALF OF HIS JUNIOR HIGH SCHOOL STUDENTS, TALOYOAK: The one thing they said was that the Inuit women (Paasa and Aanak) spoke with an American accent, as if they were from Alaska . . . One girl was actually quite funny in imitating the actors. I know that this does not speak about the writing—but it shows how a detail like the accents can really affect whether or not the students consider it a realistic and local story or not.

Language—Inuktitut and English

As Eva Colmers explains, she wanted to put what she calls "the beautiful language of Inuktitut" on stage, but not only was it difficult to "get it right" because there are numerous dialects, and even local disagreement about how things should be spelled and said, but also because she knew it would be difficult to find actors in the South who could speak Inuktitut. She describes her process of trying to get the correct translations in the script in her discussion about language.

Colmers wanted to employ Inuktitut in a way that was evocative and aesthetically powerful, rather than an accurate representation of the blend of English and Inuktitut a grandmother and granddaughter in Kangiqsujuaq would use to speak to one another. During the rehearsal process, it became clear to Colmers that Aanak should be the type of grandmother who speaks little, but with great authority. In a personal email, Colmers wrote, "This revelation worked in favour of helping possible non-Inuit actors with the difficult task of speaking the proper regional Inuktitut. Artistically, it also offered an interesting contrast to the bubbly young Paasa."

Regardless of her intentions, it is clear that students were pleased to hear actors speaking Inuktitut but found the actors' accents amusing—again, an indication that the DVD presentation was very much on students' minds when they offered their responses to the play. Bill Akerly noted that his junior high students in Taloyoak "didn't find the accents of the women actors represented them. They either found the women talked like southern Canadians, or like the 'Eskimos' from Alaska (we had Ariel Tweto visit us last fall)." Below are some additional comments about language used in the original play which were addressed in Colmers's new version.

SENIOR HIGH SCHOOL STUDENT, TALOYOAK: Me and my grandmother speak mostly Inuktitut and some English.

CHRISTINA GARRETT, ON BEHALF OF HER GRADE THREE-FOUR-FIVE STUDENTS, KANGIQSUJUAQ: Elders do not speak that slowly and are not that naïve about the modern world.

SYLVIE CÔTÉ CHEW AND PAUYUNGIE NUTARAALUK: [When] Aanak talks in broken English that is un-natural and a bit diminishing. Either she does not speak English at all or she speaks a simple English but not like this. Typically, an Elder would not speak English, and her grand-daughter would translate.

Sedna

As I explain in the scholarly introduction ("Location-Specific, Cross-Cultural Play Development Research, Collaboration, and Listening to Feedback"), Colmers's use of the Sedna myth appealed to students in Taloyoak, but the response was more diverse and complicated to read in Nunavik. When Colmers visited Kangiqsujuaq, she saw soapstone carvings of Sedna, she saw an image in the library (labelled in syllabics) that appeared to illustrate part of the story, and she worked with elementary-school students on creating a shadow puppet version of the story. She told me, "not everyone knew the Sedna story and some only knew it by a different name." Versions of the story are known in the Northern territories

Canada claims and in Greenland. Below are comments specifically related to Colmers's use of Sedna in *Beneath the Ice*.

ULAAYU PILURTUUT: Sedna is more like a Cree story not of Inuit myth.

SYLVIE CÔTÉ CHEW AND PAUYUNGIE NUTARAALUK: Sedna does not exist in Nunavik, and no "sea goddess" is referred to in that way.

I find it simplifies very much the Inuit stories I know. In any case it does not link to Nunavik. The taboos and respect for nature are expressed differently. I understand that the play has a lot of references to Sedna, but it does not really work in my opinion.

CHRISTINA GARRETT, ON BEHALF OF HER GRADE THREE-FOUR-FIVE STUDENTS, KANGIQSUJUAQ: The myth of Sedna is not believed here anymore. Inuit are Christians. The myth is not even taught as a teaching method. There is religion class and church that teaches morality and life lessons.

BILL AKERLY, TALOYOAK: Most of the class knows who Sedna is and has heard the story. They enjoyed hearing it again in the play.

MAGGIE AQQAQ, GRADE NINE, TALOYOAK: My favourite part of the play is when David wakes up after dreaming of Sedna because he learns his lesson of respecting the land and the culture of the Inuit.

HAYLEY TOTALIK, GRADE NINE, TALOYOAK: My favourite part of the story is when David learned not to take more than he needs.

CHRISTOPHER SARASIN, GRADE NINE, TALOYOAK: I enjoyed most the part where David went into the ice cave and heard the voice of Sedna—then he believed her story!

ANNIE KANAYUQ AKLAH, GRADE EIGHT, TALOYOAK: This play reminded me of when I was a little girl, I remember reading the book of Sedna.

Taloyoak High School students were asked to answer the following question after reading the play: What did you know about Sedna before reading the play? Several students offered comments like, "I never knew Sedna's English name. I only knew her Inuktitut name Nuliayuk. I can't remember how the story went but the one I know is different"; "Sedna, in my culture, is 'Nuliayuk,' she is the sea goddess. Her fingers actually turned to seals and it is her husband that tried to kill her. I'm just writing this short"; "In my language Sedna is Nuliayuk. (Nu-lia-yuk) The goddess of the sea." Several other students also used the phrase "sea goddess"; one said s/he learned about Sedna in elementary school, and many students either agreed with Colmers's retelling of the story or offered (as did the student quoted above) a different telling of the story. Some examples include:

I knew Sedna was the sea goddess of the ocean. I knew she had no fingers and filled the ocean with seals.

I knew that she lived on the land before she became the sea goddess.

I knew that Sedna took care of the animals (story).

Sedna was a sea goddess. She was an orphan that no one cared about. Her father tried to push her out of the boat and she tried holding on with her fingers but her father cut them off and each finger became different sea mammals.

She is the god of the sea. She was a normal Inuit till one of her parents cut her fingers off while she hanged onto the kayak. That how she became the god of the sea for all the animals that lives in the North.

I liked the part where Paasa was telling the Sedna story to David.

I love the story of Sedna.

David

The Southern character, David, proved to be a source of criticism regarding the play, and Colmers has altered his dialogue in this published version accordingly. Comments about David were, as mentioned, challenging to respond to with confidence because Northerners may have been responding to the actor's performance, or to other elements of their experience watching the Quest Theatre DVD, rather than the words Colmers wrote for actors and directors to interpret. Some students in Taloyoak had trouble understanding why David is in Kangiqsujuaq, or why his mother leaves him with Paasa and Aanak, and one student commented, "Never heard a story like this before." However, more frequently students found David to be offensive and his behaviour towards Aanak ignorant and rude. In my experience, if a young person says they do not like an aspect of the play or a character's behaviour, it does not necessarily mean that they wish it were absent, but that they found it upsetting or controversial. Certainly audiences for *And by the way, Miss . . .* sometimes reacted that way. However, in this case it seems likely that the students critiqued David because they felt his character was disrespectful to them, as Northern people.

They also commented on David's behaviour towards Aanak in a way that suggested that the character pushed social boundaries too far for a believable relationship with an elder. As one Taloyoak high-school student put it, "I did not like the boy's attitude. I think it was too much to take for a grandmother and granddaughter." Andrea Iqilliq, a Taloyoak grade eight student, even argued that the theme of the play centred on how problematic it was for David to be so disrespectful. She wrote, "This play made me feel that if you're not careful with your life, the last memory your family will have of you could be negative." David's inappropriateness was also a source of pleasure for Northern students: when students were asked if there was anything they particularly liked about the play, often it was when David couldn't plug in his iPod (and looked foolish), when Paasa saved him, or when David learned lessons about his own arrogance at the end. After reading the students' feedback, Colmers noted that the Quest Theatre video and the actors' performances may have intensified the impression of inappropriate behaviour. She also noted, "Kids were appalled by David's initially rude attitude but this is my intent as we watch David change and grow into a more compassionate human." Nevertheless, Colmers wanted to be sensitive to the feelings of the Northern students. In response to those comments and the feedback below, David is less arrogant and is more interested in the North and the people around him in Colmers's revised text, which you read here.

CHRISTINA GARRETT, ON BEHALF OF HER GRADE THREE-FOUR-FIVE STUDENTS, KANGIQSUJUAQ: My students did not like the character of David. They found him too spoiled and rude . . . They found it very rude when David was trying to say the name Kangiqsujuaq and then said "oh . . . somewhere up north."

SENIOR HIGH SCHOOL STUDENT, TALOYOAK: . . . But I don't like David because he is too loud, hyper and it's rude to yell at elders and he needs to calm down.

SENIOR HIGH SCHOOL STUDENT, TALOYOAK: I didn't like the boy yelling at Aanak and thinking that he knew it all.

SENIOR HIGH SCHOOL STUDENT, TALOYOAK: I feel like David is too much for old lady Aanak. He shouldn't be treating them like that, just cause he wants to know about the north.

SENIOR HIGH SCHOOL STUDENT, TALOYOAK: I liked the part where Paasa went under the ice. When she came back David asked her why so little? Don't take more than what you need.

SENIOR HIGH SCHOOL STUDENT, TALOYOAK: The part where he went under the ice, then Sedna came to him then saved his life.

SENIOR HIGH SCHOOL STUDENT, TALOYOAK: I don't like the way David acts.

When Paasa saves David after his foolhardy decision to go under the ice, Raymond Manniliq seemed to find it particularly satisfying—almost as if it were a kind of comeuppance. He wrote:

RAYMOND MANNILIQ, JUNIOR HIGH SCHOOL STUDENT, TALOYOAK: The scene where David is saved by Paasa after the tide came up beneath the ice was my favourite.

SENIOR HIGH SCHOOL STUDENT, TALOYOAK: I think that part where Paasa mentioned who she was living with. I liked the part at the ending when the boy learned to learn from his experiences.

SENIOR HIGH SCHOOL STUDENT, TALOYOAK: I like the ending when David apologized.

Grandmother-Granddaughter Relationships

Colmers created the characters of Paasa and Aanak in part based on what she observed in her brief visit to Kangiqsujuaq. Dramaturgically, it was important to confirm that the way the grandmother and granddaughter interacted made sense to Northern young people. After looking at the script and the Quest Theatre DVD, the grade three-four-five students in Kangiqsujuaq argued that Paasa seemed too childish and Aanak too naive about the modern world. Were these comments an example of a reaction to the script? To the performance? To the way we gathered feedback? Except occasionally when Bill Akerly's class responded to our questions by taking time for additional class discussion, we were unable to clarify or probe more deeply: one of the challenges with listening well is that we do not know exactly what we "heard."

The Kangiqsujuaq students chose not to discuss the relationship between the two female characters, but the high-school students in Taloyoak answered these questions:

> The characters Paasa and Aanak are granddaughter and grandmother. Did the way they interact make sense to you? How does it compare to your own relationship with your grandmother/grandfather? Did you like the characters?

All of the students who answered these questions said that Aanak and Paasa's interactions were believable and that they had a similar relationship with their own grandmother, or that they knew people in Taloyoak who did. A few elaborated, especially emphasizing their love for their grandparents and their respect for their knowledge:

Yes, the way Paasa and Aanak interacted made sense to me . . . when I was younger she took care of me now and then.

Me and my grandmother only used to live alone and go on the land and speak about legends. The characters are good.

Yes, Paasa and Aanak made sense to me, by how they reacted. Paasa learned a lot from her Aanak which compares me to me and my grandmother. Aanak is very smart just like my grandmother and teaches her granddaughter a lot of things just like my grandmother.

Paasa and Aanak show that they love each other that is similar to how we interact with our grandmother.

I like the characters. They did make sense to me and my grandmother and I sort of compare to Aanak and Paasa. I learn new things from her just like Paasa does with Aanak. I listen to my grandmother about what to do and what not to do, just like Paasa does.

Paasa and Aanak's relationship is close to my grandmother Aqnaoyok and my relationship. I always listen to what my grandmother says because she knows a lot of things . . .

I liked that you must always listen to your grandparents.

I liked when Paasa said that Aanak liked living the old ways; when Aanak said too many things more worries.

I like the part where Paasa and Aanak were throat singing and then they laugh.

CREATIVE JOURNEY

When my children were little, one of their favourite bedtime stories was *Very First Last Time* by Jan Andrews and Ian Wallace. Because I am a writer/director, I wondered how to make such a magical Northern setting come alive on the stage. I imagined how a child from the city with a very different lifestyle would perceive such a "foreign" place. Without any geographical references in Andrews and Wallace's book, I had no idea where this place would be, but the seed for the story of *Beneath the Ice* was planted right then.

When I approached dramaturg Tracy Carroll with my concept, she was immediately intrigued and on board. In our communication with Jan Andrews, we learned about an old *National Geographic* issue that featured Kangiqsujuaq and the community's practice of gathering mussels underneath the frozen ocean. Amazingly, it is the only place in the world with a big enough tide and cold enough temperature to be able to gather mussels that way.

From the outset, authenticity and respect for the community was of utmost importance to my play development. But, as my character David also discovers, there is only so much you can learn from book research. A much-appreciated exploration grant from the Canada Council for the Arts made it possible for Tracy and me to fly to Kangiqsujuaq, and I could see for myself the people and the land I was writing about.

After many emails and phone calls, we were able to identify contact persons in Kangiqsujuaq at the Arsaniq School, the Nunaturlik Landholding Corporation of Kangiqsujuaq, and at the mission with the Inuit scholar, Father Jules Dion. Rather than arriving with nothing but requests and questions, I wanted to present a mutual exchange with the community where everyone learned something from the other. As an experienced shadow puppeteer, I offered a workshop in which students at the local school learned how to make shadow puppets and scenery to tell the myth of the sea goddess Sedna.

So, with a portable shadow screen and all the necessary puppetry material in my heavy luggage, we arrived in Kangiqsujuaq on January 9 after a twenty-six-hour journey and multiple stopovers. Our simple co-op accommodation was right at the shore of the frozen ocean, where we heard and witnessed the daily groaning rise and fall of the frozen ocean's ice cap.

Our days were *very* full: translation meetings at the mission with Father Jules Dion and his assistant Paasa, shadow-puppet workshops and myth development with students of grade four through seven, recording sessions of voices and environmental sounds, visits to the traditional kamik bootmaking group, throat-singing practice with Elisapi, and a guided tour with Johnny out onto the frozen ocean to experience the traditional mussel-picking under the ice.

Although our hopes were high, we could not go down under the ice ourselves. Fluctuating temperatures in the past few months had negatively affected the density and thickness of the ice layer. We watched Johnny disappear through the hole he had chiselled in the ice and he even took pictures from underneath with my camera, but it was not meant for us to witness this. Just like my character David, I needed to wait . . . for another time . . . maybe next year. And just like David, I was disappointed. At the same time, it brought home to me the effects of global warming and our interconnectedness.

With a first draft of the play with me in Kangiqsujuaq, many of my questions regarding translation, habits, contemporary life, and traditions could be addressed during my stay. But, intentionally, my script was not too finalized to prevent me from incorporating new, first-hand experiences, like the gnawing of the raw hide.

In March 2009, my freshly completed *Beneath the Ice* received its first production under the skilful direction of Tracy Carroll with Cookie Theatre at the Edmonton International Fringe Theatre Festival. We were delighted to share the news about our well-received production with our friends in Kangiqsujuaq, and it even made it into their local newspaper. The success of this first production led to an invitation to produce the show for Ice on Whyte during a winter festival in Edmonton in January 2011.

Meanwhile, Alberta Playwrights' Network had supported our request for a workshop to refine the lead character of David and to explore greater use of shadow imagery to make the magic of Kangiqsujuaq come alive. The contributions by the initial cast and particularly those of dramaturg and director Tracy Carroll were extremely valuable, and in summer 2011 Tracy received a Sterling Award for Outstanding Artistic Achievement for her work on *Beneath the Ice*.

Early in 2013, Nikki Loach of Quest Theatre in Calgary directed the play in a beautiful, more projection-driven production. As a touring company, Quest Theatre took *Beneath the Ice* to many schools throughout Alberta and Saskatchewan. There was a long waiting list of schools whose booking request could not be accommodated, which prompted Quest Theatre to tour *Beneath the Ice* again in the fall of 2013.

Also in 2013, Heather Fitzsimmons Frey approached me about including the play in this book. As I am neither Inuk nor have lived in Kangiqsujuaq for a significant period of time, questions of accuracy and appropriation were key points of our discussion. How would the community of Kangiqsujuaq feel about my play? Once again, I explored the possibility of bringing the cast and crew of *Beneath the Ice* for a performance to Kangiqsujuaq, but with a ticket price close to $5,000 per person, this was simply impossible.

Heather tried very hard to find people in the Kangiqsujuaq area who were comfortable with reading and willing to look at my script and provide feedback. The teachers I worked with during my 2009 visit, unfortunately, had moved to other communities or the South. In the end, Heather was able to gather feedback from three people who read the script (though not all Inuk nor from Kangiqsujuaq). Heather was also able to acquire permission from Quest Theatre to send a DVD of their *Beneath the Ice* production for viewing at Northern schools. Three teachers and their students (one teacher at Kativik School in Kangiqsujuaq and two teachers at Netsilik School in Taloyoak, Nunavut) viewed the play recording and provided written feedback as listed by Heather Fitzsimmons Frey in the previous Creative Collaborators section.

It is important to point out that the DVD was an archival recording, never intended for a public audience, which means the camera is set up at the back of the theatre in a static position and the sound quality is rather poor. While I very much appreciate the encouraging feedback, I have some doubt whether teachers and students could accurately assess my script by watching a hard-to-hear and wide-shot DVD recording. The comments by one of the teachers in particular indicate that she and her students must not have been able to accurately hear everything the actors were saying.

Overall, I am delighted that so many Inuit students found the close relationship between Paasa and her grandma very realistic and reflective of their own experience. Also very interesting was the fact that students and teachers in the North greatly disapproved of David raising his voice towards old Aanak. This is in cultural contrast to the audience in the South of Canada who interpreted David's action more as a forgivable moment of frustration and anger.

Most surprising to me were the comments of two women (one non-Inuk, the other Inuk, but from a different community) who questioned my choice of the Sedna myth. The story of sea goddess Sedna is known throughout the North but there are indeed different versions of the story and different names given to the sea goddess, depending on the geographic region. While other myths may perhaps be more common in Kangiqsujuaq, teachers and students there told me that they know of Sedna, though more commonly as Nuliayuk. The school librarian in Kangiqsujuaq showed me a myth compilation that did indeed include a picture story similar to the Sedna myth but with a different name and written in syllabics. Reading different versions of the Nuliayuk myth, the similarity and likely identity between the Sedna and Nuliayuk story becomes evident. In the co-op store, too, I saw soapstone sculptures of Sedna on the shelf. Hence, it is neither incorrect nor implausible that my fictitonal grandma Aanak, a soapstone carver herself, loves to share the Sedna myth.

For a while, I did indeed consider incorporating a different, local myth into my play, but there were various obstacles. Traditionally, Inuit culture is passed on orally and the syllabic writing system was not established until the early 1900s, when missionaries moved up to the Kangiqsujuaq area. Of the few written Inuttitut stories, only a small number were translated, and mostly into French. One afternoon, the school librarian at the Arsaniq School proudly showed me some popular local myths—all in the syllabic printing. I found only three myths translated into English, but none worked with my dramatic intent.

My artistic reason for choosing the Sedna myth and not another lies in its message of moderation, to not take more than one needs. This stance against overconsumption or greed is a valuable point to be heard.

I carefully assessed all the comments we've received and took the time to personally respond to each and every one. The hardest task was to achieve consensus on the proper choice of Inuit words and their spelling due to slight regional differences. In most cases, the community feedback led to further email discussions, to clarifications, re-evaluation, appreciation, and changes to my script.

As a non-Inuit writer and somebody who has visited Kangiqsujuaq for a limited time only, I wrote the story from the only perspective I can write it and that is one of a *quallunaaq*—through the eyes of the "white" person, in particular through the perspective of the city boy, David. As with other plays, I began my writing process with extensive research, a visit to the actual community, and, in this case, more feedback from the community to ultimately arrive at this version of the script. My main concern was and remains that all the facts in my play are accurate and that the portrayal of characters is done respectfully and are completely plausible. But I am a fiction writer and as such I have embellished my characters with qualities that not all members of the community in Kangiqsujuaq—nor all young boys from the city—may share.

What you have in your hand now is the revised final script of my *Beneath the Ice* in which I have incorporated feedback from the community. It was written with the creative, factual, financial, and emotional support of many people and organizations around me.

Beneath the Ice was first produced by the Cookie Theatre in Edmonton in March 2009, with the following cast and creative team:

Aanak: Alison Wells
Paasa: Lisa Truong
David: Brendan Meyer

Director/dramaturg: Tracy Carroll

Sound design: Dave Clarke and Matt Skopyk

Set and costume design: Marissa Kochanski
Lighting design: Guido Tondino.

INUTTITUT WORDS USED IN BENEATH THE ICE

During my eight-day stay in Kangiqsujuaq in January 2009, all the Inuktituk or Inuttitut words I used in *Beneath the Ice* were originally translated by recognized Inuit language scholar Father Jules Dion (known also as Pirtiu), who has been living in Nunavik and Kangiqsujuaq for the past sixty years. While I was in Kangiqsujuaq, a recommended local English- and Inuttitut-speaking woman named Paasa read the Inuttitut words into a tape recorder; this recording was later used by the actors in Southern Canada as an audio reference for the proper pronunciation.

Before publishing *Beneath the Ice*, editor Heather Fitzsimmons Frey and I wanted to have the accuracy of the Inuttitut words in my play verified. Despite extensive searches through Inutittut dictionaries and websites, I was unable to find a definitive translation or spelling for all of the words. Each English word seems to have several different Inuttitut translations depending on the geographic Northern region. Trying to connect with people in the Nunavik region to ask them directly also proved to be very tricky. Teachers at the school I had visited seemed to have moved.

Eventually, editor Heather Fitzsimmons Frey was able to connect with Ulaayu Pilurtuut, a teacher and artist who was born in Kangiqsujuaq, and with Pauyungie Nutaraaluk, originally from Inukjuak and now working for the Avataq Cultural Institute in Montreal. These two sources live rather far apart and—not surprisingly—their communities speak, translate, and write words slightly differently. Several of Pauyungie's comments suggested changes in the English spelling of words, specifically to replace the letter "q" with the letters "it." For example, she suggested the word "mittens" to be written as "pualuit" rather than "pualuq" or "pualuk," or the word for "mussels" to be spelled "uviluit" rather than "uviluq."

Getting consensus on the choice and spelling of Inuttitut words by all of my three sources (Ulaayu, Pauyungie, and Father Dion) was nearly impossible. Therefore, I decided to use those words verified by the majority of my three sources, with a slight preference given to the translation by Father Dion. Despite considerable effort, I cannot say that all the chosen words and their spelling are perfectly accurate. I sincerely hope that the community of Kangiqsujuaq and other Inuktitut speakers forgive me any inadvertent errors in their beautiful, complex language.

No doubt, it would have saved me much trouble, time, and exposure to criticism if all of my characters spoke in English. But to hear this rare, beautiful, old language is a joy I did not want to withhold from the audience. It is an important aspect of the overall experience I hope *Beneath the Ice* offers.

Uumajusiurtiit qajanga kivivallialaurtuq usijualuugami iqalunnut imarsi-urinillu (Father Dion); iqalliatiup qajanga iqalunnut uqumaittualuulirami kivivallialaurtuq (Pauyungie): The fisherman's kayak was so heavy with fish that it dipped into the cold sea water.

Iqalualuit (Father Dion and Ulaayu): many fish.

Aa (all three): yes.

Auka (all three): no.

Naammagijarpit ungataanut pitsanak (Ulaayu and Pauyungie); sunagan-nik atulaan ngitarnik pisunguviit (Father Dion): Do not take more than you need.

Atsunai (all three): goodbye.

Pualuk (Father Dion and Ulaayu); pualuit (Pauyungie): sealskin mitten.

Piujuq (all three): good, nice.

Kamik (by two): boots.

Qinuittuq (Father Dion and Ulaayu); qinuisaarniq (Pauyungie): patience.

Uviluq (Father Dion and Ulaayu); uvilluit (Pauyungie): mussels.

Nakurmiik (all three except one spells it "nakurmiiq"): thank you.

Qallunaaq (all three except one spells it "qallunaq"): white man.

Inuksuk, plural inuksuit (all three): stone marker (in English mostly inushuk).

Uliniq (all three except one spells it "uliiniq"): tide.

Ilaali (all three): you're welcome.

SETTING

Beneath the Ice takes place in the small Inuit community of Kangiqsujuaq in Nunavik, Northern Quebec. Snuggled in the hollow Wakeham Bay, the freezing temperature, shallow ocean floor, and huge tides provide the optimal conditions for a unique way of harvesting mussels.

In Kangiqsujuaq there is a school, a small hotel, three churches, and a co-op where one can buy imported food (apples, oranges, milk, Coke, all for very high prices). Fishing is still a very important part of daily life for most Inuit families.

The next small community lies hundreds of kilometres away and there are no connecting roads. Planes and, in the summer, boats are the main transportation for long distances. Within the community, everybody gets around by skidoo, on foot or—to a much smaller degree—by dog sleds.

Many extended family members live together in one house. It is very common to have a "shack" or simple hut outside the community for hunting or to "have it quiet." Within Kangiqsujuaq, electricity and Internet is available. Not all hunting huts have electricity and the simple hut in my play does not.

White is the dominant colour. Like the small community itself, the set should be minimal, with simple creative lighting and sound. Sheets of fabric or plastic have served previous productions well. In such a vast open space, sounds appear heightened: the footsteps on the crunchy snow, the howling of the dogs, the "groaning" of the moving frozen ocean, etc., which should all become important elements in the play.

It is still common practice to eat or work sitting on the floor. There may be no tables in the play and all activities can be done on floor or low boxes (ice chunks).

Please feel free to update cultural references and replace noted Southern cities with one close to the production to create relevance for the audience.

CHARACTERS

David: an eager city boy who—like his scientist mother—is genuinely interested in the world around him. An only child, he knows lots from books and computers but has little real-life experience.

Aanak: an Inuit grandmother who carries the wisdom and knowledge of the land with her. She speaks in a direct manner, with a dry sense of humour. Even with limited English, she knows how to get her point across.

Paasa: a young Inuit girl who loves her grandma's old ways. She deeply cares for her land and people. Always cheerful and giggly, she is very observant and insightful.

The sound of city traffic increases.

Somewhere on stage, a small area of DAVID'*s room lights up: there is an open suitcase and a terrarium with a tree frog.*

DAVID *plugs in his iPod as he talks to his pet frog in the terrarium.*

DAVID: . . . and there are not many cars there, you know . . . 'cause, what's the point . . . *no roads.* Well, maybe one or two? But not as many roads as we have here in Edmonton. Now skidoos, that's what they have up North . . . excellent for all the snow and ice . . .

DAVID *revs the engine of an imaginary skidoo:* BRRRRM-BRRRRM.

Cool, eh?—I read all about it. And Mom always talks about her research and the people in Kanga . . . Kangi . . . Kangiqi . . . aaah, that place up North.

Wouldn't be for you, Pete. You, my little tree frog, like it warm, don't you? You need water to survive, not ice. Ice is good for polar bears but you'd freeze to death in the cold.

DAVID *puts his face against the terrarium glass.*

You're better off here with Dad. But I'll be back in no time . . . with lots of awesome pictures of thick ice, and polar bears, and skidoos, and . . .

MOM'S VOICE: Done packing, David?

He quickly shuts his suitcase.

DAVID: Done and ready, Mom!—

MOM'S VOICE: Time to leave for the airport!

DAVID: Coming!

He puts on his down jacket and slips his camera into his pocket.

He salutes with an excited gesture.

Your research assistant David is ready for action!

He exits his room. Blackout.

***

Howling wind.

In the dark, the bright full moon gradually appears.

The faces of old AANAK and her granddaughter PAASA are illuminated by the light and appear as shadow silhouettes in the circle of the moon. AANAK's hands bring alive shadowy characters from the old Inuit myth of Sedna, the goddess of the sea animals.

AANAK: Uumajusiurtiit qajanga kivivallialaurtuq usijualuugami iqalunnut imarsiurinillu. [The fisherman's kayak was so heavy with fish that it dipped into the cold sea water.]

PAASA: The fisherman's boat must have been sooo full and heavy. That's dangerous!

AANAK: Iqalualuit [Many fish] . . . too many iqalualuit in kayak.

PAASA: Why didn't he throw some fish over board?

AANAK: Aa! [Yes!] Fisherman want much . . . too much!

PAASA: Ooh, Sedna does not like that.

AANAK: Auka! [No!] *(shakes her head)* Sea goddess Sedna teach him lesson: Sedna make big, big waves . . . so hunter will drop iqalualuit.

PAASA: And? Did he drop some fish?

AANAK: *(shaking head)* Auka! Fisherman hold on more tight to fish. And his heavy kayak . . . *(sways downward with her hands and arms)*

PAASA: . . . sunk to the bottom of the ocean. And then . . . did Sedna show herself?

AANAK: Aa! Sedna reach out of ocean . . .

PAASA: *(interrupting excitedly)* Goddess Sedna without her fingers, right!?

AANAK: Aa!

She makes a fist that creates the shadow of a club hand.

And she speak: Naammagijarpit ungataanut pitsanak. [Do not take more than you need.]

PAASA: *(contemplating)* Do not take more than you need.

Daylight has come and bleaches away the silhouettes of grandma and granddaughter. A beautifully coloured sunrise illuminates the white, frozen surrounding.

* * *

Tall white hills appear in the distance.

The sound of an engine rises as a small plane descends.

In the twilight PAASA *and* AANAK *rush by.* AANAK *is out of breath and rests on an ice block. She motions* PAASA *to continue. The sound of the plane engine stops.*

PAASA re-enters, waiting for the visitor to catch up.

DAVID, with headphones covering his ears, pulls his suitcase with one hand and eagerly takes pictures with the other.

PAASA: And this, David, is my grandma . . . Aanak. David?—David!

DAVID: O . . . yes . . . nice to meet you, ma'am. My mom told me all about you.

AANAK: Aa-nak.

DAVID: What?

PAASA: She wants you to call her Aanak.

DAVID: Aanak. Okay. Good morning, Aanak . . . or is it afternoon? Hard to say with the sun always low in the Arctic, right?

PAASA and AANAK exchange a look and PAASA hides a giggle.

AANAK: Much learning for young David.

DAVID: Actually, I know a lot about the North—from my mom, books, and the Internet.

AANAK: *(teasing)* Fishing net?

DAVID: Internet! I learned a lot about your place from the Inter-net. So, don't worry. I can take care of myself while Mom is off doing her research.

PAASA: Well . . . then let's go.

PAASA helps AANAK up.

DAVID tries pulling his suitcase but the wheels buck on the icy ground. He struggles.

AANAK: Your wheel . . . good for city, bad for Kangiqsujaq.

DAVID: Well yuh . . . I thought you all drove around in skidoos here.

DAVID clears ice from the little wheel.

AANAK: Skidoo broken.

PAASA: The repair part will be flown in from Montreal . . . in three weeks.

DAVID: Three weeks?

AANAK: So we walk.

DAVID: How far?

PAASA: Oh, just down to Uncle Lucassi's. He'll drive us with *his* skidoo.

DAVID: Good!

DAVID's suitcase gets stuck again. He yanks hard on the handle, causing it to come off.

Oh no! *(embarrassed, he tucks it away)*

AANAK: So, Dr. Cooper, your mom, she need a go to Upper Research Station?

DAVID: Yes. And I would have loved to come along but . . .

AANAK: Upper Research Station no place for young boy.

DAVID: I could have helped her.

AANAK: Your mom want you safe . . . with us.

PAASA: It's just for a few days, David. Then your mom will be back here, in her Kangiqsujuaq office.

We hear the noise from the departing plane.

The shadow silhouette of the distant plane taking off moves across the hills.

AANAK and PAASA wave excitedly after the disappearing plane.

Have a good time looking at our ice, Dr. Cooper!

AANAK: And we good time looking at your David.

DAVID: I'm counting the days, Mom.

AANAK: Now, time to walk.

AANAK exits and PAASA starts to follow.

PAASA: *(excitedly)* Come! We'll be at Aanak's cabin on the bay!

DAVID sighs.

DAVID: My mom said you have Internet in . . . Kangiq-so . . . here. Right?

PAASA: Right. But not at Aanak's cabin. She likes the old ways.

PAASA notices DAVID's disappointment.

But there are lots of other things to do here. You'll see.

PAASA exits. DAVID is alone and takes in the foreign place.

DAVID: I see . . . nothing but ice and snow . . . a huge sky . . . oh . . .

He notices the magnificent sunset and pulls out his camera.

. . . a colourful sunset. *(flash)* Very . . . *(flash, checks picture in camera, surprised)* very beautiful, actually.

DAVID puts away his camera and picks up his suitcase.

Hey . . . little girl . . . wait for me.

The sound of the howling wind rises as the stage turns black.

***

Inside the small, bare cabin a flame flickers under the kettle on the stove.

PAASA helps AANAK with the sewing of sealskin mitts. They quietly speak in Inuktitut.

DAVID sprawls on his makeshift bed, listening to music through his headphones and playing a handheld electronic game.

PAASA: *(putting on a half-finished mitt)* Look, David, pualuk [sealskin mittens]! Look!

PAASA looks at AANAK and shrugs.

David? Strong mitts from sealskin . . . really warm.

AANAK cups her hands over her ears, mimicking DAVID with his headphones.

AANAK: Why talk to person who has no ears.

PAASA: But I want to show him our things.

AANAK hands PAASA the sealskin and cheers her up by making a funny gnawing noise with her teeth.

PAASA giggles and starts chewing carefully on the hide.

AANAK: Piujuq! [Good!]

AANAK gently strokes the hair of chewing PAASA when DAVID suddenly jumps up.

DAVID: O noooo!!! I almost had it. Darn!

PAASA: David?

AANAK and PAASA stare at him, alarmed.

DAVID: Batteries dead. Just when I was so close!—

(rummaging through his backpack) Battery recharger—environmentally friendly—where is it? Ta-da! Just need to plug it in and I'm good to . . . go.

Holding the plug of the battery charger, he looks around for an outlet. He realizes the futile situation and drops down defeated.

PAASA: *(holding up the half-finished mitt)* Look, David! Pualuk mitts, from sealskin.

DAVID: Very nice.

He packs away his electronic game and battery charger.

PAASA: Seal skin is very tough and hard to sew. See how I make it soft . . .

PAASA chews demonstratively.

DAVID: I know! Mom brought back a pair and told me all about it.

PAASA: *(to AANAK)* Dr. Cooper wears our pualuk mitts in Edmonton.

AANAK giggles, amused, and continues sewing.

PAASA watches DAVID.

Your Edmonton must be very different than our place here . . .

She waits for a response but DAVID just crosses his arms and sighs.

I've heard about your hockey team, you know. And you have malls, and many cars, and trees, right? I've never touched a tree.

DAVID: Really? I've got pictures from home on my camera. I can show you, if you like?

PAASA: *(jumps excitedly)* Yes. I want to see your Edmonton.

DAVID takes out his camera and PAASA moves closer. They both look at the camera screen.

DAVID: Okay, then. Here . . . This is my house.

PAASA: A big house! How many people live there?

DAVID: Just me and my mom and dad.

PAASA: In my house I live with two grandpas, *(pointing)* one grandma, two parents, one uncle, three cousins, two brothers, and one sister.

AANAK: *(laughing)* Very noisy there!

DAVID: I bet. And this is my backyard . . . in the summertime.

PAASA: Oh, trees! How beautiful, and each very different.

DAVID: That's because they are different tree species.

PAASA: We don't have any tree.

DAVID: Too cold, I know. And this is me in my room . . . *(pointing)* with Pete.

PAASA: This green, little thing is Pete?

DAVID: Pete is a Brazilian tree frog . . . from the Amazon region.

PAASA: And Pete-Tree-Frog sleeps with you in your room.

DAVID: Well, he has his own bed, a terrarium to be precise . . . *(pointing)* the glass box . . . in the corner here.

PAASA: I see.

DAVID: And this is me and my best friends at the rock-climbing centre.

PAASA: I like the colourful stones.

DAVID: Actually, they're spray-painted climbing holds.

PAASA: Oh.

DAVID: Here I am at the top of the climbing wall . . . ringing the bell. And this is me in my full hockey gear at the rink.

PAASA: I play hockey, too!!!

DAVID: You do? . . . *(takes time to imagine it) Cool.*

PAASA: And this? Is this Dr. Cooper?

DAVID: Yes. Mom and I at the lake.

PAASA: Funny, Dr. Cooper without her red parka.

DAVID: And this is me on my computer . . .

PAASA: In your bed!?

DAVID: Yuh, it's a laptop . . . which I wanted to bring along but Mom said no. I guess there's no point when there's not even electricity to . . .

PAASA: *(appalled by his ignorance)* But there is! We DO have electricity in Kangiqsujaq . . . and some Internet. Just not here at Aanak's cabin! And I told you, David: Aanak likes the old, simple way.

AANAK: Many things, many worries; few things, few worries! *(laughs)*

DAVID: Well, I like many things: my new Xbox game, my bike with front suspension, I LOVE my new skates and my cool hockey stick, and . . .

PAASA: You have a lot, David!

DAVID: I have a lot . . . because I need a lot.

AANAK: *(to herself)* Many things make kayak sink.

PAASA: Why?

DAVID: Because . . . well, because I'm pretty smart and I don't like to be bored.

PAASA: I don't like to be bored either! That's why I sing and carve and help Aanak make pualuk or kamik or . . . or other things—using my own imagination—having lots is not always better, David Cooper!

DAVID: I know! And I didn't mean it that way.

PAASA: And that's not how your mom talks to us!

DAVID: I KNOW! But I'm not a saint like my mom!

AANAK: *(clicking tongue disapprovingly)* Qinuittuq! [Patience!]

DAVID: *(putting camera back into backpack)* I didn't mean to hurt your feelings. All I wanted to say is . . . that . . . oh, forget it!

AANAK: Patience.

DAVID: I'll just go to bed, now.

DAVID *stores away his belongings and crawls into bed.*

PAASA: Good night, then.

AANAK: Sweet dreams, David!

DAVID: Thank you! Sweet dreams . . . sure.

PAASA *cuddles up to* AANAK, *who strokes her hair as the light goes down.*

It is night now and a huge full moon appears.

Beautiful northern lights come alive against the white hills— dancing and moving like characters from an old story. The northern lights take on the expressionistic shape of a woman lifting up a bundle and speaking with a mystical distorted voice: Naammagijarpit ungataanut . . .

DAVID *moves and rolls in his nightmarish dream.*

***

The howling wind subsides and the sound of a carving knife becomes audible. In the dimly lit cabin AANAK *works on a soapstone sculpture.*

DAVID *enters drowsy and yawning.*

AANAK: *(in exaggerated English)* Hellow-hellow.

DAVID: *(startled)* O . . . good morning!

AANAK: No morning. Is noon time, now.

DAVID: But the sun isn't even . . . *(suddenly recalls)* I know: we are far North . . . here, the sun barely comes out during winter . . . am I right?

AANAK: Yes, young Dr. Cooper. Good time for being inside and carving stone.

(thrusting the stone towards him) Sedna!

DAVID: The stone . . . it's called Sedna?

AANAK: *(clicks tongue disapprovingly)* Stone *become* Sedna. She is sea goddess watching over sea animals.

DAVID: I've heard of her. *(inspecting more closely)* A fish tail on the bottom . . . a person on top.

O . . . you forgot to carve her fingers.

AANAK: *(clicks tongue and raises her fist in front of his face)* Fingers of Sedna become whale, seal, walrus, beluga . . .

PAASA *enters from outdoors. She turns up the lamp light.*

PAASA: Sleepyhead, David, you're finally up?

DAVID: Well, yuh, it's dark even in the morning and . . . I had this crazy dream.

PAASA: What did you see in your dream?

DAVID: I don't know . . . a strange lady . . . talking to me in a strange voice.

AANAK: Somebody want tell you something.

DAVID: Well, I couldn't understand a word. And she was doing this . . . *(pushes hands upwards)* as if she was lifting something? I don't know.

PAASA: Sometimes, the same dream comes back until we understand.

DAVID: No thanks! It was a freaky dream!

The dogs start howling and barking outside.

PAASA: *(to dogs outside)* Qinuittuq! [Patience!] They go crazy when it's full moon.

AANAK: *(mysteriously)* Is full moon, today. Right time for collecting uviluq [mussels]. You know "uviluq," David?

DAVID: I only know one Inuit word: nakurmiik—thank you.

PAASA: Uviluq means mussels. So now you know two words.

DAVID: *(practising quietly)* U-vi-luq. Uviluq.

AANAK: Sweet Paasa, go soften sealskin.

PAASA grabs some seal hide and turns to DAVID.

PAASA: You want to see how we soften the seal hide in the snow?

DAVID: Could be interesting.

He grabs his jacket and follows PAASA out the door.

AANAK continues carving the sculpture.

The sound of the dogs and the outdoors increases.

***

Outside the cabin DAVID sits on a stone and watches PAASA stomp energetically on the seal hide on the ground.

DAVID: You're sure all this stomping is good for the leather?

PAASA: Very sure. It softens the animal hide. Makes it easier for Aanak to sew. Touch it. Feel how soft it is now.

DAVID touches the leather hide, then takes out his camera.

DAVID: Crazy!

He takes some pictures—FLASH, FLASH.

So, why are you here, at your grandma's and not with your family?

PAASA: Aanak is my family! She looks after me when Mom and Dad are off working in the nickel mine . . . on the other side of those mountains.

DAVID: That sucks.

PAASA: Two weeks on, two weeks off.

DAVID: That really sucks!

PAASA: *(thinking it over)* No! Not really. *(pointing)* Now stand here, on this corner, David.

DAVID steps onto the hide as PAASA continues stomping.

I like it at Grandma Aanak's. She teaches me the old ways, how to listen to the land and to be safe.

DAVID: *(amused)* C'mon, there's nothing "un-safe" here . . . *(gestures)* no busy traffic, no robbers hiding in a dark alley. I'm sure it's way safer here than in a big city.

PAASA: You have no idea what it's like. There are many important things you must learn to be safe here. Aanak teaches me how to read the sky . . . how to listen to the cracking ice . . . what to do when there's a heavy snow storm and you can't see anything but white around you. Here, if you don't respect nature, you will die. So, David Cooper, you better watch and learn from Aanak!

> PAASA *angrily stomps on the leather hide around* DAVID, *who realizes that he has pushed her too far.*

DAVID: All right, all right, your grandma knows things.

PAASA: *And* she's a respected carver.

DAVID: Okay! I saw her carve that Sedna sculpture but she didn't make her any fingers.

PAASA: *(appalled)* Sea goddess Sedna *lost* her fingers!

DAVID: Hmh . . . and how exactly did she "lose" her fingers?

PAASA: *(hesitant)* A long story.

DAVID: I've got time.

PAASA: It's an old story Aanak learned from her grandma. You may not get it.

DAVID: I'm not stupid . . . Paasa. Please? I really want to hear it.

> Reluctantly, PAASA *stops working the hide.*

PAASA: Sedna was a beautiful Inuit girl with beautiful, long hair. When she came of age, her parents wanted her to marry. But Sedna refused every-body. One day, a well-dressed, strong man arrived. Sedna was so smitten, she happily went with him to his place. But: he was disguised and turned out to be . . . a bird man.

DAVID: A bird man. So, he could fly . . . like Batman?

PAASA gives him a look and abruptly turns away to work.

PAASA: Qallunaaq [White man].

DAVID: I'm sorry. I do wanna know. Tell the story . . . please.

PAASA: *(takes a moment to continue)* The "bird husband" dropped Sedna in his nest on top of a cliff and left. Sedna was very unhappy and cried and cried. Far away, Sedna's father heard her cry and he took off to rescue his daughter.

DAVID: He heard her . . . from far away?

PAASA: DAVID!! It's a magical story and it wants to tell us something!

DAVID: Okay. Okay. I'm listening.

PAASA steps onto a snow block to use it as imaginary kayak.

PAASA: When Father arrived, Sedna quickly jumped into the kayak. Father paddled off as fast as he could. Then—woooosh—Sedna's bird husband flew down. He was soooo angry: "Give me back my Sedna."

"No, no. You leave my daughter alone," said the father.

The bird husband got even angrier. He flapped his wings like this, *(flaps arms)* making huge waves.

DAVID: That'll make for a bumpy ride.

PAASA: Ssssh! In their kayak, Sedna and her father feared for their lives. The mean bird man threatened the father to give him back Sedna or to sacrifice her to the sea.

So, in horror, Father threw his own daughter into the storming sea. "Aaaaah!" Sedna grabbed on to the side of the kayak. With the paddle,

Father whacked Sedna's cold, frozen fingers and they snapped off . . . one at a time . . . and she sank to the bottom of the ocean.

DAVID: *(outraged)* Oh no!! I can't believe he did that. And she sunk to the bottom of the ocean? That's horrible!

PAASA: That's not the end of the story, David.

AANAK: Children. Time for uviluq! Come!

PAASA: Coming, Aanak!

(to DAVID) Things happened for a reason.

DAVID: So, what happened to Sedna?

PAASA: Later, David.

DAVID: Did she freeze to death?

PAASA: Later, later . . . !

DAVID: *(as they all exit)* . . . I really want to know now . . .

The wind increases and fog fills the stage.

***

Through the fog and wind, AANAK with a pole, PAASA with a bucket and lantern, and DAVID walk one behind the other.

PAASA points out a heard of caribou far away on the horizon. DAVID snaps pictures—FLASH, FLASH.

The fog clears as they stop in front of a towering inuksuk. DAVID is in awe with the landmark, while AANAK and PAASA inspect the hole in the ice next to the inuksuk. AANAK starts chiselling with the pole.

DAVID: Wow, a real inukshuk! . . . I read all about them.

AANAK: Inuk-*suk*!

DAVID: Inuk-shuk.

PAASA giggles and shakes her head.

AANAK: *(close to his face)* Inuk-suk. Mark way for people . . . inuksuk.

DAVID: Inuk-suk. Okay. I get it!

PAASA: This one marks our spot for collecting mussels from the ocean floor.

DAVID: *(amazed)* So, we are not on land now . . . but *(stomping)* but on top of the ocean?

PAASA: The *frozen* ocean, yes. And way out there . . . *(pointing)* is a popular spot for polar bears.

DAVID: I wanna go there! See the polar bears and take lots of pictures.

AANAK: No more!

DAVID doesn't understand and turns to PAASA for an explanation.

PAASA: Polar bears don't come here anymore. They changed their route . . . they go now further North, where it's colder.

DAVID: Because of stupid climate change?!

AANAK: *(as she continues chiselling)* People change.

DAVID: *(to AANAK)* What?

PAASA: Aanak believes it's the people who've changed. She thinks climate change is because people in the South pollute so much more now.

AANAK: Making things change here . . . up North.

DAVID: Well, I . . . I recycle at home . . . I turn off the light when I don't need it and . . . I'd like to become a scientist, like Mom.

AANAK: *(triumphantly pulls out pole)* Piujuq! [Good!]

PAASA moves closer and inspects the hole.

PAASA: Piujuq! Time to collect mussels.

PAASA picks up the bucket and lantern.

DAVID: *(peering down the hole)* But I don't see any water down there.

PAASA: That's how we want it when we go under.

AANAK: We wait for ocean water go out . . . when is uliniq.

PAASA: Tide! She means: we wait till it's low tide.

AANAK: You know t-i-d-e?

DAVID: Of course, I know t-i-d-e! *(scientifically)* Tide occurs daily when the ocean water rises or falls!

AANAK: Tide very far, far out, when moon is full. Full moon is right time to collect uviluq.

PAASA: I'm ready, Aanak.

AANAK: Aa! Safe to go, now.

PAASA and AANAK affectionately rub their noses.

Then PAASA slowly descends through the hole in the ice.

DAVID watches in awe.

DAVID: Won't she freeze under the ice?

AANAK: Auka! No icy wind down there.

AANAK sees the lantern light signal three times through the ice and nods.

She fine, now.

AANAK takes her guarding position above the hole—motionless, just like an inuksuk herself.

DAVID pulls out his camera and takes shots of the inuksuk (FLASH), the stacked ice (FLASH), the surroundings (FLASH), and the hole in the ice (FLASH).

DAVID: *(hollering into ice hole)* Hey, Paasa! Smile for the camera.

AANAK: Quiet, David! Ice can fall!

DAVID: Crazy! I wanna go down there too.

AANAK shakes head without losing her observation position.

I can do it!

Pause.

I know I can!

AANAK: Is dangerous.

DAVID: You let Paasa go.

AANAK: You not ready!

DAVID: But I'm older than her! And way taller than her. Just let me go under, take a couple of pictures . . . and I'm out again.

AANAK: Maybe next time.

DAVID: Tomorrow?

AANAK shakes her head.

Then when? When?

AANAK: Maybe . . . *(long pause)* . . . next winter.

DAVID: You're kidding? I may not be back here again . . . ever! Mom will return to do more research—but not me. So, let me go, now . . . please.

AANAK: You qallunaaq! [White men!] . . . wanting more than is good.

DAVID: *(stunned)* Qallunaaq?

AANAK does not look at him and holds her observation position.

Qallunaaq—that's us white people. You know, my mom is a qallunaaq, too. And you let her look at your ice, measure it, research it . . .

AANAK: Dr. Cooper, she respect nature.

DAVID: Me too!!!

AANAK: Your mom care for *all* of us . . . like Sedna.

DAVID: The goddess without fingers?

AANAK: Sedna care for *all* sea animals.

DAVID: And my mom?

AANAK: Your mom, she care for *all* weather—our weather in Kangiqsujuaq, your weather in Edmonton. She know we connected.

DAVID: And if she'd be here, she would let me go.

AANAK: *(with a twinkle)* But your mom not here. And I am substitute to care.

DAVID: Arrgh! I don't need any substitute inuksuk mom!

DAVID stomps off angrily and plops down onto a mount. He pulls out his music and wrestles to put the headphones over his hat.

He presses the play button several times madly but can't get it to work.

PAASA's head pops up from the ice hole. AANAK helps her out.

PAASA: *(lifting bucket to AANAK)* Still lots of mussels left.

AANAK: Good! Naammagijarpit ungataanut pitsanak.

(smelling the mussels) Mmmmh!

PAASA: Do not take more than you need. I know.

PAASA senses that something is bothering DAVID.

Uhm . . . it felt really warm down there. Had to take off my parka . . . funny, hmh?

DAVID: Warm? Underneath the ice?

PAASA: Hard to believe. But you see, there's no icy wind down there.

DAVID: I sooooo wanted to go down there but Aanak said . . .

He quickly glances at AANAK.

. . . well, she said a lot of things.

AANAK: Time to go.

AANAK exits.

PAASA: Coming!

Sulkingly, DAVID gets up. He examines the hole.

DAVID: I can actually see the ocean floor. Hm, not far down at all.

(following others) Hey, Paasa? How dark is it down there? Can you actually see anything or is it . . .

A slow fade as night falls and the fat moon becomes more visible. Wind mixes with the distant sound of throat singing.

***

The profiles of AANAK and PAASA move rhythmically back and forth in front of the glowing moonlit window as they throat sing to one another.

Lights up inside the cabin. Finished dinner plates still sit on the ground. PAASA and AANAK laugh over a mistake. DAVID is still sulking.

DAVID: Weird! Technically, I wouldn't even call this singing. You hardly moved your mouth . . . you just breath in and out.

AANAK: Too cold opening mouth wide. Make icicles grow on teeth.

DAVID: *(unsure)* I don't think so.

AANAK: Maybe . . . when is freezing cold?

DAVID: *(hesitant)* I've never heard of that.

AANAK: Maybe is better not to open mouth wide but just breath . . . aa-ha—aa-ha—aa-ha.

PAASA: She is teasing you, David!

AANAK bursts into jolly laughter and surprises DAVID with an affectionate pinching of his cheeks.

She walks over to her sewing area and continues stitching.

PAASA slurps up one last mussel and cleans up the plates.

Did you like our fresh uviluq?

DAVID: Honestly?

PAASA: Of course: honestly!

DAVID shakes his head.

Must be different than what you eat at home.

DAVID: Correct! Raw mussels are not what we eat in Edmonton.

PAASA: Oh, do you have more pictures of your Edmonton? I want to see them.

She picks up DAVID's backpack and holds it up expectantly.

Please!!!

PAASA takes out his camera from the side pocket of the backpack and swings it in front of him.

Pretty please?

DAVID: Careful!

He grabs the camera from PAASA, checks it, and drops it into his jacket pocket.

PAASA: But . . . I want to learn more about your big city.

She notices the tree frog stuffy attached to his backpack and unclips it. She changes her voice to animate the stuffy.

(animating the stuffy) "Don't be so grumpy, David! Show sweet Paasa your photographs?"

DAVID: No!

PAASA: *(animating)* "Just a few pictures?"

DAVID: Maybe another time.

PAASA: "How very sad. Oh . . . hello, Aanak. I am Pete, the tree frog."

AANAK: *(playing along)* Hello Pete-Frog.

PAASA: "Do you know why my master David is so grumpy?"

AANAK: David grumpy because things not go the way he want.

DAVID laughs it off.

PAASA: Pete-Frog, do you like uviluq?

DAVID: No, he doesn't. Tree frogs have a sensitive digestive system. They can't eat mussels. And you really shouldn't hold him like that. The oil in your hand . . . tree frogs can't handle it, it blocks their breathing.

PAASA: But he's not *real*, David.

DAVID: I know but . . . he reminds me of my real frog.

AANAK: He inuksuk—stand-in for real frog. Like I stand in for your mom?

DAVID: Not really. My mom would have let me go under the ice. *(holding out an open hand, upset)* Can I have him back—now!

PAASA hands back the stuffy to DAVID who reattaches it to his backpack.

PAASA: I'm sorry, David. I was just kidding.

DAVID: *(finally bursting out)* I could have taken important pictures for my mom's research!

PAASA: David?

DAVID: *(towards AANAK)* It could have helped "all of us"—but you, you didn't let me go!

AANAK stays focused on stitching the mitts.

DAVID grabs his jacket and mitts.

Excuse me. I need some fresh air . . . clear my head!!

PAASA: David!

AANAK: Stay calm. And stay close.

DAVID: Won't be long.

DAVID dashes out.

***

The big full moon shines brightly on the night sky.

In the distance we can see the inuksuk.

DAVID: . . . treats me like a baby . . . as if I know nothing!!!

(zipping up his jacket) I mean, if Paasa can go down there, then *I* can handle it for sure. Hmh, I can actually see the inuksuk. *(waving at distant inuksuk)* Hello! It's showing me the way . . . Maybe, I should just go . . . now. *(slips hand into his pocket)* Oh, a flashlight . . . handy! *(tests switch)* And it's working . . . a good sign. *(reaches into other jacket pocket)* And my camera. Hmh, I gotta do this. There may not be another chance. Now or never.

DAVID walks off quickly.

***

The moving circle of the flashlight guides DAVID across the frozen ice and to the inuksuk. This scene can be staged with the perspective from underneath the ice.

DAVID: *(shining flashlight up onto inuksuk)* Hello, old inuksuk guard. Still watching over the "holy" entrance? Guess what, I'm gonna go down there. Just for a very short time . . . for a few pictures.

Feet first, DAVID slowly wiggles his way down the ice hole.

Where is the ocean floor? Where is it?

(with a final jump he lands) AAAH! Made it!

> *He slowly circles his flashlight around. The whole cave-like under-water world becomes illuminated and sparkles brightly in absolutely magical, beautiful ice reflections.*

Holy moly . . . this is . . . amazing . . . unreal . . . icicles under the ice . . . beautiful . . . so—COOOOOOL! *(echo-echo)*

> *We hear the sound of cracking ice.*

(imitating AANAK) "Quiet, David. Ice can fall." *(chuckles)* Paasa was right, it feels warm down here . . .

> *He takes off jacket and mitts and places them on a big rock. DAVID looks up and listens. He hears the sound of rushing water very faintly in the distance, and it gradually increases throughout the scene.*

Water? *(shakes off his wet boots)* . . . that's strange . . . I thought the tide is still far out . . . Oh well, I won't stay long.

(pulls out camera) Just a few important pictures . . . "Scientists must always record their findings," Mom says.

> *FLASH, FLASH.*

(in a "scientific" voice) "And here, ladies and gentlemen, we have some beautiful icicles hanging from underneath the ice . . .

> *FLASH, FLASH, FLASH.*

"And here are some . . . tide pools . . . or maybe puddles from the melting ice above."

(walking along further) O, unvi . . . no, uviluq. Paasa could have taken way more . . .

He breaks off one mussel, smells it, and chucks it.

Yuck!!!

He takes pictures of uviluq. FLASH, FLASH.

Nice!

The FLASH sounds of the last pictures seems amplified by a strange female voice.

Hello . . . somebody there?

He listens but it's quiet again, except for the sound of waves moving closer.

Crazy . . . I could have sworn I heard something . . . or someone.

(turning and listening) I better go.

DAVID lifts his flashlight to light up his way.

My jacket? . . . Where did I put it? . . . Where is it? . . .

He looks around frantically.

In the frenzy of his movement, DAVID's camera slips out of his grip and SPLASH, drops into a puddle.

O nooooo!! My camera . . . not in the water . . . all of my pictures for Mom . . . my important research pictures . . .

(searching on hands and knees) I *must* find it . . . expensive camera . . . darn water . . . my pants are soaked.

(jumping up) Water? . . . rising . . . the tide is coming back!?

SEA VOICE: Naammagijarpit ungataanut pitsanak. [Do not take more than you need.]

DAVID: Who is that?

He swirls his flashlight around and starts to run off in different directions.

This is crazy! I gotta get out . . . stupid hole . . . where is it? . . . How do I get back?

SEA VOICE: Naammagijarpit ungataanut pitsanak. [Do not take more than you need.]

DAVID: Mom? . . . is that you?

The underwater environment is filled with splashes of coloured light and the vague image of a woman swimming with the sea animals.

That can't be . . . I must be dreaming?

SEA VOICE: Naammagijarpit ungataanut pitsanak. [Do not take more than you need.]

DAVID: Sedna! Is that you? You're really down here? SEDNA? Listen, I don't need my camera, or my coat, mitts . . . keep the stuff . . . not important, really . . . just get me out . . . back to Aanak and Paasa . . . I'll wait patiently for my mom's return and . . . the right time.

The flashlight flickers and then dies.

Nooo!!! Don't go out, flashlight! Noooo. Not now.

HELP—somebody, HELP ME!!

The shadowy woman shape lifts her hands upwards repeatedly.

PAASA'S VOICE: *(muffled and distant)* David. Daaaaa-vid. DAVID!!!

DAVID: HELP ME—PLEEEEASE!

A gigantic white FLASH fills the whole stage.

Aaaaaaahh!

***

DAVID: *(nightmarish in his sleep)* Aaaaaaahh!

PAASA sits next to the bed watching DAVID finally wake up.

His wet pants are drying on a clothesline.

(startled, pops up in bed) SEDNAAAAA?

PAASA: No, David . . .

DAVID: Mom!

PAASA: No. It's me . . . Paasa.

DAVID: Where did she go?

PAASA: David, you're here at Aanak's cabin.

DAVID looks around, trying to make sense of his "dream."

DAVID: But where is she? . . . Who saved me?

PAASA: Well, when you didn't come back, Aanak knew right away what you were up to. She was *very* worried and we both went out looking for you.

DAVID: So, *Aanak* saved me.

PAASA: No.

DAVID: Then who?

PAASA looks at him demonstratively with a big gesture and smile.

You?

PAASA: Yup! I got you out.

DAVID: You did!

PAASA: Just in time. The water was already up to your knees. Your pants were totally soaked.

DAVID: I don't quite remember.

PAASA: We had the sled with us . . . and Aanak wrapped you up in her warm polar-bear blanket.

DAVID: She did?

PAASA: Well, yes. If you are wet, you freeze to death, David! We all know that.

DAVID: Paasa? *(long pause, sincerely)* Nakurmiik [thank you].

PAASA: Ilaali! [You're welcome!]

DAVID is coughing strongly.

DAVID: You know something? I heard a voice.

PAASA: What did you hear?

DAVID: A voice said: Naamagija . . . ungata . . .

PAASA: Naammagijarpit ungataanut pitsanak. Do not take more than you need.

DAVID nods knowingly.

DAVID: But . . . I didn't really take too much?

PAASA: Well . . . you wanted more than was good for you, David.

DAVID considers this seriously and nods.

PAASA crosses over to check and turn the wet pants on the clothesline.

DAVID: Call me crazy but the voice I heard . . . it sounded just like my mom's.

PAASA: When you truly feel connected to someone, you can hear her or him—no matter how far away that person happens to be. I often hear my mom and dad . . . even when they work on the other side of the mountain.

DAVID: *(nodding)* Yes, I could hear her . . . And I could feel somebody lifting me, too . . . and then . . . then I must have passed out . . . I can't remember a thing after . . .

> AANAK *enters with a mug for tea and a bushel of herbs in her hand. She is still very upset about* DAVID's *escapade.*

AANAK: Crazy boy awake?!

> *She goes and dips herbs into the mug to make tea.*

You very lucky boy, David!! You know?

DAVID: I know.

AANAK: You not ready to go under.

DAVID: I know.

AANAK: And waiting for right time is not waste of time, David!

DAVID: I know . . . I know.

> *Pause.*

PAASA: He heard Sedna talk to him.

AANAK: Good! Maybe now David listening.

DAVID: I . . . I'm sorry for upsetting you, Aanak.

AANAK: Aa! Is okay being curios *(pronounces it a bit funnily)* but never okay put danger on life. *(hands him tea mug)* You drink cloudberry tea . . . for good strength.

DAVID: Thank you, Aanak!

Pause.

Thank you for caring and trying to teach me . . . and for being a good inuksuk mom.

AANAK: *(surprised)* You learning, David. Good! Now, drink tea!

DAVID drinks tea under AANAK's watchful eye.

PAASA: So, did you take good pictures for your mom's research?

DAVID: Yes, but . . . I lost my camera . . . and my mitts . . . and my jacket.

PAASA: Oh no!

AANAK: Aa, Sedna way of teaching.

DAVID: Maybe she did teach me. And I am learning, even without any photographs as evidence.

AANAK: *(clicking her tongue)* You true son of your mother . . . always search for evi-dence. And one day, you be good scientist like her.

AANAK gives DAVID a big, noisy hug. He can't help but smile and enjoy the moment.

DAVID: Thank you, Aanak.

AANAK: Maybe next time right time for beneath ice.

DAVID smiles but is overcome by the same nasty cough.

Aa . . . aa. Now you rest! Must be strong when real mom pick you up.

PAASA: Sweet dreams, David.

DAVID: Yes, sweet dreams . . . Nakurmiik [Thank you].

AANAK and PAASA sit down at the sewing table.

PAASA: One day, maybe I will go to Edmonton . . . help people there.

AANAK: Maybe one day you be like Dr. Cooper . . . caring for *all* of our nature.

PAASA: Maybe.

PAASA tries on the now-completed mitts. She shakes her hands within the mitts.

Too loose, Aanak.

AANAK: Maybe not for you?

PAASA is surprised, thinks about it. Suddenly, she smiles and looks over to the sleeping DAVID. AANAK nods knowingly.

PAASA tiptoes over to DAVID's backpack, zips it open, and places the beautiful, warm mitts in it.

DAVID: *(half asleep)* Aanak?

PAASA scurries back to the table.

AANAK: Aa!

DAVID: *(sleepily)* I'd really like to know the rest of Sedna's story. Can you tell me how it ends? Please?

As AANAK tells the final Sedna chapter, beautiful northern lights dance on the sky like the sea animals in the story.

AANAK: Sedna, she live at bottom of ocean. With seal . . .

PAASA & DAVID: . . . seal, beluga, whale, fish, and walrus.

AANAK: She care and protect *all* sea animals . . . When hunter greedy, Sedna not let him catch a thing. Then, hunter need go down to ocean floor and comb Sedna long hair . . .

DAVID: *(sleepily from his bed)* Because Sedna has no fingers to hold a comb.

Surprised, AANAK *and* PAASA *look up at* DAVID.

AANAK: Greedy hunter must comb Sedna hair and must promise be fair and not take more than needed.

(with PAASA *and* DAVID *joining)* Naammagijarpit ungataanut pitsanak. [Do not take more than you need.]

> *During the end of the story, the stage has slowly turned black—except for the big full moon hanging low.*

> DAVID *crosses in front of the low moon with his new mitts on his hands. He waves goodbye. Before he exits, he runs back and gives his tree frog stuffy to* PAASA *and another hug to* AANAK.

> *The silhouette of a departing plane crosses over the moon. When the sound of the plane engine has faded, we hear* DAVID's *letter.*

DAVID: Dear Aanak and Paasa,

Thank you for the gift. Aanak's handmade pualuk are the best. My hands are never wet or cold.

Yesterday, I gave my science class presentation about Kangiqsujuaq. Everyone thought it was really cool and asked many questions about your way of life. Many kids want to know what they can do to help the polar bears come back to your place. Some kids want to learn your throat singing and maybe I can record your voices, next time I visit. Yes, I actually would like to come back to Kangiqsujuaq—IFFF you take me in again.

I promise to listen better next time.

I hope you are well.

Your . . . inuksuk son, David.

The end.

ABOUT THE CONTRIBUTORS

Bruce Barton is a performance maker and research/creation scholar located in Calgary, Alberta. His stage and radio plays have been produced across Canada, celebrated with regional and national awards, and anthologized. He works extensively as a director, playwright, dramaturg, and designer with numerous devising and intermedial performance companies across Canada and internationally. He is also Artistic Director of Vertical City, an interdisciplinary performance hub. Recent Vertical City projects include *2YouTopia*, *All Good Things*, and the award-winning *Trace*. Bruce taught playwriting, dramaturgy, devising, and intermedial performance at the University of Toronto for fifteen years. In January of 2015 he became the first director of the School of Creative and Performing Arts at the University of Calgary.

Eva Colmers lives in Edmonton where she works as a writer and director in theatre and film. From early on, Eva was fascinated by different places, people, and their stories. After moving to Canada, she studied theatre at the University of Calgary and received an M.A. in Drama in Education with Theatre for Young Audiences as her main focus. Eva has written and produced five youth plays (among them *Down By the Brook*, *A Suitcase Full of Stories*, and *The Visit Next Door*) and has taught drama to youth, teens, and adults at the Citadel Theatre, Northern Light Theatre, and St. Albert Children's Theatre among other organizations. She has also translated *Shakespeare's Will* by Governor General's Literary Award–winning playwright Vern Thiessen into German. Eva has written and directed a dozen award-winning short films (including *2.57k*, *Granny Baby*, *The Weightless Traveller*, and *End of the Rope*), and three documentaries for the National

Film Board of Canada (*We Regret To Inform You . . .* , *The Elder Project*, and *The Enemy Within*). Her latest youth play, *Beneath the Ice* (produced by Quest Theatre, Calgary, and Cookie Theatre, Edmonton) played in theatres as well as schools to an appreciative, combined audience of six thousand people. The production by Cookie Theatre was honoured with an Elizabeth Sterling Haynes Award.

Alan Dilworth is known for his award-winning direction of contemporary tragedies and reinvented classics. He has brought over thirty new Canadian plays to the stage including his own SummerWorks Jury Prize–winning *The Unforgetting*, Erin Shields's SummerWorks Jury Prize and Governor General's Literary Award–winning *If We Were Birds*, Andrew Kushnir's Toronto Theatre Critics Award–winning *The Middle Place*, Pamela Mala Sinha's multiple Dora Award–winning *CRASH,* and the acclaimed Stratford Festival production of Kate Hennig's *The Last Wife*. These, along with his work on Edward Bond's epic masterpieces *The Bundle* and *Human Cannon,* have established Alan as a director of sometimes harrowing but always humanizing productions, known for their stage imagery and "operatic minimalism." In 2013, he was awarded the inaugural Christopher Plummer Fellowship Award of Excellence for his contribution to work on classical text. Alan is a resident director and Drummond-Dorrance Fellow at Soulpepper Theatre Company.

Heather Fitzsimmons Frey is a director and dramaturg, and holds a Ph.D. from the University of Toronto Centre for Drama, Theatre and Performance Studies. Her current research interests include contemporary and nineteenth-century theatre for young people, and performing youth, girlhood, and cultural identities. She has presented in Canada, England, Germany, and as a keynote speaker at One Theater World in the United States. Her research appears in *Canadian Theatre Review* and *Youth Theatre Journal*, and she has published several book chapters including "Canadian Chocolate War: Imagining, Depicting, and Fearing 'Youngster' Power" in *Nationalism and Youth in Theatre and Performance*. She also co-edited a collection of essays with Art Babayants called *Theatre and Learning*.

Kathleen Gallagher is a Distinguished Professor at the University of Toronto. Dr. Gallagher's books include *Why Theatre Matters: Urban Youth, Engagement, and a Pedagogy of the Real* (2014); *The Theatre of Urban: Youth and Schooling in Dangerous Times* (2007); and *Drama Education in the Lives of Girls: Imagining Possibilities* (2000). Her edited collections include *In Defence of Theatre: Aesthetic Practices and Social Interventions* (in press, with Barry Freeman); *Drama and Theatre in Urban Contexts* (2013, with Jonothan Neelands); *The Methodological Dilemma: Creative, Critical and Collaborative Approaches to Qualitative Research* (2008); and *How Theatre Educates: Convergences and Counterpoints with Artists, Scholars, and Advocates* (2003, with David Booth). Dr. Gallagher has published many articles on theatre, youth, pedagogy, methodology, and gender and travels widely giving international addresses and workshops for practitioners. Her research continues to focus on questions of youth civic engagement and artistic practice, and the pedagogical and methodological possibilities of theatre.

Andrew Kushnir is a Toronto-based playwright, actor, director, dramaturg, and community arts worker. He is Creative Director of Project: Humanity, an organization raising awareness of social issues through the arts. Drawn to questions of justice and community, Andrew's writing has been described as "more than dramatized social work." His produced plays include *Captain Princess, foto, The Gay Heritage Project* (co-created with Damien Atkins and Paul Dunn), *The Middle Place, Small Axe,* and *Wormwood.* Since 2011 Andrew has been playwright-in-residence at Tarragon Theatre. Andrew is currently developing a new verbatim play *The Teacher* (in collaboration with Dr. Kathleen Gallagher) that explores how the high school drama classroom provides an inimitable window into the lives of young people. A four-time Dora Award nominee (twice for writing, twice for performance), Andrew is a graduate of the University of Alberta's BFA Acting program as well as a Loran Scholar. In 2013 he received the University of Alberta's Alumni Horizon Award in recognition of his verbatim theatre practice.

Michelle MacArthur teaches at the University of Toronto, where she completed a Ph.D. from the Centre for Drama, Theatre and Performance Studies in 2013. Michelle edits the book reviews section of *Theatre Research in Canada*; has published articles in *TRiC*, *Canadian Theatre Review*, and *alt.theatre*; and has contributed to several edited collections as a writer or editor. She is also the lead researcher for the Equity in Theatre initiative, a campaign focused on redressing gender inequities in the Canadian theatre industry. Her report, entitled "Achieving Equity in Canadian Theatre: A Report with Best Practice Recommendations" (2015), can be found at http://www.eit.playwrightsguild.ca.

The women of URGE have created as a collective since 1991. URGE's mandate has always been to co-create original musically driven performance works, which use the variety of skills, techniques, and sound worlds of the members of the ensemble. In 1993 *I had an Urge to write you* included percussionist Beverley Johnson, clarinetist Lori Freedman, and composer/clown Lisa Karrer, as well as core members Marie-Josée Chartier, Linda Caitlin Smith, Joanna McIntyre, and Fides Krucker. *She promised she'd bake a pie* (1995) brought in pianist Eve Egoyan, actor/flamenco dancer Anita La Selva, and performer and eventual core member Katherine Duncanson. *Trousseau/True Nature* (their second show to go to Calgary's High Performance Rodeo) introduced actor Gabi Epstein to the process.

Each member of URGE brings with her a mature art form, sophisticated craft, and personal history. These become the tools for a shared training period during the development phase of each new work. It is also the mandate of URGE that each woman brings what is most current in her life. These fresh and surprising impulses—ranging from the repetition of a daily chore, the unusual use of every day and sacred objects, the darker tones of life-chafing and changing events, or situations to the unfolding landscape of a night's dream—become elements for improvisation in rehearsal. An important aspect of the work in URGE is the structuring of improvised "play" into the fabric of each public performance ensuring an ever-changing, evolving landscape of sound and image.

Currently Marie-Josée Chartier choreographs and directs in dance, opera, and multi-media; Katherine Duncanson teaches yoga and voice; Fides Krucker teaches, creates, and writes about voice; Joanna McIntyre is a facilitator in transformation; and Linda Catlin Smith composes concert music. They each incorporate their URGE-y ways into a wide variety of performance and creation contexts.

Anne Wessels's doctoral research analyzed performances of the suburb and the intersection of youth, pedagogy, drama, and place. After graduating from the Ontario Institute for Studies in Education at the University of Toronto, she won the Canadian Association for Curriculum Studies Dissertation Award and the ARTS Doctoral Graduate Research Award. She has published in *Theatre Research in Canada*; *Research in Drama Education: The Journal of Applied Theatre and Performance*; *Pedagogy, Culture and Society*; *Youth Theatre Journal*; *Journal of Adolescent and Adult Literacy*; and *Ethnography and Education*. A graduate of the National Theatre School of Canada, Anne now works as the Education Director at Tarragon Theatre in Toronto.